THE
GIANTS
OF
IRISH RUGBY

JOHN SCALLY

MAINSTREAM
PUBLISHING

EDINBURGH AND LONDON

To the memory of my grandfather

First published in Great Britain in 1996 by
MAINSTREAM PUBLISHING COMPANY (EDINBURGH) LTD
7 Albany Street
Edinburgh EH1 3UG

ISBN 1 85158 834 5

Me 9337.   Me -> F G

A catalogue record for this book is available from the British Library

Typeset in Janson Text
Printed and bound in Great Britain by Butler and Tanner Ltd, Frome

CONTENTS

INTRODUCTION

Since Ireland's first ever international, against England in 1875, Irish rugby has produced many exceptional players and fascinating characters. The most difficult part of writing this book was to decide which forty players to feature. I was spoilt for choice and acutely conscious that no matter what route I took I was not going to please everybody. Ollie Campbell objected to the inclusion of Colin Patterson amongst the giants of Irish rugby on the basis that Patterson is only five foot five inches!

Even if I had cast my net to include 140, perhaps 240, stars of the past and present I would still have to exclude a number of wonderful players. In no way am I implying that the forty 'giants' in this book are the greatest Irish players. Several of them certainly are but equally some of them are definitely not. I have interpreted the term giants of Irish rugby liberally to include not only the acknowledged best players but also some of the great characters of the game.

My priority was to get as much diversity of stories as possible – players from different periods, positions on the pitch, geographical regions as well as different personalities. This led me to make a number of difficult decisions, for example Nigel Carr merited serious consideration for inclusion by virtue of his sterling performances in Ireland's 1985 Triple Crown victory but his career dovetailed so closely with his old school pal Philip Matthews that I had to reluctantly overlook him. Likewise, Willie Duggan would have been an automatic choice had I not interviewed his back-row colleagues on the 1982 Triple Crown side, Fergus Slattery and John O'Driscoll. However, Willie still fills more inches of print in this book than most of the people profiled!

In recent years the phrase 'democratic deficit' has gained popular currency. The selection choices I made have been primarily personal ones. To redress the balance somewhat I invited four of my interviewees to make the final four choices.

Acknowledgements

Thanks to Willie Anderson, Gerry Casey, Mick Doyle, Kevin Flynn, Ciaran Fitzgerald, Simon Geoghegan, Tom Grace, Moss Keane, Michael Kiernan, Donal Lenihan, Sean Lynch, Willie John McBride, Barry McGann, Hugo MacNeill, Philip Matthews, Mick Molloy, Brendan Mullin, Con Murphy, Phil Orr, Bill Mulcahy, Phil O'Callaghan, John O'Driscoll, Colin Patterson, Fergus Slattery, Dick Spring and Pat Whelan.

Special thanks to David Deering, Mick English, Jack Kyle, Noel Henderson, Johnny Moloney, Jim McCarthy, Jim Glennon, Des O'Brien, Paddy Reid and Mick Quinn.

Very special thanks to Ollie Campbell and Tony Ward.

I am grateful to my good friend Noel Coughlan of RTE Radio Sport for his practical assistance.

Thanks also to Inpho for the cover pictures.

My gratitude to all at Mainstream, especially Judy Diamond, Avril Gray, Lorraine Kemp and Peter MacKenzie. Above all I appreciated the interest and encouragement of Bill Campbell.

1

WILLIE ANDERSON

Don't Cry For Me Argentina

You ask me if headquarters worry about change. Well, hardly –
everything is paid for by cheque.

RFU official on BBC Radio

In sporting terms he is one of a kind. He is famous in the rugby world
for playing the bagpipes. Whatever that indefinable quality called
charisma is, this guy has it in buckets. He has a keen appreciation of the
black humour of life, an easily discernible kindness and sensitivity,
particularly for those down on their luck, and his smile signals a warm
affection for friend and stranger alike. He lacks one thing – a capacity to
dissemble. Despite his 27 caps for Ireland and his record of 78 caps for
Ulster, Willie Anderson will probably always be remembered as the
player who precipitated an international diplomatic incident. He was on
a tour of Argentina with the Penguins in 1980 and took a shine to the
Argentinian flag and decided to claim it as his own.

'Myself and another player were walking home to the hotel around
midnight. I liked the look of the flag and its colours. Shortly after that
six guys came through the door with machine guns. They said:
"Someone in here has an Argentinian flag." I immediately handed it
back and said I was sorry. I was quickly told saying sorry was not good
enough in this situation. As I was brought down to the jail two Irish
internationals, David Irwin and Frank Wilson, volunteered to come
with me for moral support. For their consideration they were both
thrown in jail with me for three weeks!

'I was strip-searched and had 30 sets of fingerprints taken. I was

7

literally in the interrogation chair for a day. Anyone who has seen the film *Midnight Express* will have an idea of the naked terror you can experience when you are in prison and there's a gun to your head. Things got worse before they got better. I was put into this box which is the most frightening place in the world before being taken to my cell. The cell was six foot by four and had nothing but a cement bed in the centre. The people who had been there before me had left their excrement behind. It was pretty revolting. The only blessing was that I wasn't put in the "open" cell with a crowd of prisoners because I would have never survived.

'The next day I was taken out in handcuffs which is the ultimate in degradation. I was taken up the stairs and was stunned to discover that there were about 60 or 70 reporters and journalists waiting for me. For three or four days I was not just front page news in Argentina, I was the first three pages. To me the press were not much better than terrorists. As I had a British passport they tried to whip up a nationalistic frenzy and portray me as an imperialist. They didn't print the truth. Some said I had urinated on the flag. Others said I had burned it. Yet more said I had done both. My lawyer got death threats.

'It was much more serious than anybody realised here at the time. I know for a fact that two or three army generals wanted to have me executed. Others wanted to make sure that I served at least ten years' hard labour. The whole episode cost my parents ten thousand pounds in legal fees and so on, but you can't put a price on the mental anguish that they had to endure. I remember one letter I sent home that I would hate to have to read again because I had struck rock bottom.

'The two lads and I were taken back to a cell where we came into contact with two South Koreans. They had tried to smuggle some Walkmans into the country. David Irwin taught me how to play chess and we had the World Chess Championships: South Korea v. Northern Ireland.

'One of the guards looked like a ringer for Sergeant Bilko. At one stage he was marching us in the yard and Frank roared out: "Bilko." I said: "For Christ's sake Frank just keep your mouth shut." Thankfully the guard didn't know who Bilko was. I think things could have been much worse had not the warden wanted to learn English. His colleagues would have been happy to throw away the keys to our cell. In that country we were guilty until proved innocent.'

Although Anderson uses the analogy of *Midnight Express*, perhaps a more obvious comparison is with the experiences of a fellow Northerner, the Beirut hostage Brian Keenan. Keenan describes his dark moments as that of 'a man hanging by his fingernails over the edge of chaos feeling his fingers slowly straightening. It is a humiliating stripping away of every fibre of your being.' This also serves as apt summary of the darkest chapter of Anderson's life and his sense of utter despair and isolation. In adversity he found out who his friends really were. It was evident in the difference between the concerned and the simply curious.

'After three weeks Frank and David were sent home. It was the loneliest day of my life. I had to wait for a further two months before my trial and release. Someone arranged a hotel room for me. I wouldn't wish what happened to me on my worst enemy. All rugby players contributed via the clubs to a fund to pay for the legal expenses. The people of Dungannon rallied around and raised a lot of money also. I owe them a lot. I wrote to my then girlfriend, now wife, Heather, every day. The following year we got married. I think the Argentinian experience consolidated our relationship. I also learned a lot about myself. In the beginning of that experience I prayed intensely but I gradually realised that I could not leave things to God. I had to take control of things myself. I ran every day and made a great effort to learn something about the culture and the political system. Bad and all as things were for me, it was a real culture shock to visit the town square and see all the women who were frantically looking for their sons. It was part of the way of life there that people disappeared and were lost forever. If you were seen as any kind of threat to the state you were eliminated.

'In rugby terms I was to pay a heavy price for my indiscretion. I was perceived as a rebel and was quietly told later, by a prominent personality in Irish rugby, that my first cap was delayed because of the incident. In fact, I was 29 when I first played for Ireland.

'I met Dennis Thatcher some years later and told him that I could have told his wife the Argentinians were scrapping for a war. There was another amusing postscript to the incident many years later. I was attending the Bermuda Classic and the Argentinians were playing the Americans. The ball went out of play and came in my direction. As I went to retrieve it I heard one of the Argentinians say: "Give us back the ball there Willie and while you're at it give us back our flag as well!"'

Patrick Kavanagh in one of his poems, *From Failure Up*, poses the question: 'Can a man grow from the dead clod of failure?' He goes on to speak of moments 'where the web of Meaning is broken threads'. Yet, however bleak the situation, there are always new possibilities:

Under the flat, flat grief of defeat maybe
Hope is a seed.

Anderson is the living proof of the truth of this penetrating analysis of the human condition. In rugby terms he made his international debut against Australia in 1984. As a player he had many highs and lows: the highs being the 1985 Triple Crown and the night he captained a scrap Irish side to a famous victory over France at Auch in 1988 – Ireland's only victory over France on French territory in over twenty years. Playing for Ireland was the fulfilment of a childhood dream.

'I have a clear memory of watching Ireland play the All Blacks in 1972 and wanting to play for my country after that. The players I most admired were Ken Goodall and Mervyn Davies. I even grew a moustache to look like Mervyn! I was fortunate in that my brother Oliver represented Ireland at both the discus and the shot. I was very impressed with his Irish tracksuit and this spurred me on even more.

'Nowadays players are getting paid a lot of money to play for Ireland. If those terms had been around in my day I would have earned about two hundred thousand pounds. After I was chosen for my first cap my father gave me an old fifty punt note. Every time I took out the note to buy a drink nobody would let me split the note so I had never to pay for any drink. At least my first cap saved me a lot of money!

'I can still feel that tingle that went down my spine when I first heard the national anthem as an Irish player. People couldn't understand how an Ulster Protestant could feel this way. It was an even greater honour to be chosen as captain. The flip side of the coin was that I had to make the speeches at the dinner. A lot of drink is consumed on those occasions and not everyone wants to listen to a speech. One of my earliest dinners as captain was after a Scottish game. During my address I looked down and I could see Kenny Milne with his hand over his mouth trying to hold back the vomit. I can only hope it was from drink and not from listening to my speech! I shouted down to him: "I know how you feel." I seem to have an effect on Scottish players. At another Scottish dinner I was sitting beside a prominent player all night. At the end he had to be carried away on one of the tables!

'After captaining Ireland to a defeat against England I was talking to Will Carling at the dinner in the Hilton. It was a very serious atmosphere so I asked him to come downstairs with me for a wee drink. I asked him what he wanted and he said a gin and tonic, so I ordered two. I nearly dropped dead when the barman charged me ten pounds. When I asked him if he could charge it to my room he said no. Then I pulled out two Northern Ireland five pound notes. The barman immediately said he couldn't take this. I said to Will that he would have to pay for the drinks. When he pulled out his wallet I think there was a combination to it! Although we lost the match at least I had the satisfaction of making the English captain buy me a drink!'

As captain he was also known for a famous piece of sporting theatre before Ireland played the All Blacks, when he led the Irish team literally up to the noses of the All Blacks in an effort to intimidate them. Whose idea was this ploy?

'It was a joint effort between myself and our coach, Jimmy Davidson. After the match, Wayne Shelford was asked if he was scared. He answered that he was absolutely petrified. When asked why, he answered: "I was terrified that Willie Anderson would kiss me!" In fact I once got a kiss on the top of my head in an international from Donal Lenihan after I made a try-saving tackle. Years later when we played New Zealand in the Bermuda Classic the guys knew I would have something special planned for the "haka". The New Zealanders were led in the haka by their lady physiotherapist. I kept my hands behind my back until they had finished when I walked up to her and pulled out a big bunch of flowers. Another time we faced the All Blacks and theatrically swung over our legs. They weren't sure what we were up to until we started singing: "You put your left leg in and your left leg out … " The whole place cracked up.

'More seriously, a few days before that famous match against the All Blacks a good friend of mine was killed as part of the Troubles. He died just because he was a builder. At my after dinner speech I spoke about the importance of keeping perspective. While you want to win at rugby there is more to life. Not everybody appreciated my comments but a number of All Blacks spoke to me afterwards about how impressed they were by the sentiments.

'Jimmy Davidson was ten years ahead of his time. He had a crucial role in my development as a player. It was he who pointed out what was wrong with my game. The feeling we had when we ran out to play for Ulster you could have cut with a knife. We had great players, like Nigel Carr. I've never met anyone who could match Nigel for fitness and commitment. He used to do a thousand sit-ups when watching *Top of the Pops* and a thousand press-ups when watching some other programme.'

Anderson is grateful for all the opportunities rugby has provided for him, particularly in relation to touring. Despite the apparent glamour of travelling abroad, it can be a very isolated existence, wherein the only thing you see of the country is a hotel room, a few bars and many rugby grounds – though in which precise order varies greatly depending on the team.

'Rugby has been my passport to travel the world. Most of the time it has been very pleasurable. When we toured Romania with Ulster, though, it was horrifying to see the scale of the poverty. I have one clear image of that trip. We passed by what must have been a thousand-acre field and there were lines of women with hoes working away. They all looked about a hundred but they were probably no more than thirty.

'Even when things are at their blackest, from a rugby point of view, on tour there are moments of comedy. After we lost to Australia in the World Cup in 1987, Donal Lenihan rang home. As a result of the time difference the match was shown live on Irish television at 6 a.m. His mother had seen the match and knew the result already. Instead of offering him sympathy she said: "Anyone stupid enough to play rugby at 6 o'clock in the morning deserves to lose!"

'In 1994 I was back in Australia as assistant coach to the Irish touring side. At one stage our seconds played the Australian thirds. We were lucky to keep the defeat down to 60 points. Ken O'Connell had just joined the Irish touring party. I went into the dressing-room afterwards and the boys were in a state of shock at such a hammering. I told them not to worry, they would get another chance and asked Ken how he had got on. He answered: "I sidestepped one guy five times. The only problem was that he had the ball each time!"

'Once, when I played in the Hong Kong Sevens, Jonathan Davies and I decided we would go out for a real Chinese meal. After we had finished, Jonathan said he was going to do a runner. I told him not to be crazy because there were six guys at the door with machetes precisely to discourage people from leaving without paying their bill. Jonathan could do the 100 metres in about 10.5. I could do it in 16.5 so sprinting off was not a realistic option for me! When Jonathan ran out I carefully considered my options. Eventually I took the decision and paid for both of us. When I went out I found Jonathan hiding behind a dustbin!

'People over here don't realise just how big the Sevens are. It gave me the most terrifying moment in my rugby life. There were 100,000 people watching when we played Australia. At one point there were 12 players in a small corner of the field and what seemed about 35 acres with just two players – David Campese and me. I was petrified about having to try and tackle Campo when he had so much space so I screamed my head off to get some cover.'

At a time when Ireland's rugby fortunes were at an all-time low, Anderson was brought in to be assistant coach in 1993, and is credited with the revival of the Irish team which led to victory over England in consecutive seasons in 1993 and 1994. He resigned from this position for 'personal reasons'. What exactly did this mean?

'Because of Argentina and other disappointments I think I have a very clear idea of what is important to me. My number one priority is my family. I have three young kids and I wanted to be there for them at a time when they needed me. I got tired of driving three hours up and down to training sessions. My great ambition is to coach Ireland. I'm still learning about rugby but I have a clear idea of the type of game I want to play which incorporates a mixture of the Australian-French approach. It's a total game, technical but Irish. The traditional Irish spirit must never be lost.'

For the moment he is channelling all his energies into coaching Dungannon, the club he captained to Ulster Cup glory in 1993. His evocative reminiscences of the halcyon days when he wore the green jersey are provided in a spirit of inimitably witty celebration.

'After we beat England to win the Triple Crown, my wife, Heather, met Seamus Heaney's wife, Marie, which was a big thrill for her as she's an English teacher. A few weeks after that we were at the dinner to mark our Triple Crown victory. It was the night of one of Barry McGuigan's big fights and I went upstairs to see the contest on the television. Heather was there on her own and was trying to make polite conversation. She was chatting to Ciaran Fitzgerald, who was the best captain I ever played under, and made a bit of a *faux pas* by telling him that she had met James Joyce's wife after the English match. Fitzie turned around and asked Hugo MacNeill what age would Mrs Joyce be. Hugo answered: "About 150!"'

2

OLLIE CAMPBELL

Campbell's Kingdom

> When you are number one there is only one way to go – stay at
> number one.
>
> Barry Hearn

Following the sensational decision to drop Tony Ward, in Australia in
1979, in favour of Ollie Campbell, both players found themselves
unwittingly embroiled in the long-running Ward–Campbell saga.
Records and adulation meant little to Campbell, a quietly spoken fly-
half, who would rather have melted into the background than be the
centre of attention. A reluctant star, he was far from the norm, with no
time for the arrogance or pretensions associated with such a label. Off
the field he tried to portray himself as an ordinary guy; on it he could
not disguise his skill.

Rugby was in his genes. His maternal uncles, Seamus and Michael
Henry, won Leinster Cups with Belvedere College. Seamus (also Ollie's
godfather) captained one of the famous seven-in-a-row Old Belvedere
Senior Cup winning teams in the 1940s, as well as captaining Suttonians
to their last Metro Cup win in 1947 when they were only a minor club.
Ollie's father was also on that team – as prop. His father played minor
football with Louth but after he left school he went to live in Howth and
joined Suttonians club, where he met his wife Joan. It was his father who
bought Ollie his first leather ball.

'I was only five or six and he said: "If you can catch this you can keep
it." I did! He only missed one international between Ireland and
Scotland in over 40 years. The gap was caused by the birth of my sister.
I always thought it was a very weak excuse! My father was hugely

supportive right through my career. It was he who taught me the skill of tackling.'

An impressive framed painting of Belvedere College graces Campbell's trophy-laden apartment and offers a tiny clue as to the affection he feels for his Alma Mater.

'To my shame I mostly associate Belvedere simply with rugby. I remember when we lost a first round Junior Cup match, 6–3, against Newbridge, I cried for three days. (When I became an adult and played for Ireland I was much more mature about the whole thing. Whenever we lost an international I only cried for one day!) Winning the Leinster Cup in both 1971 and 1972 were incredible thrills. After the first victory I took off the mud from Lansdowne Road from my boots and kept it in a plastic bag as a souvenir. I only threw it out a few years ago. Although she never missed her brothers playing, my mother only ever saw me play three times. I was small as a kid and the first time she saw me play she was afraid I would be killed. When I became an international she would turn on the radio from time to time during the game to see if my name was mentioned. When it was she knew at least I was still alive. That was really all she was concerned about.

'At school not only was I not a kicker in terms of kicking for goal but I hardly kicked in play at all, and was not even responsible for 25-yard drop-outs or kick-offs or restarts. Times change! When I played my first game for Old Belvedere firsts after I left school and we scored a try, the captain assumed that because I was playing fly-half I was a kicker. So I just did what other fly-halfs do and it sailed through. And that's how it started. After that, it became something of an obsession to perfect the art of place kicking and I practised endlessly. I figured everybody else had been taking place kicks right through their school days so I had to make up for ten years' lost ground. There is also a strong perfectionist streak in me, I have to admit.'

One of the few occasions when Campbell's kicking let him down was in his international debut against Australia in 1976.

'It was one of the biggest disappointments of my life. It was everything you want your first cap *not* to be. I was dropped from the side straight away which was the only time in my career I was ever dropped, off any team.'

It would be three years later before Campbell regained his place in the Irish team, on the Australian tour at the expense of Tony Ward. The following season he set a new points record (46) for the Five Nations Championship. Campbell's next close encounter with Ward was on the Lions tour in 1980.

'With the first Test looming and with both out-halfs, Gareth Davies and I, injured, a fit one was needed. Who was flown out? A.J.P. Ward. Not only did he play in the first Test he scored 18 points which was then, and remains, a Lions individual points scoring record in a Test match. Was there to be no escape from this guy?'

Ward was a sub to Campbell in the third Test in Port Elizabeth. To his horror he discovered in the dressing-room that he had forgotten his boots. It was too late to retrieve them from the team hotel. His problem was exacerbated by the fact that nobody had a spare pair of boots to lend him. He consoled himself with the thought that he probably would not need them. The seating arrangements for the subs that day were bizarre to say the least. They were to sit on the very top row of the stadium. As the match began Ward was making the long journey up countless flights of stairs with John Robbie when he heard somebody shouting for him. Campbell jokes about a lost opportunity to scuttle his rival's career.

'I was injured in the very first moments of the match and was pumping blood. [Campbell still has a small scar on his face as a "souvenir".] It was panic stations all round. John Robbie got a pair of boots from a ballboy for Wardie to wear. At size nine they were too big for him but an even more serious problem was that the studs were moulded. The pitch was waterlogged that day and even if they had been the right size they would have been a disaster in the conditions, but they were all he had at the time. If only I had known I was straight off and he was not getting my boots! It would have been Wardie's ultimate nightmare and his reputation would have been destroyed at a stroke!'

Campbell has more pleasant memories from his trip to South Africa.

'We were preparing for what was effectively a fifth Test against one of their top provincial sides, Northern Transvaal. One of our centres that day was Ray Gravell from Wales. He always got very nervous before big matches and tried to cope by singing nationalistic Welsh songs, crying and getting sick – but not necessarily in that order. Before that particular match his gum-shield went missing. He basically gave an ultimatum to the team that he was not going to play unless it was found. The result was that instead of the normal serious preparation for the match, every member of the touring party was emptying bags and looking under benches for Ray's gum-shield while he cried, sang and got sick. Unfortunately we did eventually find it – in Ray's own gear bag!'

In 1981 Campbell was moved to the centre to allow for Ward's return as Irish out-half. How did he react to the change?

'I never minded the idea of playing in the same team as Tony – provided I was at out-half. Playing in the centre is a very different position and to be honest I was never really comfortable there. In 1981 we lost all four matches, by a single score after leading in all four at half-time. It was Ireland's best ever whitewash! I remember at the time Tom Kiernan kept telling us repeatedly that whatever the results, if there was to be a Lions tour that year the country that would have the most representatives would be Ireland. I'm not sure if that was true but it certainly kept our morale and self-belief up. That summer we toured South Africa. It was a non-event for me – concussion and a broken wrist keeping me down to about 50 minutes of rugby.'

The following season things came together for the Irish side. A record score from Campbell, kicking all of Ireland's points (with six penalties and a drop goal) in their 21–12 victory over Scotland, allowed the Irish to clinch the Triple Crown in 1982 and end a 33-year famine to take their first Triple Crown since 1949. One of Campbell's enduring recollections of the game was of the fans.

'Probably my abiding memory of that whole season was the reaction of the crowd during the whole of the second half of that Scottish game, particularly in the East Stand because much of the half seemed to be played there. I think it was really the start of *Molly Malone* becoming the "anthem" of the Irish team. The atmosphere was just incredible. I heard a piece of radio commentary of the game for the first time last year and it really brought goosepimples down the back of my neck. An interesting postscript to the match came when my aunt, in Scotland, asked me to send on my autograph for a local lad showing a lot of rugby promise. Later he would be a star for both Scotland and the Lions. His name – Craig Chalmers.

'There were a lot of great moments that season – I suppose most famously Ginger's celebrated try against England. On a personal level I remember a break I made which set up Moss Finn's first try against Wales; the virtual touch-line conversion of Ginger's try in Twickenham and the drop goal against Scotland. That score came from a special loop movement we had devised in January with David Irwin, but kept under wraps. It should have led to a try but I gave a bad pass to Keith Crossan and the move broke down so we had to settle for three points. Life for that team was never really the same afterwards. Most of the team had grown up with no international success. There was a huge sense of achievement and a bonding that has lasted since.

'When we won our first match, all we were trying to do was to bring a sequence of seven consecutive defeats to an end. Two weeks later we won at Twickenham and suddenly we were in a Triple Crown situation. It was something, as a team, we had never thought about. But we knew we were on to something big when we saw the huge crowds watching us in training. That was something we had never experienced before. It was a very exciting week as we had a general election at the time following the fall of Garret Fitzgerald's first coalition government, but nobody seemed to care about it. Everybody was more excited about the possibility of a Triple Crown – Ireland had never won one before at Lansdowne Road.

'The tension mounted, but when Tom Kiernan, the Irish coach, decided to have a closed practice session, on the Thursday before the game, suddenly the Triple Crown match became just another game, and I have never felt so at ease and comfortable going into a game. It was a master-stroke as far as I was concerned. Two weeks previously I had missed a penalty against England that would have sewn the game up. On the Sunday afterwards, I went to Anglesea Road, with my five balls, and kicked for two hours from the same spot I had missed from the previous day. Ninety per cent of all the kicks I took in practice over the next two weeks were from this spot. After just three minutes of the Scotland game, when the first penalty arrived, I relaxed. Amazingly, it was from exactly the same spot. I felt I would have kicked it with my eyes closed but I didn't take the chance. We were on our way and, for me at least, never before had the value of practice been more clearly demonstrated.'

After the Lions tour to New Zealand in 1983, in which he scored 124 points, Campbell's career never reached the same dizzy heights again. His retirement from international rugby was, through no fault of his own, shrouded in mystery. He is delighted with the opportunity to set the record straight about his decision to bid a reluctant farewell to the game he loves.

'The general perception was that New Zealand tired me out. Nothing could be further from the truth. New Zealand rejuvenated me. As far as I was concerned I had been to rugby's Holy Grail. When I returned I was brimming with enthusiasm and new ideas about rugby. I did get some bug for a short time but that was a relatively minor setback. The real problem was hamstrings. I strained my hamstring in the penultimate game of the Lions tour and shouldn't have played in the final Test under any circumstances, but we were so decimated by injuries that basically anyone that could walk was selected. In fact I had to come off in the match after half an hour. We were losing 12–3 at the time but ended up losing 38–3. I asked the lads later what happened after I went off!

'I began the 1983–4 season feeling keen, healthy and eager with the confidence of a mature player but the hamstrings got worse and worse and worse. My problems were compounded by the fact that both my hamstrings were affected but I struggled through that season. I trained harder than I had ever trained before in the summer of 1984 but the following season was a disaster because of the hamstrings. I trained even harder the following summer but the hamstring went in the first ten minutes of the season. By this time I now had a chronic problem and a lot of scar tissue. I visited practically every specialist in the business. It was even suggested to me that I should consider ripping them out completely and/or having them operated on. To be honest if I thought it would have worked I would have gone for it but I was not convinced.'

When he pulled out of the England game in 1984 it was suggested by some that Ollie was giving up rugby and joining the priesthood!!!

'I've absolutely no idea where this particular rumour emanated from. To this day, though, John Robbie still calls me Fr Campbell! To highlight just how absurd that fabricated story was, two weeks later after Ireland played Scotland I turned up dressed as a priest at the post-match dinner! Not only that, I persuaded a female friend of mine to accompany me dressed up as a nun! I went around all night with a fag in one hand (and I've never smoked) and a pint in the other (and at the time I didn't drink) and danced away with this "nun" although I've never been much of a dancer. All of this was so out of character for me that I assumed that people would immediately see that the priesthood story was entire nonsense. What staggered me was the amount of people who came to me and, apologising to "sister" for interrupting, sincerely congratulated me on my big decision! Instead of putting this little fire out all I succeeded in doing was to pour fuel on it!'

Even after his retirement from rugby Campbell still found his name linked with Ward's.

'I was invited on Mike Murphy's radio show at one stage. Before the broadcast I was asked if there were any subjects I did not wish to discuss. I said: "Tony Ward and South Africa" because I thought they had been flogged to death. The first question Mike asked me was: "I see here, Ollie, that the two areas that you have said you do not want to be questioned about are South Africa and Tony Ward. Why is that?"

'I was at a meal in the Oyster Tavern in Cork after Munster played the All Blacks in 1989 and sat down beside a great stalwart of the Greystones club, Eric Cole. I was aware that when I did that some people started whispering and nudging each other. I continued talking away to Eric and we had a great chat but there were a lot of comments being made which were going straight over my head when people pointed us out, like: "Ollie give Wardie a break". It was only after I discovered that Tony had being going out with Eric's daughter, Louise, for months and they got engaged shortly after that. Afterwards some typical Greystones mischief-makers put out the story that not being content to "steal" Wardie's place on the Irish team I was also now trying to steal his girlfriend!'

Contrary to popular opinion Campbell has other interests apart from rugby. In 1995 the hottest ticket in pop music, the family group from Dundalk, The Corrs, released their debut album *Forgiven Not Forgotten* which quickly rocketed up the American charts. On the credits 'special thanks' are expressed to Ollie Campbell. Is this the former Irish out-half?

'I'm afraid so. The thanks is there for the musical direction I've given them! Seriously, the Corrs are managed by one of my closest friends, John Hughes. With his brother, Willie, he formed the group Minor Detail which attracted a lot of critical acclaim in the mid 1980s but never got the commercial success they deserved. As I do not have a note in my head the truth is I'm probably the least musical person ever to have been mentioned on an album sleeve!'

After the Irish squad were awarded professional contracts Campbell jokingly thought of establishing a petition of ex-international players asking that former internationals be rewarded retrospectively. Although he would appear an obvious choice, Campbell has declined to enter the media world as a rugby analyst. What is behind this reticence?

'Firstly, my main love is coaching. Secondly, when you are a media commentator you cannot sit on the fence. You have to be critical. That means that your relationship with any particular Irish team suffers.'

Talking to Campbell is like opening a Pandora's box as the rugby stories flow out of him. He has many anecdotes which illustrate the funny side of the game.

'John O'Driscoll was a very committed, driving player but a real Jekyll and Hyde character. His party piece was to hang out of windows late at night. During Ireland's tour of South Africa in 1981 this got a bit boring after a number of weeks. For the sake of variety he decided he would hang someone else out of the window, so one night he dangled Terry Kennedy by the legs as he held him outside the hotel window – 17 storeys up. It's the only time I've ever seen Terry quiet. My feeling was that this had gone too far. Then Willie Duggan came into the room, puffing his cigarette, with a bottle of beer in his hand and his matted hair that hadn't being combed since the tour started! As Willie was such a senior player and a close friend of John's I assumed he would talk some sense to him. All he said to John before turning and walking out was: "O'Driscoll, you don't have the guts to let him go." He was right too!

'In 1981, after Tony Ward was brought back onto the Irish team and I was at the centre, John went out with me for a walk through Stephen's Green just before the game. Suddenly John told me that he was delighted I was playing there. My morale lifted straight away and I inquired why. He said: "Now at least we will have somebody at out-half who can make a tackle!"

'Freddie McLennan was the ultimate practical joker. In 1980, when Leinster toured Romania, Paul Dean was making his debut on that tour and was desperate to become one of the "lads". At dinner one night Paul McNaughton asked Deano to go up to Freddie and ask him what size shoes did his mother wear. Paul was a bit suspicious but eventually agreed to do so. As soon as he did Freddie turned away and put his hand over his face and started to sob. Deano didn't know what to make of this and asked some of the other players what was the matter. They replied: "Did you not know? Freddie's mother was in a horrific car crash a fortnight ago and had both her feet amputated." Deano's face turned a whiter shade of pale and a number of times he tried to apologise to Freddie that night, but every time he got near him some of the players headed him off. The result was it was well into the night before Deano found out that it was all a con job and he had fallen for it hook, line and sinker!

'Tom Kiernan is an accountant by profession and has a great head for figures – most of the time at least! After the All Blacks were beaten by Munster in 1978, Tom, as their coach, was asked by a local journalist if it was a one-off. In all earnestness Kiernan is reputed to have replied: "You could play the All Blacks two or three times and they would beat you nine or ten times!"

'Mick Doyle was a very shrewd coach. My only experience of him was as coach of Leinster. We played Romania when they toured Ireland in 1980. We arrived at the ground well over an hour before the game. I thought then we had mistimed the arrival. The previous week Romania had hammered Munster and Doyler had noticed in the lead-up to the match the Romanian players were constantly in and out of the toilet. Being the cute Kerry man that he was Doyler gave a newspaper and a match programme to each of our substitutes and told them to lock themselves in the toilets until the game began. We demolished the Romanians in the match. The next day the phrase that was used in the newspapers was: "The Romanians were strangely heavy and leaden-footed." Was it any surprise?'

On the basis of the interviews for this book it appears that rugby players judge their colleagues on the basis of four criteria: skill, contribution to the team, commitment to rugby and personality. For the older players who saw Jack Kyle in his prime he scores the perfect ten on all counts. All the interviewees for this book had either played with or seen Campbell in action. Uniquely he unites all the generations of Irish rugby in their total admiration for him. Who then are the players he would most have liked to play with?

Campbell's biggest difficulty was leaving Simon Geoghegan out of the team. His dream Irish team is as follows:

15. Hugo MacNeill
14. Trevor Ringland 12. Mike Gibson 13. Brendan Mullin
    11. Keith Crossan
10. Jackie Kyle
 9. John Robbie (capt.)
 1. Phil Orr 2. Ken Kennedy 3. Ray McLoughlin
 4. Willie John McBride (vice-capt.) 5. Moss Keane
 6. John O'Driscoll 8. Ken Goodall 7. Fergus Slattery
Manager: Tom Kiernan
Coach: Dr Ollie Bourke (President Mary Robinson's brother)

He prefaced his discussion of his dream world team by pointing out that he could have picked out an equally strong one without picking any of those who made it onto his dream side, for example great players like Sella and J.P.R. Williams.

15. Serge Blanco (France)
14. Gerald Davies (Wales) 13. Tim Horan (Australia) 12. Mike
    Gibson (Ireland) 11. David Campese (Australia)
10. Barry John (Wales)
 9. Gareth Edwards (Wales)
 1. Ray McLoughlin (Ireland) 2. Tommy Lawton (Australia)
    3. Graham Price (Wales)
 4. Colin Meads (New Zealand, capt.) 5. John Eales (Australia)
 6. Ian Kirkpatrick (New Zealand) 8. Murray Mexted (New
    Zealand) 7. Michael Jones (New Zealand)
Manager: John Hart
Coach: Carwyn James (Wales)

3

MICK DOYLE

Odd Shaped Balls

Don't ask me about emotion in a Welsh dressing-room. I cry when I watch Little House on the Prairie.

Bob Norster

The most startling thing about Mick Doyle's office is that it is situated immediately opposite the Naas Christian fellowship. I wondered immediately if this would be a mellowing influence on Doyler? A few hours later, having being exposed to more than a handful of expletives, my question was firmly answered in the negative! Yet despite the perception of him as a hard man there are shafts of tenderness and generosity in everything he says. As the conversation progresses the old cliché of a lamb in wolf's clothing springs readily to mind.

His first love was the GAA, though when he began his secondary education as a boarder in Newbridge College rugby exploded into his life.

'In a strange way it was only then that my father became the biggest influence on my rugby career. Whenever I was at home I would have big question and answer sessions with him about what options should be taken in specific situations during a match. It was from him I got my philosophy of the game and in those sessions my "give-it-a-lash" approach was born. As we had such a small pool in Newbridge, and there were no subs allowed in a match at the time, I played in a wide variety of positions: in the centre, wing-forward, out-half, full-back and as a number eight.'

He made his international debut against France in 1965 and scored a try on his debut. What are his memories of that game and of his international career?

'If I had died after that match I would have gone to my grave happy.

Noel Murphy and Ray McLoughlin were a great help to me in adjusting to the demands of international rugby. I always looked up to Bill Mulcahy. He always made you aware of what it was to be an Irish player and the standard you had to reach to do justice to the green jersey. I loved every single game I played for Ireland. The highlights for me were beating South Africa in 1965, playing against England with my brother Tommy, also playing on the other flank for Ireland, scoring a try against Wales in the ninth minute of injury time in 1968 and touring with the Lions to South Africa in the same year.

'The great thing about my rugby career was that it gave me the opportunity to meet so many great characters, like Ken Kennedy. He has a great irreverence. I would describe him as a macho David Norris. I have great respect for him as a person. Of course you could write a book about Phil O'Callaghan. He's a panic. Sam Hutton of Malone was another great character not least because he had the best chat-up line I ever heard: "Excuse me darling, haven't you met me somewhere before?" The late Jerry Walsh was a great Irishman and a fabulous tackler. Willie John has a great sense of humour and I love Syd Millar's ready wit. Both of them could take it as it came.'

The year 1968 marked his retirement from international rugby. The decision was prompted by non-rugby factors.

'I was 28. I had been a perpetual student up to that time. It was time for me to settle down and to build up my veterinary practice.'

The rugby bug bit again and he made a comeback with Naas, initially as a coach and then as a player. 'I got so hoarse from shouting on the sideline that I used up less energy by joining in on the pitch.' As Leinster's coach he took them to five interprovincial titles between 1979–83 (1982 shared). There was controversy about the manner in which he was appointed as Irish coach with Willie John McBride being cast aside after just one year. What prompted him to throw his hat into the ring for the position?

'After Ireland lost to Scotland in 1984, Moss Keane and Willie Duggan came to me and persuaded me that I should run for the job of Irish coach because they felt we were going nowhere fast.'

On his office wall hangs a picture of the Irish team in the famous pose where they linked arms in Cardiff Arms Park. There is no disguising the pride in his voice as he talks about the Triple Crown in 1985.

'From time to time I look back at the videos of the games and I still get very emotional. I had built up a huge dossier of information about each player. I had made up my mind if I ever was made a coach of a representative side I would give players responsibility for their own performances. The only thing I would not tolerate is players not trying. I think it is fair to say I gave straight answers to players and there was honest selection which helped to build up the right spirit.'

The highs of 1985 were dramatically reversed the following year when Ireland were whitewashed in the Five Nations championship. 1987 too was a year of missed opportunities and some rumours of discontent within the Irish camp.

'We should have won the Triple Crown in 1987. We let the game against Scotland slip through our fingers. Things were sometimes misinterpreted. After we lost that match the then chairman of the selectors, Eddie Coleman, asked if he could sit in on our team meeting. I told him I would have preferred if he didn't but because he was chairman of selectors I couldn't stop him if he really wanted to. During the meeting I was very critical of the players' performances and told them so in forthright terms and what I expected of them. I also stated that what I had said was not for repeating outside. Some people obviously thought I was putting on a macho display for Eddie's benefit and was trying to show them up. Within a week, a journalist, David Walsh, had the story. I didn't think the "affair" did lasting damage. The mood was brilliant after we beat Wales in Cardiff and the guys, in a show of affection, threw me in the bath!'

In doing the interviews for this book it became evident that there were some players from the 1985 team who felt that Doyle was taking too much of the glory for the Triple Crown victory for himself, and losing some of his focus giving speeches at dinners and being a celebrity. When I mention this, and that a former player has told me that Doyler was less tolerant of players towards the end of his stewardship than at the beginning, he answers with an ascending level of raw emotion.

'I think that it's probably fair to say that I was less tolerant towards the end particularly during the World Cup in 1987. My period as Irish coach cost me about £750,000. Before we left for that tournament my business was going down the tubes. I didn't have time to keep my eye on the ball in terms of my business. I had never experienced stress until then but literally up to the last minute before going down under I was frantically trying to salvage my business. I was also hitting the bottle too hard and it wasn't doing me any favours. It was the darkest hour of my life because everything I had worked for was disappearing before my eyes. Of course, what made it much worse was that I was worried about not being able to provide for my family.

'I suppose we didn't have the same off-the-cuff attitude we had in 1985. On the rugby side things were not going right in the build-up. We lost Nigel Carr in that horrific bomb blast which was a huge blow. I always take too much on and I was trying to do everything I could for the players on the organisational side. Philly Orr told me I was doing too much.

'Within 24 hours of getting to New Zealand I had my coronary "incident". I should have been sent home after that. I was on tablets to sleep, tablets to wake up, tablets for hypertension and God knows what else. Most of the three or four weeks I was there I was edgy and irritable and in no way a suitable candidate for being a coach. The guys deserved a better coach than I was. I was less understanding than I should have been. Syd Millar and Mick Molloy were probably too kind to me at the time. They should have shook me up a bit. When I came home I was on the point of having a nervous breakdown but I never quite went over the brink. That phase lasted for about six months until I started to put the pieces back together.

'I learned a lot about myself in that period. I discovered I wasn't invincible. The one thing I will say is that if you can't control stress it will control you. Two exercises which I found helpful were to firstly think of the blackest possible scenario that could happen to me in my worst nightmare. Once that wasn't happening I was already winning. Secondly, I learned to live in the daytide, that is, to forget worrying about yesterday or tomorrow and just worry about today.'

Doyle's philosophy of life is also indicated in a message that is displayed in both his office and in the reception area which states: A journey of a thousand miles begins with a single step. He rebuilt a new business, Doyle International Marketing, which is at the cutting edge of the fast-changing world of international agri-business. The company's primary role is in the areas of research and development and niche marketing. Now his main ambition is to move his family to Kerry. As if to underline his commitment to the county of his birth he is wearing a Kerry cricket club tie – which is made curiously in England.

After he had restored his professional and emotional life on an even keel he wrote his autobiography which was described by one observer as 'a good love guide'. There was some very hostile reaction as it recounted in vivid detail some of his sexual conquests. Did he expect the reaction?

'No. The best story I heard about it was about the two women in a taxi who were discussing it. One said: "I can't understand how anybody wrote a book like that while they were still alive!"'

He does a more than passable impersonation of Charlie Haughey to recount another memory about that time.

'I rang up Charlie to see if he would be willing to launch the book. He asked me what it was about. I said 20 per cent is about rugby and 80 per cent is pornography. He said: "You got the balance just right!"

'CJH opened his speech on the night by saying "I always like people who expose themselves in public!" Later that night I asked him if I could write his biography. He answered: "No way. I've seen what you've been prepared to write about yourself. Where would you stop if you started writing about me!"

'Some time later I was doing a book signing in O'Mahony's bookshop in Limerick. Garret Fitzgerald had been there the night before. In the front window they had photographs of both of us. As I prepared for my signing I noticed this religious brother in his white collar walking up and down past the shop shouting "Get that bastard off the window." One of the shop assistants went out and asked him: "What's wrong with Mick Doyle?" "Nothing. He's a grand fellah. It's that other so-and-so that I can't stand!"

'Then we moved on to Galway. Two of my mates came to the signing dressed up as nuns. (One of the scenes in the book relates how Doyler was caught in a state of undress by a nun after performing the "marital act".) They hid all my books in the science section where no one could find them.'

He continues to air his views trenchantly through his weekly column in *The Sunday Independent*.

'In 1988 P.J. Cunningham, sports editor of *The Evening Herald*, asked me to write a column for his paper. The two points I had to resolve in my own mind were: Was I good enough to write authoritatively? If I was going to write, I would have to write honestly: was I prepared to write about mates? I was paid to give my opinion, not to interview players, so I had to wear my heart on my sleeve. Initially I found it very hard to criticise players I had coached. However, there were players who were not reaching their potential. Players just going through the motions really switch me off.'

There is a perception, though, that he has personalised his criticism notably in relation to Neil Francis. Has his writing style cost him friends?

'I'm as fast to praise as to blame. I'm still very passionate about rugby though I'm not promoting any agenda. It's not my wish to be right every time. In the main I'm trying to stimulate debate. I've no antagonism towards anybody and there are checks and balances in *The Sunday Independent* to ensure I don't go over the top. Sometimes I might be asked to take another look at an article to see if that is really what I want to say about a player. The only thing I am super-critical about is coaches promulgating rubbish.

'I think people who know about the game basically respect me and what I'm trying to do in my column. There are a few people who don't talk to me any more but I don't give two f***s what they think of me. The vast majority of people do talk to me. I know there are people who think of me as being big-headed and arrogant. All that matters to me is that my family and my friends know who I am. There is no way I'm going to change my style just to keep people happy. Moss Keane once said to me: "Thanks be to Jaysus I don't play any more. Otherwise I'd be afraid to open the paper on Sunday because of what you'd say about me!"'

4

MICK ENGLISH

Natural Born Thriller

Perhaps my best years are gone … but I wouldn't want them back. Not with the fire in me now.

Samuel Beckett

Mick English has three claims to fame. Firstly, he was an accomplished Irish out-half succeeding to oust no other a person than Jack Kyle in the number ten jersey. Secondly, he has been immortalised around the world in after dinner speeches by Tony O'Reilly. Playing against Phil Horrocks-Taylor during a Wolfhounds match in Limerick, English was asked what he thought of his opponent who had scored a try that day. English replied: 'Well, Horrocks went one way, Taylor the other and I was left with the hyphen.' In the O'Reilly version, though, this exchange happened after an Ireland-England international at Twickenham. English never played opposite Horrocks-Taylor in an international.

Thirdly, he might be said to be the architect of Richard Harris's acting career. When the actor Anew McMaster was touring Limerick he stayed in English's home. He required some extras for his stage production of the Dickens classic *A Tale of Two Cities*. English supplied him with some of his friends including Harris and the horse trainer Teddy Curtin. They were paid a half-a-crown each per performance to do the mob scenes. Subsequently, Harris spent hours talking about acting in Mick's kitchen with McMaster. Harris was badly bitten by the acting bug and McMaster persuaded him to go to London and join an acting school. Appropriately, Harris went on to win an Oscar nomination for his role in a film called *This Sporting Life*.

English's rugby career began in 1946 when he attended Rockwell College. Up to that point his time at Sexton Street CBS had ensured that he had never even seen a rugby ball, and that his sporting interest was hurling. In fact he played with minor hurling for Limerick in 1950, as well as with the famed Claughan club. In the environment of the time he had to sign a form at the beginning of that summer declaring that he would never play rugby again. When the rugby season began in September he broke his promise and switched his allegiance to rugby.

'I started one game at scrum-half and moved to out-half after 20 minutes and remained there for the rest of my days. The skills of kicking and dropping goals were honed at lunch breaks and evening times when, in pairs, we played "drop goals". This consisted of one set of goal posts and to score three points you had to drop one over the bar, and the ball had to hit the ground before the opposition caught it. I was lucky in that we had an acre of garden at home which had a large chestnut tree in the centre. After a year or so I was able to kick a rugby ball over this tree. My up-and-under kicks started there.

'At Rockwell I was fortunate to be on a Junior Cup winning team in 1949 and also played against Crescent College in the senior final that same year. We lost 8–0 and, having started at out-half, I moved to first centre, second centre and wing – not a good day! Richard Harris played in the second row for Crescent that day. We became good friends after we left school. We met on a daily basis at Sarsfield bridge and walked together to work. I went to my clerical job at the Insurance Corporation of Ireland and Dickie to his father's flour store in Henry Street, where he was chief mouse catcher! He was always an actor and the centre of all "divilment". We played junior interpro for Munster together and I have no doubt that if he had not gone to London he would have gone all the way in rugby. After he left to pursue his acting career the next time we met he was on stage in Brendan Behan's *The Hostage*. Free seats for the pals from Limerick!'

The following year English added the Senior Cup to his collection. By this time he had added a new training routine to his repertoire. While on holiday in Kilkee, Co. Clare, he developed his running and swerving technique down the potentially treacherous Chimney Bay Cliff.

'When I left school I played junior rugby with Shannon for a year. My mother was advised by Shannon's Christy Quilligan that senior rugby was unsuitable for one so young. Little did I know that in fact junior rugby was *much* tougher than senior.'

In 1952 English began what was to be a very happy ten-year association with Bohemians. He almost immediately acquired cult status especially for his performances at Thomond Park. The ground is famous for the 20 foot wall which was insufficient to prevent the ball from leaving the ground from time to time. When balls were lost the crowd were wont to shout: 'Never mind the ball get on with the game.' English was famous for deliberately kicking the ball over the wall when his side was defending a narrow lead near the end of a game.

In 1958 he was central to Bohemians success in winning their first Munster Cup in 31 years. Part of the gloss was taken over the Bohs' victory when the Cup went missing for four days. The strong suspicion was that it was a 'local job'. Eventually the Cup was left outside English's home and discovered by his sister, Philomena, on her way home from Mass. English also won Munster Cup medals in 1959 and 1962. He reached an important milestone when he became a Munster player in 1955.

'I have fond memories of training in Thomond Park with four or five players, some Garryowen, some Bohemians, all playing for Munster and hoping to go further. Paddy Reid, one of the all-time greats, would put us through our paces two or three nights weekly. The only lighting came from the street lights outside the ground. Training was followed by a cold shower. Paddy had returned from professional rugby and was an accomplished hockey player with the Lansdowne hockey club in Limerick. Such was his great interest in rugby that he gave unselfishly of his time to help others to gain the breakthrough. We all remain greatly in his debt. He even allowed "Pa" Whelan, the current Irish manager, to marry his daughter Deirdre!'

English won final trials in 1956 and 1957 but had to wait until 1958 for his first cap for Ireland. Ireland lost 9–6 after John O'Meara retired injured. The match was the final curtain call for Cliff Morgan's distinguished international career. No substitutes were allowed. English received notification of his selection in the following way:

TELEGRAPHIC ADDRESS	IRISH RUGBY FOOTBALL UNION
"FOOTBALL, DUBLIN."	14, WESTMORELAND STREET
TELEPHONE Nos 77984 & 79707	DUBLIN
SECRETARY: R. W. JEFFARES	

M.A. English, Esq., Rosehill, O'Callaghan Strand, Limerick. Date 4/3/58.

Dear Sir,

I have pleasure in advising that you have been selected to play for:–

Ireland v Wales. At Lansdowne Road on Sat. 15th Mar. '58. Kick Off 3.00 p.m.

and shall be glad to receive your acceptance BY RETURN POST. If following acceptance you find that through injury or illness there is a doubt about your fitness, kindly advise Secretary by 'phone without delay.

Headquarters Shelbourne Hotel, Dublin.

Your jersey will be supplied, and must be returned immediately at the conclusion of the game.

The Irish Rugby Union provides transportation and pays Hotel Expenses covering table d'hote meals only. (Gratuities, telegrams, 'phone calls, etc., etc., being of a personal nature, MUST NOT be chargeable on the I.R.F.U) Should you, however, incur any legitimate expenses kindly furnish particulars on attached Form to the Treasurer within one week of Match. Please bring your Dinner Jacket.

As a member of the team or travelling substitute, you are entitled to two East Stand tickets, which will be sent to you on receipt of £2. : 0s. 0d. received within seven days. Later applications cannot be considered.

Each travelling player or substitute should provide himself with training togs, clean white knicks, towel and soap and see that his boots are in good playable condition. Kindly let me know size of boots so that we can arrange stockings for you.

Yours truly,

R.W. JEFFARES,

Secretary and Treasurer.

Kindly travel to arrive Dublin 14/3/1958 in time for luncheon, departing for home morning of 16/3/1958. Team Meeting, Shelbourne Hotel, Friday, 14/3/1958 at 2.15 p.m. Bus departs Shelbourne Hotel 3.30.p.m for Irish Team's training – Dublin University F.C. Ground – College Park.

My hearty congratulations and good wishes!

'I recall this correspondence vividly, especially after so many letters arriving telling me that I had been selected as substitute. I think I had nine or ten of those before the real thing. I suppose that is the greatest moment in any rugby player's career.'

He was tickled by a letter written to him by the late Mai Purcell of *The Limerick Leader* when he won his first cap. The letter read:

> Mick. I should like to impress on you that I'm spending a whole week's wages to visit Dublin just to see you play and I beseech you not to make an idiot of yourself on this occasion.
>
> I furthermore request that on this auspicious occasion mindful of your duties and responsibilities not only to your club and the people of Limerick but to your country as a whole, that you keep your bloody eye on the ball. Good luck and God Bless.

The following year came the highlight of his career when he dropped a goal to help seal a 9–5 victory for Ireland over France and book his place on the Lions tour of New Zealand and Australia. Note the greeting in his letter of notification.

FOUR HOME RUGBY UNION'S
TOURS COMMITTEE
7, HAYMARKET LONDON S.W.1

PEB/JUM.   22nd March, 1959.

Dear English

I am requested by the Four Home Rugby Unions' Tours Committee to invite you to join the British Isles Rugby Union Team 1959 to tour Australia and New Zealand.

I hope that you will be able to let me have your acceptance of this invitation by return of post.

The attached memorandum is for your immediate guidance.

Yours sincerely

P.E.B. Bradforth

The Lions won the two Tests in Australia but lost 3–1 to the All Blacks. 'Unfortunately, due to injuries to stomach muscles, I played only twice and with six weeks remaining, and unable to play on, both Niall Brophy and I departed the scene by luxury liner for home. Niall had sat his accountancy exams in Melbourne in the first week of the tour and passed. He played against New South Wales and injured his ankle after just five minutes. No more rugby for him. Our itinerary included stops at such places as Sydney, Melbourne, Freemantle, Suez Canal, Cairo, Naples, Marseilles, Gibraltar and finally to Liverpool.

'One of the stars on that tour was Tony O'Reilly who was truly magnificent on the left wing. He was top try scorer and a huge influence on those around him. It was often said that the Lions tours saw him at his peak and when playing for Ireland the small matter of making a living got in the way of his rugby. His time was not wasted!

'Another to shine was David Hewitt whom the New Zealanders thought was one of the best and fastest centres to play New Zealand. In some matches David, who was a keen photographer, was very taken by the strange cloud formations one sees in New Zealand skies, and at times when he should have been concentrating on the play was admiring the clouds.'

English's international playing career from 1958 to 1964 had many interruptions, some through injury, some by being out of favour. He was capped in every season of his six-year international career. However, in that period seven other out-halfs were also capped for Ireland: W.J. Hewitt, Seamus Kelly, Ken Armstrong, Dion Glass, Gerry Gilpin, Gerry Hardy and John Murray. English was also in trouble with the IRFU for non-playing reasons. He got in hot water because of his 'excessive' expense claims.

M.A. English, Esq.,   8th January, 1958
"Rosehill,"
O'Callaghan Strand,
LIMERICK

Dear English,

Your letter of the 7th inst. received confirming acceptance as travelling reserve for our Game against Australia. I note that you will let me know, in the course of the next few days, if you require the 2 East Stand Tickets, I further note that your size in boots is 9.

I am returning your slip for expenses in connection with the Trial Match as I believe you inadvertently charged £3. 10s. 6d. for your rail fare Limerick/Dublin return when a 2 day return i.e. Friday/Saturday is £2. 17s. 7d. Will you kindly amend and return when cheque will be forwarded to you.

Congratulations on your excellent Game last Saturday.

Yours sincerely,

R.W. Jeffares
Secretary.

Which Irish out-half impressed him the most?

'It has to be Ollie Campbell. He's as close to perfection as you get. He had it all – a superb tactical brain, wonderful place kicking, great tackling ability, an outstanding team player and his kicking for touch was first class. In my view a close second was my good friend Barry McGann who was an extremely accomplished tactical player.'

In 1962 English moved to Dublin and joined Lansdowne chiefly through the influence of the late Gordon Wood and Paddy Berkery. He has a unique record with the club. After winning a cup medal in 1965, he played on all teams right down to 3rd Ds.

'My last match was for Lansdowne 3rd Bs in Maynooth in 1977, at the age of 44! The field was a converted Gaelic pitch and surrounded with barbed wire to keep the sheep away. After the game I gashed my leg on the barbed wire and ended up in hospital for anti-tetanus injections – not the finale I would have wished for!'

5

CIARAN FITZGERALD

Captain's Log

Success comes before work only in the dictionary.

John Virgo

The beauty of television coverage of sport is that it can occasionally capture an image which offers a telling insight into a sporting hero. For the Irish rugby fan an enduring image will always be Ciaran Fitzgerald's efforts to rally the Irish team as they appeared to be letting the Triple Crown slip from their fingers, in 1985, against England in the wake of their dazzling and stylish victories away to Scotland and Wales. Even those who had no experience of lip-reading could clearly make out his plea from the heart (as he temporarily put aside the good habits he acquired as an altar boy with the Carmelites in Loughrea). 'Where's

your pride? Where's your f***ing pride?' His record speaks for itself –
Triple Crown and Championship in 1982, a share of the Championship
in 1983 and the Triple Crown again in 1985. Fitzgerald, though, was a
rugby virgin until his late teens.

'As a boy growing up in Loughrea the only social outlet available was
the boxing club. I won two All-Ireland boxing championships. My
heroes at the time, though, were the Galway football team who won the
three-in-a-row in 1964, 1965 and 1966, and I attended all three finals.
At Garbally my main game was hurling. The highlight of my hurling
career was playing in an All-Ireland minor final against Cork in 1970.
Our team had been together from the under-14 stage and featured
people like Sean Silke and Iggy Clarke. Initially I played at half-back but
for some reason for one match they moved me to the forwards and I
scored three goals. The problem was that when I played at full-forward
in that All-Ireland final I was marked by Martin Doherty who
subsequently made it big with the Cork senior team. Big was the word
for Martin. I would have needed a step-ladder to have competed with
him in the air! I was moved out to centre-forward but who followed me?
Only Martin. He destroyed me. That Galway minor team went on to
win an Under-21 All-Ireland and most of them formed the backbone of
the senior All-Ireland winning team in 1980. After I left school, though,
rugby became my main game.

'It was not until my final year in Garbally that I became a rugby
player. The previous year we had qualified for the All-Ireland colleges
hurling semi-final, losing to St Peter's, Wexford. In my Leaving Cert
year, though, we went out of the competition early so I had time on my
hands. The school was stuck for a hooker and felt I looked the part. At
the time we did not take part in any competitions. The local bishop felt
that the rugby ethos was a corrupting influence on our Catholic
sensibilities. We just played friendlies. My first game was against
Blackrock College. I remember spending the journey to Dublin on the
back of the bus reading the rule book because I was still a rugby novice.
I couldn't figure out this off-side law.

'After I left school I joined the cadets. We played in the Leinster
towns Cup for a season. In my first match I made the fatal mistake of
winning two balls against the head. The next thing I knew I was being
carried off. I quickly learned how to survive in the rugby jungle. I did
my degree in Galway where I played for UCG in the Connacht League
and quickly found myself playing for Connacht against Ulster. We had
an all ex-Garbally front five, my front-row colleagues were Ray and
Fedhlim McLoughlin, with Mick Molloy and Leo Galvin in the second

row. I was up against the great Ken Kennedy. It went well for me and I found myself in the Irish squad taking part in squad sessions which, as you can imagine, was a great thrill especially because I was literally just out of my teens.

'When my university days finished I joined St Mary's in 1973 because I enjoyed their style of play. This caused me some problems. My superior in the army at the time was a great Monkstown fan. In almost our first conversation I was marched into his office and he said in his most authoritarian style: "You're joining Monkstown aren't you."

'I answered meekly: "No sir I'm not." I subsequently had another interrogation with him on the reasons why I hadn't joined Monkstown.

'My early years with Mary's were a bit of a disaster when I was constantly injured. There wasn't the specialisation in sports injuries then that you get now. Basically, there were three strategies: "Bandage it, rest it or give it up." I was so keen to play that I made things worse for myself because I was returning far too early. I would say, though, that when I did play, Sean Lynch was a great help to me. He was a great man to bind a scrum.'

It was not until 1977 that he got his career back into groove, captaining the Irish B team in the 1977–8 season. Then, on the controversial tour to Australia in 1979, he made his international debut, playing in both Tests although he went out as number two to Pat Whelan.

'At the time there was an incredible fuss about the fact that Tony Ward had been dropped and Ollie Campbell was chosen in his place. I was totally oblivious to it all. I heard my own name mentioned when the team was announced and nothing else registered with me. A tour is a great place to win a first cap because you are sheltered from all the hype, press attention and distractions that you get at home. I was able to hold my place the following season. I never felt threatened but I never felt comfortable. All you can do is perform to your very best and forget about the lads who are challenging for your position.'

In the 1980–1 season Fitzgerald sustained a serious shoulder injury in a club match.

'A bad situation was made worse by a doctor during the match. Immediately after the injury he tried to "yank" my shoulder back into place. Then I was assisted off the pitch. He put me on the flat of my back on the side line and tried a second time. As a result of the injury and the "cure" I missed the entire international season.'

The following season not only did Fitzgerald regain his place on the team but he found himself taking over the captaincy from Fergus Slattery. What was the secret of his success?

'I think I'm very sensitive to people and curious about them. I was still a relatively inexperienced player in comparison with most of my pack. I knew there was no way I could use my army style to deal with these guys. You have to remember there were a lot of world class players in the forwards like Orr, Keane, Slattery, O'Driscoll and Duggan. The previous year Ireland had won no matches and those guys were fed up hearing from people who knew virtually nothing about rugby: "You're only a shower of . . . " That really annoyed them and they were fired up to prove just how good they were.

'Whatever you say to players of that calibre has to be effective. Every player is different. The most important thing is to find out how to bring out the best of each player and find a strategy appropriate to his personality. In 1982, before the decisive Triple Crown match against Scotland, *The Irish Press* wrote a very critical article about John O'Driscoll who was a superb player and central to our success that season. The day before the match I quietly went to him in the Shelbourne Hotel and expressed my sympathy about the article. He knew nothing about it and asked to see it. He read it but said nothing. The next day he played like a man possessed.

'The most difficult players to handle are those making their debuts. They get distracted by the press and the hype. The worst of all though are relatives who want to socialize with them and fill their head with all kinds of nonsense. The best way around this is "the buddy system", that is, to get them to room with one of the more experienced players. At the time the young players looked up to Moss Keane as if he was God. As everybody knows Mossie speaks in a broad Kerry brogue which at the best of times can be difficult to understand but the new players from the north found it virtually impossible. We had a little ritual for those new players.

'I especially remember Trevor Ringland's initiation. We put him beside Moss for dinner and Trevor was in awe of him. We primed Moss to speak for two minutes in fast-forward mode! He was talking pure gibberish. Then he turned to Trevor and asked him what he thought of that. Trevor answered lamely: "I think you're right", not having a clue what Moss had said! Then Moss launched off again only faster. I can still see the panic on Trevor's face. He was going green! All the lads were killing themselves trying to keep a straight face until Trevor found out he was being wound up. The sense of camaraderie was very strong which made my job much easier.

'As captain, no matter what position you play in you can't see everything that is happening on the pitch. You need guys you can quickly turn to in the heat of battle who can read the game and tell what is needed in their area. Fergus Slattery was a great player in those situations. Ollie Campbell, apart from being an outstanding player, had a great rugby brain and I relied on him to control the game for us. His partner at scrum-half, Robbie McGrath, also played a crucial role. He was a very underrated player who never got the acclaim he deserved. Later in his career Hugo MacNeill developed into a very tactically astute performer.

'Our coach, Tom Kiernan, was always two moves ahead of you. I often heard myself saying things which I would later get a flashback and see that Tom had discreetly planted the thought in my mind either the previous day or a week earlier. He was a great man manager. He was always prompting you. He wanted the ideas to come from the players themselves because they took more responsibility for their own decisions. Tom was not called "The Grey Fox" for nothing. I wanted the players to do more physical work but Tom always subjected everything to a cost benefit analysis and asked: "Was it worth it?" He always said that what exhausted players was not training sessions but constantly travelling up and down to Dublin. P.J. Dwyer, as chairman of selectors, was also somebody who was a great prompter of ideas.

'My clearest memory of 1982 was when Gareth Davies limped off in the Welsh game. We could see it in their eyes that they knew we were going to beat them. The England game really established that we were a side to be reckoned with. I remember travelling on the bus back to the hotel. When everybody else was ecstatic, Willie Duggan was sitting at the back of the bus working out the practicalities of what was needed for a Triple Crown decider in terms of extra tickets for players and so on. There were a lot of myths about Willie and Moss Keane at the time in terms of drinking and lack of training. That's rubbish. I was living beside Moss at the time and was training every other night with him. I'm not exaggerating one bit when I say I was going flat out just to keep up with him.

'Moss's contribution was crucial on many levels, in my view not least of which was in telling Ginger McLoughlin: "I'm not going back." I know this is very technical but basically, to put it as simply as I can, if the prop-forward retreats the second row normally has to as well, otherwise the prop's back is arched up. Ginger knew that this would be his fate if he didn't hold his line which meant that he went in there fighting like a tiger. It's things like that which make the difference between victory and defeat and only someone of Moss's stature could have pulled it off.

'I believe we should also have won the Triple Crown in 1983. We should have beaten Wales but we lacked discipline. The French match was like World War Four. World War Three was the previous year. Both sides had a lot of physical scores to settle in the first ten minutes of the game.'

The year 1983 also saw Fitzgerald selected as captain of the Lions.

'It was like a whirlwind. I first heard about the captaincy when I got a call from a journalist. I was very surprised to hear the news because the strong rumour, coming from the English press, was that Peter Wheeler was getting the job. It was a tremendous honour and I didn't give a tuppenny damn about who was disappointed. There was so much media hype it was hard to focus. It was like getting a first cap multiplied by ten with all the receptions and media interest. I had to take ten days off in Mayo to regain my focus and kept in shape by training three times a day.

'I underestimated the ferocity of the campaign that would be waged against me. I couldn't influence what was said about me so I just tried to do all I could to get the best possible performance out of the team. It's part of the psychological war that goes on when the Lions tour New Zealand that both media "talk up" their respective squads. In New Zealand, though, they were stunned to see that the British media were trying to outdo each other in terms of rubbishing me. By the time we arrived everybody wanted to know: who is this fool of a hooker? It got to the stage where I expected the first question of every interview to be: "What kind of ape are you?" I was amazed that the New Zealanders knew everything about me. It shows how fanatical they are about the game. Gradually they discovered that in my case what you see is what you get and they largely turned on my side so we ended up with a bizarre situation of the British press against me and the Irish press and sections of the home press for me.

'The tour was a roller-coaster for me. As captain I was asked to attend all kinds of receptions and press events which I was determined to do because the PR aspect is so important. The result, though, was that I never got a day off and couldn't get away from the press. There was one day, though, I was determined to get away for a break. The Irish guys had arranged a game of golf so I decided to join them. We pulled a fast one by having our team car parked outside the front of the hotel as a decoy but arranged to have a car pick us up and discreetly whisk us away. I'm not a golfer but was just managing to relax at last at the fourth hole when I heard a rumpus behind me. It was the media scrum!

'The press have to fill their columns. There were all kinds of stories about splits in the camp which were absolutely untrue. There was a story about fights on the team bus which was a blatant lie. At the end the English players threw some of their journalists into the swimming pool they were so disgusted by the untruths. As a result of all that was written about me I developed a very tough skin. You are judged by your results and at the end of the day we didn't win our matches, which was a huge disappointment for me. I think we could have won the first Test which would have changed the shape of the tour. I have to take part of the blame for that defeat because my throw-ins were poor. The only consolation for me was that the squad stuck together throughout which is not easy when you are losing.'

After the Lions tour Fitzgerald's misfortunes accelerated when he was dropped from the Irish team for the English game after the defeat to Wales in 1984. Was he a fall guy for Ireland's slide?

'I don't know why I was dropped. Nobody ever told me. Maybe I deserved to be axed. The one beef I had was the way the whole thing was handled. It was said that I was not available for selection because of injury but in fact I played for Mary's that day. I wish they had been straight about it and said I was dropped. The one thing, though, was that I was determined I would come back and play for Ireland in 1985, though I had no thoughts about the captaincy.

'When Mick Doyle took over in 1984 he brought me back as captain. Doyler made an enormous contribution to our Triple Crown win. He won the psychological war in terms of keeping all the media attention on him and away from the players. He was the crown prince making edicts but was also very tactically astute. His chairman of selectors, Mick Cuddy, was a peculiar character. He was an insider in the IRFU but got on exceptionally well with Doyler and the players. His great gift was that he got things done. If we wanted new gear he made the phone calls and got it for us. For my part I got on exceptionally well with Doyler. Ours was much stronger than a rugby relationship. There was a deep friendship between us and we complemented each other in lots of ways.

'I would say, though, Doyler's contribution was not nearly as positive the following season. There were some crazy selection decisions, for example dropping Phil Orr was madness. Doyler's focus was not as clear. I'm not sure why that was but I felt his heart wasn't in it as much. Having said that, I was not as focused myself because I had left the army and taken on a new challenging job with James Crean.'

In the end, business commitments led to Fitzgerald's premature retirement, forcing him reluctantly to forego the opportunity to play in the inaugural World Cup, but he was back at the heart of the action as coach to the Irish team in 1991.

'If I had the chance to do it differently I would in terms of my time as coach. I was reluctant to take the position but the IRFU pressed me. There was a good buzz early on in that we brought in a lot of new players and we played an exciting, expansive game. Although we played an attractive brand of rugby we were always nearly winning. That's not good enough. Eventually you have to win otherwise morale and confidence start to sap. The tour to New Zealand in 1992 was a bit of a disaster. We faced an impossible task because so many key players were unable to travel. For business reasons I shouldn't have travelled but out of loyalty I went because there were so many defections. We made a superhuman effort and again nearly won the first Test but it was downhill all the way after that. Later that year I had to step down for business reasons. It was not the ideal time to go because I would have liked to go out on a winning note.'

For the first time there is a note of reticence in Fitzgerald's voice when asked about the difficulties of balancing his rugby and other duties as Irish coach.

'The job of Irish coach is a full-time one. There was a cost to me in business terms. I'm not prepared to elaborate. Likewise there was a cost in terms of family life.'

Fitzgerald continues to play a significant role in Irish rugby as coach of St Mary's and as media analyst.

'The one thing I've learned is that there is no shortage of experts out there who have instant solutions for all the ills of Irish rugby, and who have no qualms about giving me the benefit of their wisdom. At one stage of my army career I worked with Paddy Hillary when he was president. He always said: "There's only one of you. There's hundreds of them." I've found that a nod and smile covers a multitude and gets me off the hook.'

6

KEVIN FLYNN

Centre of Excellence

In my time I've had my knee put out, broken my collar-bone, had
my nose smashed, a rib broken, lost a few teeth, and cracked my
ankle, but as soon as I get a bit of bad luck I'm going to quit the
game.

J.W. Robinson

It is said that when a prominent ex-Irish international, who shall remain
nameless because of the libel laws, dies, the presiding clergyman will
have to break with liturgical convention. Such is his liking for publicity
that instead of saying: 'May perpetual light shine upon him', the vicar
will probably say: 'May perpetual limelight shine upon him.' In the
modesty stakes at the opposite end of the spectrum is former Irish
centre Kevin Flynn. He shows the same discomfort with generous
compliments that Mother Theresa would be expected to show in a
brothel.

'Flynner' was capped 18 times in the centre for Ireland, initially
between 1959 and 1966. After a gap of six years his good form in
Leinster's win in the interprovincial championship catapulted him back
into the Irish side. He was capped a further four times in the 1972 and
1973 seasons, becoming part of an élite group of Irish players to play in
three different decades, the others being Syd Millar and Tony O'Reilly.
A product of Waterford and Kilkenny parents, he did not come from a
rugby background.

'My father took me to Lansdowne Road to see Ireland play when I
was seven. My hero was Louis Jones, the great Welsh winger. It was my
school, Terenure College, which has to take the credit for my

development as a rugby player, especially Fr Grace and Mick Pender who were great influences on me. After I left school I played for Terenure College Past for a year and then moved on to Wanderers, and in my first year there won my first cap when I was 19. The great Ronnie Kavanagh was a huge influence on me. Although I played in the final trial, and there was a good bit of talk about me knocking at the door, my international call-up came as a surprise to me.

'Of the match itself I particularly remember the Lansdowne Road roar. You hear about that but you have to really experience it first-hand to appreciate how special it is. The whole thing had a dreamlike quality. The thought flashed across my mind: "What am I doing here?" I probably remember more about that game than any other. Everything went well for me personally and for the side and we won 14–9. It was a dream debut. I made a break which set up a try for Niall Brophy.

'As the game went on my confidence grew and we were on top but nobody would pass the ball to me. I kept shouting for the ball to Mick English. Eventually he turned to me and told me in no uncertain terms to "f*** off" and that there was no way he was going to pass the ball to me. It was nothing personal but he was not going to take the chance of losing possession.

'Mick tells a good story in the same vein about Mick Doyle. Doyler was playing his first match for Munster in the centre and English was the out-half. They were playing Connacht during a downpour. Mick himself describes the conditions more colourfully. Munster were on top all through the game and English was kicking everything. Doyler was going mad for a pass and eventually Mick gave him one but his new centre dropped it and Connacht broke right up to the other end of the field. Mick screamed out: "Doyler, that's the last f***ing time I'm passing to you until you can drop it further than I can kick it!"

'I was to pay a price for my success on my debut because the following year my immediate opponent, who had a very unhappy afternoon against me, laid me out in an off-the-ball incident. Players were not sent off in those days for thuggery as they are today.

'There was a postscript to the match that I hadn't expected. A week or so after, I got a bill from the Union for sixpence for a phone-call I made to my family after the match!

'The approach then was very amateurish. It was almost naïve in terms of warm-up. In fact I can't even remember if we had one at all. Walking into the dressing-room was a big culture shock. It was like having an apparition. Here were all the great players that I had almost worshipped from afar and what were they doing but covering themselves in layers of strapping.

'I came on the scene for the last game of the season which meant I was too late for consideration for a place on the Lions tour. Hamstring injuries restricted my appearances for Ireland.'

These injuries made it difficult for Flynn to feel he was a settled international but simply being in the company of so many great players was a very enriching experience for him.

'There were many great characters on the team, like Gordon Wood who was very vociferous. And of course there was A.J.F. O'Reilly who was a class player and had an aura about him. What people forget, though, was he was a bit like Simon Geoghegan: he seldom got the ball. Tony played many matches for Ireland when he never got a pass. With the ball in his hands, though, he was a sight to behold but he was not above passing the buck! In the early days you didn't have the organised defences you have now. Normally it was man-to-man marking. You took up your opposite number. In my first game against France one of their wingers, who was O'Reilly's opposite number, came through like a rocket between David Hewitt and myself and scored a try. O'Reilly came up to me afterwards and said: "He was your man!" I was lucky in that my partner in the centre, David Hewitt, was an exceptional player and had great pace.'

Hewitt was capped 18 times for Ireland between 1958 and 1965 and toured with the Lions in 1959 to Australia and New Zealand and to South Africa in 1962.

One victory had special significance for Flynn. Crushing victories over England in great matches are not a commonplace occurrence for the Irish rugby team. There are certain famous exceptions – notably a 22–0 victory in 1947 and an 18–5 win in 1964 – a match memorable for the magical "criss-cross" try when Mike Gibson ran from his own twenty-five diagonally left, transferred to the late Jerry Walsh, who ran crossfield to the right before in turn passing it to Pat Casey who scored underneath the posts.

'The most satisfying win was against England in 1964 when we ended a 16-year losing sequence at Twickenham. We hockeyed them by playing a running game and so did they.'

Flynn neglects to mention that he scored two tries himself on that occasion.

'Another clear memory for me is that in 1962 our game against Wales was postponed due to the outbreak of foot-and-mouth disease. Up to that time Irish sides concentrated on frustrating the opposition by preventing them from playing their game, though it was more subtle than the boot, bite and bollock approach. When you think about it we were normally up against bigger, more powerful sides but we coped with them because we always had some very intelligent players. Later, we introduced more sophisticated ploys like calling our passes. To fool the opposition we would call short which really meant long.

'Ray McLoughlin brought a new dimension to the job of captain – almost bringing in a coaching style. He was perhaps the first of the deep thinkers of the game. It was the first time we seriously discussed the game in advance and tactics came into it. He decided that initially we had to be defensive. There was a fair amount of analysis of the opposition and closing down players – Jack Charlton style.

'The regret of my career is that we never won a Triple Crown. We should have won one but let a victory against Wales slip through our fingers by missing our kicks.'

Of his five international tries he is best remembered for his grandstand score against England in Twickenham in 1972. Ireland trailed 12–7 when Barry McGann dropped a goal. Then, when everyone thought the final whistle was about to be blown, from an Irish scrum close to the English twenty-five Johnny Moloney fed McGann, who passed to Flynn, and the evergreen centre, like a prisoner suddenly bursting the confining bonds of a strait-jacket, cut through the English defence like a knife through butter for a superb try. To add salt to the English wounds, Tom Kiernan added the conversion and Ireland won 16–12.

'After having been off the team for a number of years my comeback in 1972 was against France. I went into the game with a slight calf injury and did not play with the confidence I normally had. I was a lot less ring rusty for the England game. We had great players in the side at the time. Although best known as a kicker Barry McGann was one of the great passing out-halves. He could put a ball on your belly button.'

He singles out two trends of the modern game which particularly disappoint him.

'I really dislike the highly personalised campaigns that some of the commentators in our media have resorted to. They seem to have forgotten down through the years that up to now our players were amateurs. The other thing that I regret is that rugby has become a very serious game. A lot of the fun has gone out of it. I'm worried that professionalism will accelerate this trend.'

Although Triple Crown success eluded him on the field, Flynn had the distinction of being chairman of the selectors of the 1982 Triple

Crown-winning side. The way he celebrated the historic victory speaks volumes about the man.

'I waited until things settled down and everybody had left the dressing-room and then I drove home and went for a walk.'

What is the secret of being a successful selector?

'One of the tricks of being a selector is not to pin-point the game when a player hasn't got what it takes at international level any more, but in knowing in the game immediately before the match when he shows he hasn't got it any more.'

7

SIMON GEOGHEGAN

The Winger Takes It All

There he stood, poor little chappie,
Looking lonely and unhappy . . .
When a thousand voices screamed a startled 'Oh!'
I looked up. A try or something?
Then sat gaping like a dumb thing.
My children, somebody has passed to Lowe.

P.G. Wodehouse
(who was so shocked when England's winger Cyril Lowe
actually got a pass that he wrote this poem).

Naas Botha was one of the most prodigious goalkickers of all time but attracted a lot of controversy in South Africa because of his apparent reluctance to pass the ball. After he kicked his club side's 24 points to give them victory in the Cup final he was sitting beside another man on the plane. Botha was a bit surprised that his companion said nothing to him. After half an hour of total silence he turned around and said: 'I don't think you realise who I am, I'm probably the most famous rugby player in South Africa.'

His companion quietly said: 'I don't think you realise who I am. I play for your team. I'm your first centre!'

Simon Geoghegan would have readily understood that centre's frustration because he has spent much of his international career waiting for a pass. Indeed, it is surprising that he never got the nickname Cinderella because it often seemed nobody wanted to take him to the ball. David Campese once remarked: 'The only thing you're ever likely to get at the end of an English backline is chillblains.' Geoghegan again would have empathised with this scenario.

At the end of a weekend squad session on a Sunday afternoon at Lansdowne Road, Terry Kingston is the butt of jokes about Plan A and Plan B. Asked to explain what that meant in the course of a television interview Kingston explained that Plan A was for the Irish side to kick the ball high at the opposition and chase after it.

'And Plan B?' asked Fred Cogley.

'Plan B calls for us to kick it even higher!'

It is Geoghegan, though, who is the main target of the handful of young autograph hunters. Even at a training session they are treated to another piece of magic from the Irish player born and bred in England. Why does he play rugby for Ireland?

'My father is from Killimor, County Galway, a great hurling area, and growing up I spent most of my summer holidays there so I got a great love for places like Ballinasloe and all the Galway area. Because of that I always had a sense of being Irish.'

Despite his talent and speed there was a potential cloud on the horizon which could have threatened his rugby career.

'When I was 15 or 16 I discovered I had a condition known as "exercise-induced asthma". It is different from conventional asthma in that, as its name suggests, it is brought on by strenuous activity. With medication though I can cope and it doesn't inhibit me at all, really. My only problem if you want to call it that is that I don't have a great lung capacity.'

As a teenager he smoked 20 cigarettes a day, does that contribute to his problem?

'I was surprised to discover that it was not a significant factor. It's really all down to the asthma. Mind you, Willie Duggan used to run on with a packet of fags in his pocket and cadge a light from somebody in the crowd, but it didn't seem to do him any harm!'

Did he have a misspent youth? He laughs, but quickly his tone changes to that of a man who knows exactly where he is going in life.

'Well, in boarding school I was doing a lot of things I shouldn't be doing and while I was doing okay on the rugby field I wasn't going as well as I should have. I decided it was going to be all or nothing so the cigarettes went and the serious drinking went and, thankfully, I started to make my mark with London Irish, and in 1991 I won my first cap from Ireland and fortunately I think I developed a good rapport with the crowd at Lansdowne Road since.'

Great tries that season against Wales and England established the Baker Street resident as the rising star of Irish rugby. However, the following season, as Ireland lost every game, he got no chance to impress. Things went from bad to worse the following season – when he hoped to make the Lions tour to New Zealand. His ability as a defender was not just questioned it was derided – particularly after Derek Stark scored a soft try on him in Murrayfield.

'Yes, 1993 was a bad season for me. My club form was poor and that probably affected my confidence when playing for Ireland.'

His problems at the time were not just on the field. He was temporarily suspended from the Irish squad. What prompted this exclusion?

'I'm not the most diplomatic person in the world. When I give my opinion I tend not to mince my words. I was unhappy with the way the team was playing and the fact that I was getting so few opportunities, and I made my views known in a public way – but that's all water under the bridge now.'

A prominent rugby journalist openly questioned his commitment to the Irish team because of an incident in which he threw his Irish jersey on the ground. Did this type of criticism hurt him?

'Not in the least. Anybody who knows me knows of my commitment to Ireland and judge me by what I do when I am wearing my green jersey on the pitch, not by what I do with it in the dressing-room.'

Geoghegan's performance has not always been enhanced by his Irish team-mates. He was rooming with Neil Francis the night before the Fiji game in November 1995, Murray Kidd's first outing as team coach. Francis got thirsty during the night and disposed of a glass of water in the bathroom. The next morning when Geoghegan went to retrieve his contact lenses he discovered that Francis had unwittingly drunk them and the glass of water.

It is no coincidence that Ireland's best performances in recent years have coincided with the best of the flying winger. Mick Doyle is not a man to lavish praise on the Irish team with wanton abandon, so when he describes an Irish victory as an 'eighty minute orgasm' one has to sit up and take notice. The performance which prompted this vintage 'Doylerism' was Ireland's 17–3 victory over England.

In a team performance, in which all the boys in green were heroes, it is difficult to single out one player for special attention in the 1993 win, but Mick Galwey, 'Gaillimh', would have to come under that category. Six weeks before that match he lay in a Dublin hospital with his neck in a brace and his rugby future was shrouded in uncertainty. At one point he was even told that his playing career was history. A shadow on his X-ray cast an ominous cloud on his prospects. For four fear-filled days he waited for the all-clear. Then it was out of hospital onto the training field. A week later he played for Ireland against France – a game which offered promise of better things following total embarrassment in Murrayfield.

The next match saw Ireland, with Eric Ellwood making a hugely impressive debut, overcome the Welsh in Cardiff. However, it was the victory, and more particularly the manner of the victory against England which confirmed that Irish rugby was on an upward curve. The win was sealed with Mick Galwey scoring a fine try – helping him to secure a place on the Lions' squad with Nick Popplewell. For Geoghegan, though, it was a turning point because he had retained his best form. The tragedy was that it was too late for him to claim a place on the Lions tour. When injury struck it was his partner on the wing, Richard Wallace, and not the golden boy of Irish rugby, who got the call to go south.

Still basking in the glory of their win over the All Blacks, the English expected to extract retribution in 1994 in Twickenham, but a splendid try from Geoghegan helped Ireland to secure another shock win – this time on a score of 13–12.

The same year saw Geoghegan departing from his club, London Irish, for the spa town of Bath. The area around Gloucester, Bath and Bristol is a hotbed of English rugby. Bath's status in English rugby during the 1990s is comparable to that of the great Kerry team of the 1970s and early 1980s. This is largely due to the work of one man, current English manager Jack Rowell, who transformed Bath from a team of virtual no-hopers into the cream of the crop.

Rowell is renowned for his straight talking. He once described the former England prop, Gareth Chilcott, as 'green around the gills and a stranger to the lavatory'. He was also a hard taskmaster. Shortly after Chilcott got married, Rowell called his wife into the office and instructed her there was to be no lovemaking before the Pilkington Cup final and handed her a bottle of sleeping tablets to ensure that her husband had a quiet night. 'How many is he to take?' she asked. 'They're not for Gareth. They're for you,' he replied.

Rowell also thought big. Although Geoghegan was a big name acquisition, Rowell had earlier tried to bring David Campese to Bath from Milan. He got somebody to investigate how much it would cost to get Campese to sign on. When he heard the figure £200,000 he gulped but immediately did his sums and speculated that over three years it worked out at £67,000 per annum, which might just be possible. The plan was abruptly shelved when Rowell was told that Campo's contract with Milan was not for three years but for five months!

Bath is not a club for the hyper-sensitive. Jon Callard is nicknamed 'Zanussi' because his colleagues claim his head is the shape of a microwave. Geoghegan was also stepping into a very commercially advanced environment. One incident illustrates this and provides an interesting metaphor for the changing face of rugby. Steve Ojomoh picked up a nasty injury in training. Bath's team secretary informed his team-mates that Ojomoh had received a detached retina. This prompted his international colleague Victor Ubogu to say: 'I'm not happy about that. I've been here much longer than him and I'm still living in a club flat.'

Joining Bath was a move Geoghegan entered into with his eyes open.

'I knew I was taking a risk. There was no guarantee that I would get my place on the team. Reputations mean nothing at Bath. You either perform to the highest level or you're off the team. That's not a problem for me. In fact it's the reverse. I knew that if I joined Bath I would be playing consistently at a higher standard. Basically, I had the confidence in my own ability to believe I could hold my own at the highest level but believe me the work ethic is very strong in the club.'

One story which typifies the pressures on Bath's players concerns Jim Waterman. His son was doing his biology homework and asked his seemingly perpetually exhausted father if he knew what a condom was. Waterman's answer was: 'Of course I do, I've bloody well been carrying one around in my wallet for months!'

8

JIM GLENNON

Urbi et Orbi

Playing in the second row doesn't require a lot of intelligence
really. You have to be bloody crazy to play there for a start.

Bill Beaumont

Ireland has produced many players who were noted for their
commitment to the green jersey. In this category are people like Jack
MacCaulay. He was said to be the first married man to be capped in
international rugby in 1887 – according to rugby folklore he got wed
just to get leave of absence to play for Ireland! Also in this grouping
was Jim Glennon who always gave 150 per cent. Although he is not an
arrogant person he does make one proud boast: 'Nobody used his arse
better in the line-out than Jim Glennon did!' Glennon was never a
great line-out winner but was very hard to get line-out ball from. He
formed a very effective second-row partnership with George Wallace
for Leinster. They were christened 'Urbi et Orbi' by Mick Doyle.

On the Tuesday evening after Ireland's disappointing defeat to
Scotland in the opening game of the 1996 Five Nations
Championship, Glennon reflects on his playing career in a Dublin
hotel. The previous day he had been chosen as the Philips Manager of
the Month for his work with Leinster – guiding them to the
interprovincial championship and to the European Cup semi-final.
Although working hours are over, Glennon receives a steady stream of
phone calls on his mobile in connection with his work in the complex
world of medical defence – protecting doctors against litigation from
patients. A noteworthy caller is Irish team manager Pat Whelan
requesting him to defer selecting the Leinster team to play the touring

New South Wales side until he gets a chance to speak to him at greater length.

Glennon started his rugby career as a hooker at school in Roscrea because he had the physique for it, but after an explosive growth spurt he switched to the second row. His uncle, Pat McGowan of UCD, got a final trial in the 1920s and his cousins, Joe and Kevin McGowan, both were selected for final trials in the 1960s. His late father was a stalwart of the Skerries club. Glennon gave Skerries a new status when he became an Irish international during the 1980s.

He was fortunate to be in the right place at the right time. In 1962 a strong Under-14 side came through and were carefully nurtured all the way to senior level. Although he was five years behind them, Glennon fitted snugly into that team in his late teens. By the time he was 21 he had won four Towns Cups. Any one of these players could have left Skerries to go and play for a senior club, but they had an unspoken rule that no one defected because if one went more would follow. Uniquely in Dublin under-age rugby was developed in Skerries outside the school environment. In 1974 the club received another boost when former Irish captain and Lion, Bill Mulcahy, began coaching the side. Glennon was the first captain when the club went senior in 1975–6 and was capped for Leinster in 1976.

Strangely, Glennon's memories of being capped for Ireland are not as happy as his memories of playing for Leinster.

'Tragedy struck the club just after I won my second cap in 1980, when one of our players in Skerries, Bernard Healy, got a bad neck injury which devastated the club. In 1987 I broke A.J.F. O'Reilly's record for the longest gap between internationals, when I got my third cap. But by the weirdest of coincidences the joy of being recalled for me was shattered when another club-mate, Alan Boylan, sustained a serious neck injury on the eve of the game.'

Rugby tours have a number of striking similarities with a religious pilgrimage, such as uniformity in dress codes, the chanting of familiar songs and a feeling of community and fellowship throughout. The analogy does not hold true for the Wasps tour to Malaysia in 1992 when some of the tourists bared their posteriors for the world to see. Not surprisingly, in a Muslim country this cheeky behaviour caused outrage and the offenders were severely fined and deported. In 1980, the year Jimmy Carter had arranged a boycott of the Moscow Olympics because of Russia's invasion of Afghanistan, Glennon toured Romania with Leinster, under Mick Doyle and Mick 'the Cud' Cuddy, for an eventful tour.

'A vivid memory for me is of going to see Romania play Russia with Phil Orr and George Wallace. The Russians were staying in the same hotel as us but on a different floor. That night the three of us met up with the Russian captain and we invited him and his colleagues up to our room for a jar. We had stared disaster in the face earlier when we discovered that there was only one bottle of whiskey in the hotel! Worse still, that bottle was in the Cud's room and not intended for public consumption. The Cud was annoyed, to put it mildly, when he discovered it missing. He had to be restrained by Doyler. Usually it worked the other way around.

'We had a great night conversing with the Russians in French and exchanging razors for Moscow Olympic badges! The next morning the manager of the Russian team came into the lobby and asked to speak to "the leader of the Irish delegation" and invited Leinster to tour in Russia. It was a pretty strange spectacle because the Russians had KGB types following them everywhere watching their every move. I thought this invitation might provide the key to our rapprochement with the Cud so I headed in before the Russian delegation to explain the situation. The Cud was not impressed. He said: "Look Glennon, would you ever bleep off and tell them Russians to bleep off and while you're at it tell them to bleep off out of Afghanistan as well!"'

Glennon was involved in Mick Doyle's first and last representative games as coach; in 1979 when Leinster played Cheshire and in 1987 when Ireland played Australia respectively. He lays claim to an unusual distinction – he once saw Doyle speechless.

'After his heart-attack during the 1987 World Cup, Doyler rejoined us after a ten day stay in hospital. We were staying in a motel-type place. A few of the lads, known on the tour as the "amigos" were out late one night and sneaking furtively in. There was an uncarpeted stair outside Doyler's room and he was woken up by the activity. He recognised one of the voices. The next day the culprit was given a right ticking off in front of the whole squad. As Doyler delivered his attack the player in question stood and listened but when the coach had finished the bad boy said: "Jaysus, Doyler, there's none so pure as a converted hoor." Doyler was left too stunned to speak.'

There was some suggestion that Doyler must have added to some of the stories in his autobiography. Is this a fair perception?

'I don't think so. My feeling would be that they were probably slightly understated!'

After winning two caps for Ireland in 1980 he spent seven years in the international wilderness. He came out of retirement to win his final four caps.

'I had genuinely given it up in 1986. On 31 August that year I returned from holidays in Kerry. The previous night I had been out with my wife, Helen, and sister-in-law, Aileen. Aileen is married to the former Meath footballer Brendan Murray. Brendan and I were having a great chat with the hotel owner about sport. At one stage Brendan went to the loo and I told our host who Brendan was. A while later I went to the toilet and Brendan told him my history. When I returned the barman asked me how many caps I had won. I said: "Three, two in 1980 and one in 1987." No doubt I would have forgotten about that pledge but when we got home Phil Orr and his wife called to see us. Phil bet me a tenner that I wouldn't play for Leinster that season. A weighing scales was produced and I was the wrong side of twenty stone. I later learned that Phil's approach had been semi-organised because Roly Meates, who was coaching Leinster at the time, was looking for an extra bit of power in the scrum. I can tell you it wasn't for my line-out ability! The season with Leinster went really well and I found myself back in the Irish team and flying off to the World Cup.'

Glennon's impact on rugby management at the highest level was more spectacular and immediate than on the playing field. Does he have ambitions to manage Ireland?

'At the moment I have three ambitions: to retain Leinster's position at the forefront of Irish provincial rugby; to make a game with Leinster in Dublin a must for any touring team from a playing point of view rather than the social; and to win a European Cup with Leinster. I have no burning ambition to manage Ireland. The responsibilities that go with the position and the media pressures are huge, particularly for someone with a young family. As a player I knew if I was part of a winning Leinster team I had a chance of being capped for Ireland. Now in management I know that if I'm in charge of a winning Leinster team other opportunities will arise.'

Asked about the greatest character he played with he does not hesitate for a second.

'Phil O'Callaghan. I toured with Philo to Zambia in 1977 with Clontarf. The previous November I had won my first cap for Leinster. I injured my knee in the last few minutes and was replaced by Jim Bardon of Clontarf for his first cap. At the time I was one of the organisers of an annual beach game in Skerries to raise money for the lifeboats institution. I invited Jim to play the following year but we collided in the game and he dislocated his shoulder. He was due to tour

Zambia with Clontarf shortly after but his injury meant he couldn't travel, so Clontarf invited me to take his place. I then learned that Philo was also to be a guest of the club on the tour and was expected to be the entertainment content. Let's say he didn't disappoint! Everybody knows that Philo was one of the great characters of Irish rugby but what people sometimes forget is that, even then, he was a superb player. We had a fantastic tour and I was billeted out for five days in the bush with Philo. We were staying with a former Scottish international and Lion, Peter Stagg, who had a massive ranch. Staggy was 6 foot 10 inches. I learned more about touring in those five days with Philo than I learned in the remainder of my career – though I'm not prepared to elaborate!'

Even after his retirement Glennon, to his own surprise, continued to grace the world's playing fields.

'When I finished playing in 1988 I got the most unexpected invitations to tour, as the Golden Oldies idea was really taking off. I got a phone call from Moss Keane in June of that year inquiring if I was free for the last weekend in August. When I said I was he told me to keep it free. I forgot all about it until the last Wednesday in August when I got another call from Moss. He told me that he had been invited to play in an exhibition match across the water for a Lions' Golden Oldies side against a junior team and, although he had been given the plane ticket, was unable to travel. He was going to ring the organiser and tell him he couldn't make it but that he would be meeting me later that day and would attempt to persuade me to travel. Shortly afterwards I got a phone call from a panic-stricken secretary, apologising profusely for the short notice, but wondering would I be willing to play instead of Moss. I "reluctantly" agreed. On the plane over I was joined by Phil Orr, Willie Duggan and Fergus Slattery. It was a fabulous weekend. I was the only "non-Lion" on the team. We won 74–22 with Phil Bennett scoring 36 points, including a try that saw him running the whole length of the field. My partner in the second row was Alan Martin of Wales. After the match we were chatting in the bath when he asked me out of the blue: "What about Stockholm?" He went on to explain that there was a Golden Oldies match there the following weekend, Thursday to Monday, but he couldn't travel. Would I be interested? When I said yes, he told me just to leave it with him. On the Monday I rang Moss to thank him for the wonderful weekend. When I asked him why he had left it so late to tell them he couldn't make it he answered: "Because I didn't want some hoor from England to take my place."

'That Wednesday I got a phone call from a different panic-stricken secretary, apologising profusely for the short notice, but wondering would I be willing to play instead of Alan. This time I made him sweat a bit more and told him I wasn't sure if I would be able to make it because I had other commitments, but I rang him back less than an hour later and agreed to the trip. On the plane over I was again joined by Orr, Duggan and Slattery. Also on the trip were J.P.R. Williams and Jim Renwick, among others. It was an absolutely fabulous weekend. On the Tuesday morning I rang to thank Alan for putting it my way. When I asked him why he had left it so late to tell them he couldn't make it he replied: "Because I didn't want some hoor from England to take my place!"'

9

TOM GRACE

Amazing Grace

The amateur rugby union player has an inalienable right to play like a pillock.

Dick Greenwood

Dublin on a frosty winter's evening. Already some of the larger stars hang like lanterns in the sky, transmitting a magical milky radiance. I am troubled by one image. A drunk, maybe a junkie, is squatting on the steps of an office building, arms across his knees, eyes listless. Occasionally he moves his head from side to side, as if he is following some strange, self-hypnotic inner rhythm. His semi-blackened face, the result of weeks without washing, give his eyes a haunted look. His only blanket is a thin, torn sack.

In marked contrast the offices of Craig Gardener provide a welcome respite for my numb fingers. Although his profession, as a receiver of companies in financial difficulties might not suggest it, former Irish captain Tom Grace is a perfect tonic for drooping spirits. Memory is blurred and softened by time which may explain why his reminiscences of his rugby career are so happy.

'My mother often talks about my introduction to rugby. When I was six years old I was in school at Presentation College, Glasthule, and at lunchtime I was running with the ball in the yard. One of the brothers was watching me and told me afterwards that he wanted me to play for the under-9s the following week. I went home that evening and told my mother that I needed a new pair of football boots, jersey and togs. Needless to say this came as a bit of a shock to my mother. She rang the brother to check out my story. My mother had a toy shop in Dun Laoghaire and the shops were shut for a half-day on Wednesday, which was the day of my debut. While the other 14 players were brought to Presentation College in Bray on the bus and went into the changing-rooms together, I got out of the car in my gear and ran straight onto the pitch. I'm not sure where I was playing or even if I touched the ball but that was the beginning of my rugby career.'

Gracer's rugby career really accelerated when he went to Newbridge College. The highlight of his schools career was reaching the Leinster final against St Mary's in 1966, having defeated the almost invincible Blackrock College team in the semi-final.

'Beating Rock was such a thrill but the match began badly for me. A high ball was sent in which I went for but it bounced off my chest and they ran in for a try, so we were 5–0 down after less than two minutes. Rock were much stronger than us but they tried to win the game individually and we beat them because of our teamwork. The other outstanding memory I have of the game was that all the St Mary's lads were shouting their heads off for us. Mary's had a superb team captained by the great Shay Deering, and with Johnny Moloney in a starring role, they beat us 14–6. Mary's coach, Fr Kennedy, organised a dinner for the winning team and invited us as losers to the game. That gesture stuck in my mind and was probably instrumental in me joining Mary's later in my career.'

The next phase in Grace's career came when he attended university, though he found it difficult at times to see the rationale in decisions about selection: 'Strange things happened in UCD! The classic for me was the case of Joe Comiskey, who is now doctor to the Irish Olympic team. He was picked once, scored three tries and dropped for the next match. The next year he was selected again, scored four tries and was dropped again!

'We had some interesting personalities as captains. In my first year John O'Hagan was captain, who was a very innovative person, and we had a successful year. He believed very strongly that the team should get together on the night before a Cup match. So we had a cup of tea and two Marietta biscuits and he gave us an inspiring speech.

'The next year Peter Sutherland, who went on to big things afterwards on the European stage, was the captain. "Suds" put his own stamp on the captaincy. The night before the Cup matches we met in his house in Monkstown. A walk on Dun Laoghaire pier became part of the ritual. The two Marietta biscuits went out the window. For the first match we had sandwiches, tea, coffee and light drinks. As our Cup run progressed the refreshments became ever more lavish. The night before the semi-final we had a totally fabulous dinner with all kind of delicacies. Then Suds gave his speech. The food was incredibly memorable. The speech wasn't. The next day we lost narrowly . . . 28–3!

'The following year, Derek Scally was captain. He was the first to bring in a coach, former Irish scrum-half Jimmy Kelly. Jimmy produced the most successful UCD side ever. We won the colours match and the Leinster Cup. Eleven of our players made the Leinster side that year. The previous year only Fergus Slattery had made the team.

'Under Shay Deering's captaincy the next season we were beaten in the final. Deero was such a presence. He epitomised somebody who brought 110 per cent to everything he did whether it be singing a song or training. He had a gift which very few people possess. He was a natural leader rather than a follower. You felt ashamed not to be trying your best when you knew he was giving everything. When we trained in UCD we went for a two- or three-mile cross-country run. Deero would always try to be first one home. There was never doubt in my mind that I could beat him because I had a better sprint, but he never accepted this. He refused to concede that he would lose.'

In 1972 Grace made his international debut in the high pressure zone at Stade Colombes in Paris. To soothe his frayed nerves he sought consolation from an old hand.

'Team captain Tom Kiernan traditionally spoke at the team-talk with each player individually. I recall that he spent a lot of time talking with the wingers. The froth was coming out of his mouth he was so fired up. He warned us about the way the French would bombard us with high balls. The consoling thing, though, was that he assured us he would be there beside us to take the pressure off us. The match was barely on when the French out-half kicked this almighty ball up in the air between Kiernan and myself. To my horror I heard Kiernan shouting: "Your ball." So much for all that brothers-in-arms talk, but that's the captain's prerogative! I caught the ball and nearly got killed!

'In fairness to Tom, after the match I was walking off the pitch when my opposite number asked me for my jersey. I didn't want to give it to him. Tom was passing by and asked me why I wasn't parting with my jersey. I explained I was worried I mightn't get another cap. He said: "Jaysus, there's no fear of that." After I swapped jerseys Kiernan handed me the match ball which I still have.

'After the match I didn't realise how significant our victory was. I could see that players who, to me, were heroes, like Willie John and Tom Kiernan, were very emotional about the whole thing. Now I understand why. My second match was in Twickenham. I remember seeing the number of big cars going into the ground and the smoked salmon and the champagne parties and how that was used to motivate the Irish side. It was also stressed how important it was for the Irish community in England for us to win. If there was any doubt about that the Irish fans in the crowd's reaction after Kevin Flynn scored that famous try said it all.'

Grace collected his third cap against the All Blacks in January 1973 when he scored a dramatic equalising try in the right-hand corner to tie the match at 10–10. Some moments live in the memory and that try is one, when, like a salmon-leap, he sailed in a great arc through the air and scored a try in the corner with a split second to spare.

'There was a lot of speculation afterwards about whether the ball had crossed the dead ball line or not. Thankfully *The Irish Independent* had a photographer on hand to show it hadn't. Barry McGann always says if it wasn't for him I would have been famous. After I scored the try he narrowly missed the conversion which robbed us of our part in rugby's hall of fame.

'I will never forget our match against England that season. The Troubles were at their height and it was a brave gesture on the part of the English team to travel to Dublin. The reception they got when they went out onto the pitch was amazing with a standing ovation. The emotion ran through to the whole Irish team. To the credit of our coach, Ronnie Dawson, he was able to channel that emotion into performance and we won the match.'

The following year Grace was displaced by Lansdowne's Vinny Becker, a former Irish sprint champion, for the matches against Wales and France, but he was back for the matches against England and Scotland to play his part in Ireland's first Championship victory in 23 years. Grace joined Dick Milliken, Johnny Moloney, Ken Kennedy,

Stewart McKinney, Fergus Slattery and Willie John McBride on the all-conquering Lions tour to South Africa. However, he looks back on the experience with mixed feelings.

'I was very disappointed not to get a place in the Test side but before going on that tour I had sprained my ankle. I don't think most of the players recognised our achievement at the time. It was an incredible experience for me. It was also a great opportunity to meet great players, to play golf and go deep sea fishing. For three months we were treated like superstars. It was very hard when I got back home just to have beans and toast for my tea!

'Touring was always great fun. One of my first experiences of touring as an international was in 1972. A fellah came up to me in a pub and asked me if I would like to go to Bermuda. I wasn't sure if he was joking or not. Mike Gibson and Fergus Slattery were the other Irish internationals travelling. The whole thing was put together by Pat O'Riordan, Jim Doyle and Tom Gallagher. One of their players, to use a Barry McGann expression, "looked very strong". That meant that he was about eighteen stone! He had two speeds – slow and very slow.'

After the highs of the Championship win and the Lions tour the 1974–5 season proved itself to be much less satisfying. The highlights of that season for Grace came at club level. To mark the centenary season of the IRFU a special All-Ireland club competition was held in Thomond Park, with one representative from each province; that is, Glaswegians, Bangor, Garryowen and St Mary's. Grace has vivid memories of this event.

'We had won the Leinster Cup the previous Thursday night after a replay. The competition began on the Saturday but most of the guys were still celebrating. To put it as charitably as possible there were a few players on our team in no state to drive a car. We were travelling down by the train and those of us who wanted to win the tournament discovered that some of the players were using the train journey to extend the jubilations still further. The match was on at 5.30 p.m. and I remember most of us watched the FA Cup, but one of our players in particular was the worse for wear and had to sleep it off.

'Our first game was against Bangor. Both teams were travelling to the ground on the one bus. Bangor got on the team in military fashion but some of our lads looked a sorry state. They were at the top of the bus and we were at the back. One of the great characters on our team was "Tojo" Byrne. He suddenly said: "We haven't come this far to lose." Immediately the spirit of the team was transformed. We beat them and the following day we drew 9–9 with Garryowen, but won the tournament because we had scored more tries. We only realised the scale of our achievement when we looked at the stands and saw the disappointment on the faces of the Garryowen fans.'

Following a crushing 26–3 defeat at the hands of the French in 1976 Grace succeeded Mike Gibson as captain of the Irish side. He has mixed feelings about the experience: 'I don't think playing on the wing is the best place to captain a team from. Also I think my game suffered from the captaincy.'

That summer Ireland took on a formidable task with a tour to New Zealand and Fiji under Grace's leadership in the hope of helping the development of the young, inexperienced players. In the circumstances, Ireland put up a creditable performance. Initially Grace felt the pressure of the media.

'When we arrived there were two television journalists waiting for me to set up one of the interviews. I liked one of them immediately but not the other. So much for my judge of character. When we got to recording the interviews the guy I hadn't liked turned out to be extremely nice and the bloke I liked was in fact the very opposite. He began by quoting John O'Shea at me. He had written that we would have been much better off training in the hills of Kerry than going to New Zealand. Somebody must have been praying for me because I heard myself saying: "Our philosophy is that there is no better way than to learn from the best." I still don't know where I got that answer from.

'Phil O'Callaghan had been recalled for the tour. He looked a bit older than the rest of us. Another journalist asked him who he was. Philo answered: "I'm Ireland's secret weapon." There was a lot of surprise that he was selected but he played a very significant role on that tour. He earned his cap on merit. I would describe him as the traditional Irish rugby tourist. When we were being intimidated on the pitch he wasn't found wanting.

'We lost the Test against the All Blacks 11–3. I think we lost the game because both Barry McGann and I missed a string of kicks. As captain I also blame myself for not instilling sufficient belief in the players that we could win. That game was there for the taking.

'Another memory of that tour typifies the power of rugby friendships. I had marked Grant Batty when we played the All Blacks in Lansdowne Road. Grant was not involved with the Blacks in 1976 but he sent me on a bundle of New Zealand dollars to buy a round of drinks for the Irish team.'

In 1978 Grace lost the captaincy for the opening match against Scotland to his great friend, Johnny Moloney. Worse was to follow.

Although Ireland beat Scotland 12–9, in a match notable for the debut of Tony Ward, Grace was surprisingly dropped. He would never play for Ireland again. Grace was left with many happy memories of the people he played with.

'One of the great characters in the side was Willie Duggan. I always thought there was an inherent contradiction in his preparation for matches. He always had a cigarette five minutes before going out on the pitch then he took out a jar of Vicks and rubbed it on his chest. To put it at its kindest he had an unconventional approach! A lot of that stuff about his lack of training is exaggerated. He couldn't have performed at that level without training. He was considered to be lucky to make the Lions tour in 1977 but, with proper training, he came back with the reputation of being their star performer.

'Another player I have to mention at this juncture is Moss Finn. We were staying in the Shelbourne and I was sitting with him and Tony Ward in the hotel and Moss was telling us how good he was feeling. It was possibly his first trip to Dublin and he went on to say that he had been out for a lovely walk in front of the hotel to see the ducks in the Phoenix Park. He had really been to Stephens' Green but he genuinely thought that was the Phoenix Park! The great thing about Moss, and to a large part the reason he was so popular in the dressing-room, was that he always made himself the butt of his jokes.'

Grace too has the capacity to laugh at himself.

'When I played rugby I had jet black hair and a Beatles haircut, so it came as an enormous shock to me when my hair went grey. I was up in Donegal before one of the international matches with my family. RTE were showing some footage of tries from previous seasons. When they started to show a few of mine my wife rushed out to call my son, Conor, who was six at the time, to see me in my prime. When he came in she pointed to the television excitedly and showed me in full flight. Conor just shook his head and said: "No, it's not him. My dad has grey hair." Then he just turned on his heels and went out to play soccer!'

10

MOSS KEANE

The Keane Edge

When you play Munster in Thomond Park you can appreciate
how the early Christians felt in the Colosseum.

> Earl Kirton, former All Black

It is only when you meet someone like Moss Keane that you really
understand the phrase 'larger than life' – a huge bulk of a man, with a
penchant for straight talking and a treasure trove of stories and jokes,
surprisingly few about rugby, more about matters agricultural. The oft-
quoted words 'hale and hearty' come to mind immediately. He has a nice
line in self-deprecating humour: 'After I left university I found I had no
talent for anything so I joined the civil service!'

He has a high resistance to 'rugbyspeak' and is as uncomfortable with
reminiscing about his rugby days as he is about excessive compliments
about his playing career: 'I won 52 caps – a lot of them just because they
couldn't find anybody else.'

In discussion about the changing face of the modern game he winces
visibly when uttering phrases like: 'the scientific approach', 'getting the
angles right'. It is the disdainful expression you would expect the Pope
to wear if forced to utter a profanity. A smile of glee comes on his face
as he confesses to occasionally shouting 'watch your angles' to the team
he coaches in Portarlington just to annoy them. For him rugby is
basically a simple game – to be played not analysed.

While Moss was lucky enough to be on the Triple Crown winning
side in 1982 and was also on a Lions tour, a famous Munster victory was
the high point of his career.

'It's very hard to separate memories and say one match was more important than another. My first cap was a great feeling, so was my Lions' Test appearance, Ginger's try in '82 was memorable but the highlight was defeating the All Blacks. It was a great, great day though my clearest memory of the day is the disappointment we all felt when we heard that our captain, Donal Canniffe's father died immediately after the match.'

The only biblical story which the four gospels share in common is the multiplication of the loaves and the fishes when Jesus fed the multitude with a few loaves and fishes and managed to have twelve baskets of fragments left over. Munster's victory over the All Blacks has spawned a similar miracle. Although the official attendance at the match was only 12,000 – since then tens of thousands of people have said, often with the benefit of generous liquid refreshment: 'I was there the day Munster beat the All Blacks.'

The Clare Hills provided a scenic background for the New Zealanders as they performed their traditional 'haka' before the game. Somewhat against the run of play Munster took the lead in the eleventh minute – a delicate chip from Tony Ward was followed through and won by Jimmy Bowen, who made an incisive run and as he was caught from behind, he fed Christy Cantillon, who crossed the line beneath the posts. Ward kicked the conversion with ease. In the seventeenth minute Ward dropped a goal.

The home side hung on to their 9–0 lead until half-time but realised that a modern-day siege of Limerick awaited them in the second half when the men from down under would do all in their formidable power to protect their unbeaten record. Their fears were justified as the All Blacks exerted enormous pressure. Metaphorically and literally the tourists did not know what hit them as they were stopped in their tracks with a series of crunching tackles by such players as Seamus Dennison, Greg Barrett and, most notably, Colm Tucker. Jack Glesson subsequently described them as 'Kamikaze tacklers'.

As the seconds ticked by, agonisingly slowly in the second half, the crowd became more and more frenzied, sensing that here lay history in the making. 'M-U-N-S-T-E-R! M-U-N-S-T-E-R!' rang out at a volume to deafening levels. Ward got the only score in the second half – a drop goal – and Munster held on. It was an extraordinary team performance.

The Munster team that day was: L. Moloney (Garryowen), M. Finn (U.C.C.), S. Dennison (Garryowen), G. Barrett (Cork Constitution), J. Bowen (Cork Con.), T. Ward (Garryowen), D. Canniffe (Lansdowne), captain; G. McLoughlin (Shannon), P. Whelan (Garryowen), L. White

(London Irish), M. Keane (Lansdowne), B. Foley (Shannon), C. Cantillon (Cork Con.), D. Spring (Dublin University), C. Tucker (Shannon).

One of Limerick's best-known sons, film star Richard Harris, swept away by the euphoria of victory, wired the following message from a movie set in Johannesburg:

> Your historic victory over New Zealand made roaring headlines in every South African paper. I've been on the dry for 10 months, but I can't think of a better occasion or excuse to re-acquaint my liver with the drowning sensation of a drop. I wish I was there. I rang Richard Burton and although he extends his congratulations, I detected a tinge of jealousy.

One of Tony Ward's most vivid memories of Moss goes back to that match.

> We were leading 12–0 with only minutes left and there was a scrum close to the sideline. Our lads wheeled the scrum and drove the Blacks over the sideline right up against the wall. The All Blacks were not very pleased about this and a scuffle broke out. One of their players, Andy Hayden, swung out his arm to have a swipe at Brendan Foley and Moss grabbed him by the arm and said: 'Don't. You'll lose that one as well.' Hayden turned, smiled and accepted it. The meaning was clear.
>
> Moss is one of the great characters of Irish rugby. On the pitch he was a tiger but off the field a pussy-cat. I'll never forget when we played England in 1979 he took off on a run and the crowd started chanting: 'Mossie, Mossie.' He was one of those characters who lifts the whole crowd and that in turn lifts the team.

Stories about Moss Keane are more common than showers in April. Since his capture on 8 February, 1983 Shergar has been at a stud in the Middle East, galloping around the Scottish Highlands, peacefully grazing in a Channel Islands meadow, part of the mafia mob, part of a Kentucky killing and even giving riding lessons to runaway British aristocrat Lord Lucan. Likewise, if even a fraction of the stories about Moss were true he would have needed a brewery of his own to supply him in Guinness, broken down more doors than most people have eaten hot dinners and generally been responsible for extraordinary levels of mirth and mayhem.

On Test duty in New Zealand in 1977 Moss predicted the outcome of a particular match in the best tradition of Kerry talkers. 'The first half will be even. The second half will be even worse.'

Another story told about Mossie dates from the same tour. After their second Test victory the Lions threw the party to beat all parties in the team hotel. It was soon discovered that one of their players was missing. When everyone else expressed concern about him Moss said he knew where the missing person was – next door with his girlfriend. Moss was despatched to bring the guilty party back – though given strict instructions not to break down any doors. (His nickname on that tour was 'Rent-a-Storm' so the decree seemed more than justified.) The rest of the squad listened to a slight flurry next door and moments later Moss came in the door with the missing player under his arm, completely naked and squirming like a fish on a hook. Under the arm he held the player's girlfriend in a similar state of undress and embarrassment. Moss, in his best Kerry accent, boomed out: 'To be sure, did you be wanting the two of them?'

Yet a further classic story about Moss goes back to one of his tours with the Barbarians in Wales. At one stage his team went to the bar after a game of golf. Although everybody else was drinking beer Moss, with commendable patriotism, was drinking Guinness and was knocking back two pints to everyone else's one. As dinner time approached it was decided it was time to return to the team hotel. As people prepared to leave somebody shouted: 'One for the road.' Ten pints later for the team at large and twenty pints later for Moss the team was again summoned to the team bus. Moss was asked if the team should stay for one more drink. He shook his head. When questioned why he was opposed to the idea Moss replied: 'No, I don't. To be sure, I don't want to be making a pig of myself.'

Moss paid an interesting tribute to Ollie Campbell after the 1980 final trial. The Probables beat the Possibles 28–12 with Campbell giving a virtuoso performance, scoring 24 points, including three tries. Moss scored the other try to complete the team's scoring. In the dressing-room Moss turned around to Campbell and said: 'Wasn't it great that it was only me and you that got our scores all the same.'

Moss went down to Greystones to play in a match to mark their jubilee season between Greystones and the 1982 Triple Crown winning side. Former Manchester United star Shay Brennan was also down for the game. In Greystones they are well used to big names in the rugby world visiting but they are not accustomed to famous soccer personalities like Shay. Mossie was with him in the bar, having consumed a few drinks. He was a little cheesed off that Shay was getting all the attention, and everyone was asking Brennan questions but nobody was passing any remarks on him. Eventually Moss threw in a question: 'Who played soccer for Scotland and cricket for England?' There was total silence. Everyone in the bar was a sports fan and all were scratching their heads trying to figure out this riddle. Finally they were all forced to concede defeat. Moss walked out as soon as he provided the answer: 'Denis Law and Ian Botham!'

Mick Quinn has a lot of stories about Keane – though few are printable in our politically correct times. Quinn does the Keane voice and facial expression better than Moss himself.

'Ballymena were playing a Willie John McBride XV in an end-of-season match. The cast included Gareth Edwards, Gerald Davies and the Scot, Ian Barnes. Barnes, a second-row forward was from the Borders and speaks with a thick Scottish accent. His scrumming partner was Moss. Both were sorting out tactics before the match but were incapable of communicating through words. By using gestures and amid vigorous nodding of the head they seemed to have worked something out. The scrum was a total disaster. The touring side were losing by 20 points at half-time. Barnes went to me as his out-half and said: "Hey, Micky, I canna understand what he's saying. I'm pushing on the wrong side of the scrum. Would you think you could get him to swop sides with me?" A minute later Moss came up to me and said: "That bloody Scot can't speak f***ing English. I'm pushing on the wrong side." I then did the needful and the tourists were a transformed side in the second half and we won the match.

'When the Troubles in the North were at their height, Lansdowne played a match in Belfast. After the match the lads stopped for a case of beer in an off-licence because the drink was so much cheaper up there, which would set them up nicely for the train journey home. One evening, though, there was a bomb scare which ruled out travelling by train and after a long delay a bus arrived. The problem was that there was no room on the bus for Moss, Rory Moroney and me. Moss had already disposed of a couple of his beers and was not too happy with the prospect of having to wait even longer. He marched on to the bus and said: "Excuse me, this bus is going to crash." At first nobody moved but then a little old man got up and walked up timidly to the towering figure of Moss and said: "Excuse me sir, but where did you say this bus was going to?"

'When we played Fiji in 1976 the pitch had 18 inches of mud. Tony Ensor ran over for a try but there was so much mud he ran over the dead-ball line and we lost the try. It was a very hard game. At one stage they had 17 players on the pitch. It was a pretty bizarre scene. We had to tog out in the hotel but the heat in the dressing-room was unbearable. As it was the final game of the tour some of the players not involved didn't even bother going to the match. They were hanging around in the pool. As we departed we heard Moss shouting at us and thought he was just wishing well. Then we discovered he was drowning!

'I once left my own mark on big Moss. Tony Ward and I had both got 18 points in a final trial but I had outplayed him on the day and was feeling pretty good. Later that night Moss came up to me at the reception and told me that I was the best out-half he had ever played with. I was pretty chuffed with his compliment and told him so. Shortly after, I was going to the toilet and I saw Mossie talking to somebody but I couldn't make out who it was at first. As I passed them by I realised it was Wardie and I heard Mossie tell him he was without doubt the finest out-half ever to play for Ireland. I gave him a kick in the backside for his dishonesty. Mossie followed me into the toilet, put his arm around me and said: "Don't worry, Scout. I was only being diplomatic."'

The celebrated film director John Ford once observed: 'If the legend is more interesting than the truth, tell the legend.' To no Irish sports figure does this adage apply more to than Maurice Ignatius Keane. He shrugs his shoulders nonchalantly when asked about these stories. 'There's generally a tiny grain of truth in them but then it's blown out of all proportion.'

Drink no longer plays a significant part in Moss's life. He is able to completely deny two apocryphal stories that are told about him. The first is that he once said of an Irish international scrum-half 'he couldn't pass wind'. The second is that he spent months chasing a girl because he overheard two playing colleagues describing her as having loose morals. In fact, what one, a dentist, said was that she had loose molars!

11

MICHAEL KIERNAN

Uncle Tom's Champion

The World Cup – truly an international event.

John Motson

Arguably the architect of the modern science of genetics was Francis Galton. Galton was a fascinating character. Born into a family of wealthy Quaker gunmakers, he has the distinction of publishing the first weather map but, more curiously, he also produced the first beauty map of Britain, based on his secret grading of the local women on a scale of one to five. The women from Aberdeen had cause to wonder – they were at the bottom of the list! He discovered that chimpanzees have fingerprints and illustrated this by pasting the appropriate impression near that made by the prime minister of the time, Gladstone. The titles of his three hundred scientific papers indicate the breadth of his interests. They include: *Three generations of lunatic cats*; *Visions for sane persons*; *Cutting a round cake on scientific principles*; *The relative sensitivity of men and women at the nape of the neck*; *Pedigree moths*; *The average flush of excitement*; *On spectacles for divers*; *Statistical inquiries into the efficacy of prayer*; *Strawberry cure for gout*; *Good and bad temper in English families*; *Nuts and men*; and the *pièce de résistance, Arithmetic by smell*.

Galton's idiosyncrasies were also apparent in his trips to Africa. He went around measuring the buttocks of native women using a sextant and the principles of surveying! His main intellectual interest was the study of genius. No doubt the fact that he considered himself to fall into this category fuelled his interest in the topic. Were Galton to be reincarnated and make a study of rugby genius he would surely begin with Michael Kiernan.

His uncle, Tom Kiernan, was first capped at full-back against England in 1960. In 1970 he eclipsed the hallowed Jack Kyle's tally of 46 caps in the victory over Wales. He won his 54th and final cap against Scotland at Murrayfield in 1973; having established two other milestones at the time, scoring a record 158 points for Ireland and captaining his country for a record 24 times. Kiernan took over as coach of the Irish national team in 1980, succeeding his cousin, and Cork Constitution club-mate, Noel 'Noisy' Murphy.

One of the most striking facts which a study of Irish rugby uncovers is the prominence of family ties. Ireland's first ever rugby international was against England in 1875 at the Kensington Oval. Two of the organisers of the game were Edward and Richard Galbraith, who also played for Ireland in the game, beginning a long tradition of brothers playing for the boys in green. Noel Murphy is the most striking example of this trend. His father won 11 caps in the 1930s in the pack. Noel was capped for Ireland on 47 occasions in the wing-forward position and later managed the Irish and Lions' teams. His son, Kenny, was also capped for Ireland at full-back in the 1990s. This is the only time in Irish rugby history when a grandfather, son and grandson represented Ireland. Noisy's son-in-law is former Irish scrum-half and captain Michael Bradley.

Michael Kiernan's maternal uncle, Mick Lane, was part of the golden era of Irish rugby. He was first capped in the centre in the Triple Crown decider when Ireland lost to Wales at Swansea in 1947, although playing most of his rugby on the wing. Contrary to the perception that apart from the wizardry of Jack Kyle the Irish backs of that period were not up to much, Lane and Noel Henderson, his colleague in the backs, were chosen with Kyle on the Lions tour to New Zealand in 1950. Jim Kiernan, Michael's father, was an international selector from 1984 to 1987. Yet Michael was not brought up amid rugby fanaticism.

'I have four sisters which prevented us from being saturated with rugby talk. My younger brother, Peter, also played for Dolphin and is currently doing a great job training their Under-20s. My uncle Tommy was playing for Ireland when I was a boy and this obviously had a big impact on me. My uncle, Mick, left a legacy which was very apparent when I visited my grandmother because all the paraphernalia of his career was in her house, including the team photos from the 1940s and 1950s, and his caps. I grew up listening to all the stories of Jackie Kyle. Rugby was the main sport in my school, Pres, Cork. Des Barry, who subsequently coached Munster, was our coach and probably the biggest influence on my career.'

Kiernan learned more than rugby at school. The seeds of a promising running career were sown there. His natural talent was developed still further when he joined Leevale Athletics Club.

'My coach, Finbarr O'Brien, taught me a lot about athletics and showed me a different way of running on the track than on the field. The highlight of my running career was winning the national 200m title in 1981 and representing Ireland against Scotland that same year. At that stage, though, I had to make a choice between athletics and rugby – and rugby won.'

In 1981 Kiernan toured South Africa with the Irish rugby team. He played for the Munster side that beat Australia 15–6 at Musgrave Park that year and was selected as substitute for the international against the Wallabies. Tonsillitis forced him to cry off. All his Christmases would come at once in 1982. Kiernan exploded onto the international scene when he came on as a replacement for David Irwin, who broke his leg in the match, in Ireland's 20–12 victory over Wales. Irwin's partner in the centre, Paul Dean, was also injured and replaced by John Murphy.

'The first match of the International Championship was called off because of snow. I was 19 then but had turned 20 for the Welsh game. It was such a thrill for me, particularly as I was so young, to be in the company of such classy players as Ollie Campbell. I was happy just to be on the bench and felt so honoured to be wearing an Irish tracksuit. If I had been there for 15 or 20 times it would have been very different. I had enough belief in my own ability to know my chance would come sooner or later. It's very easy to make your debut coming on as a sub because you miss out on the anxiety of the night before and all the hype and distractions.

'The Triple Crown happened very fast. It was a kind of fairytale and a little bit unreal. In hindsight the senior players like Fergus Slattery, Moss Keane and John O'Driscoll had been toiling away for years without any success. I was only on the scene for four weeks and had won a Triple Crown. In the later years of my career I appreciated the memories of the good times much more. Although we didn't win the Triple Crown in 1983 it was as good a year as 1982 because we won the same number of matches, and we beat France which no Irish side has done since.'

There were a handful of begrudgers who hinted that he might have got his place on the team because his uncle, Tom, was coach. Was he troubled by this kind of talk?

'Not in the least. Anyone who knows my uncle understands that I got my place on merit. If anything the fact that I was his nephew made things even harder.'

Kiernan toured with the Lions to New Zealand in 1983.

'As a young man it was a great elation to be chosen for the Lions. It was a fantastic experience on a personal level but was not a happy tour because we lost too many matches. The tour probably took its toll on me because I was dropped for the opening two internationals in 1984. Having said that I don't think I deserved to be dropped.'

Shortly after Mick Doyle was appointed national coach in 1984 he announced: 'The age of Biggles is dead!' – a coded reference to Ollie Campbell and Tony Ward. Ireland would win playing the running game. The flip side of this was that he began his term of stewardship without a recognised specialist kicker. It was Moss Finn who was nominated as place kicker for the opening match of Doyler's reign against Australia but, following an injury to Finn, Kiernan took over and kicked three penalty goals in Ireland's 16–9 defeat. It seemed as if Ireland were going to pay a high price for the lack of a recognised kicker in the opening match of the Championship against Scotland after Kiernan missed three kicks, but then he found his range. Ireland stared defeat in the face until the 79th minute when Trevor Ringland scored a try following a great back movement. Kiernan kicked the conversion to give Ireland an 18–15 victory. In all he scored two penalties, a conversion and dropped a goal. The following match saw Kiernan kicking three penalties and two conversions as Ireland beat Wales. Another Triple Crown beckoned in the crunch match against England. The sides were tied at 10–10 in the final minute. Then Kiernan dropped a goal following a pass from Michael Bradley, who subsequently admitted that he thought he was in fact passing to Paul Dean, to give Ireland victory. How did Kiernan apparently make the transition to place kicker so smoothly when he had virtually no experience of kicking?

'Of all the players I ever played with the one I most admired was Ollie Campbell. He had it all. Playing with him was the only education I needed to take penalties. I learned from the routine he adopted, his commitment to practice, the intense concentration, his ability to strike the ball cleanly and follow through correctly.

'My kicking was only one factor that season. A number of new players came on the scene in 1984–5 which created a great buzz. Mick Doyle was very refreshing in his attitude. We felt we could try anything even when we weren't fully sure it would come off. In that first season he was crucial to our success, though perhaps his contribution drifted a bit in the following years. Having said that, there were a number of essential elements that combined to give us the Triple Crown in 1985. Our back row were incredible and Paul Dean was a genius at finding space. If you could write the script you couldn't have come up with a more dramatic conclusion.'

The Doyle dream turned sour the following season. Ireland hoped for a renaissance in the 1987 World Cup.

'It was a tournament we went into with our eyes closed in common with many other countries. We were poorly prepared for the event. Watching New Zealand at close quarters showed everybody exactly what a professional approach to rugby meant.'

A change of style was inevitable following Doyle's departure from the position of Irish coach following the World Cup.

'I have every respect for Jimmy Davidson as a person but I didn't enjoy his time as coach. We had training sessions which were boring beyond belief. Doyler's attitude had been: "Let's go out and enjoy it." The Davidson era, though, brought very much diagnostic rugby. There was far too much theory and too much coaching time spent on video analysis of games. I was very serious about my rugby but having had the success I had enjoyed I didn't relish listening to a constant series of lectures on how to play the game.'

The joke in the Irish squad at the time about tactics was: 'That will work brilliantly in practice but does it stand up in theory?' Kiernan hoped that the situation would improve dramatically with the appointment of Ciaran Fitzgerald as Davidson's successor.

'I was eagerly looking forward to Fitzie's reign. Nobody had admired him more as Irish captain than me. Yet I have to say I was very disappointed with his time as coach. Obviously Ciaran's expertise was with the forwards so he delegated the coaching of the backs to others. Putting it at its kindest . . . this coaching was not all that it might have been. Fitzie was very good at talking to the squad as a group but in my experience he didn't talk to players much on a one-to-one basis. I had expected that because he had played with me he would be able to talk to me if he was not happy with my performance and let me know if my place was in jeopardy and why I was dropped, but that was not the case.'

There is no hint of sour grapes in Kiernan's voice as he recalls this low point of his career. Does he think that 'non-rugby' factors contributed to his exclusion from the Irish side in 1991?

'I played my last match for Ireland against France in the International Championship that season. Yet I was not selected in the initial 43-man squad to train for the World Cup a few months later. I don't think my form changed all that dramatically in the interim. Draw your own conclusions.'

Kiernan played his final game for Ireland before his 30th birthday. Did he retire too early?

'I could probably have played for another few years but I had become a father at that stage and had family commitments. It's probably fair to say, without elaborating on my reasons, I didn't relish being part of the Irish set-up at the time.'

He represented his country both in the centre and on the wing. Which was his favourite position?

'I much preferred playing in the centre because I didn't like playing on the wing! You get the chance to create space and be involved in the game in a meaningful way in the centre.'

He is the proud father of two young sons. Will they be future Irish internationals?

'I don't know. At least by the time they've arrived on the scene the contracts situation will be well resolved and they could make some decent money out of it which I never did!'

12

JACK KYLE

Simply the Best

He has drained the language of eulogy and it is no use applying superlatives to him any more.
    The *Pall Mall Gazette*'s tribute to the greatest
            cricketer of them all, W.G. Grace.

According to rugby legend a great Welsh out-half was called to a premature death. He was met at the gates of heaven by St Peter. St Peter apologised profusely for bringing the rugby player to his eternal reward at such a young age but explained that the celestial rugby cup final was taking place and as a manager of one of the teams he needed a star player. The Welsh player was whisked immediately to the stadium and marvelled at the facilities. They were literally out of this world. Such was the excitement of the occasion that the recently deceased forgot about his death and played the game of his eternal life. With just two minutes to go St Peter's side were leading by 19 points when the Welsh player noticed an athletic sub coming onto the opposition side and, in an accent that was immediately identifiable as Northern Irish, giving instructions to his side. The new arrival got the ball four times and scored four tries – each more stunning than the other. He did not bother with the conversions but had the game restarted immediately and his team won by a point.

After the game St Peter rushed on to console his dejected star player. The ex-Welsh player asked: 'Tell me, when did Jack Kyle die?'

'That's not Jack Kyle. That's God. He just thinks he's Jack Kyle!'

This little story illustrates the esteem with which Jack Kyle is held in rugby circles. Such was Kyle's impact when he won 46 caps that he literally defined the age. His glory days, when Ireland reached its rugby zenith in the late 1940s, were known throughout the rugby world as 'the Jackie Kyle era'. According to William James the world is a theatre for heroism. Kyle made every rugby pitch he graced a theatre of dreams – dwarfing all who trailed in his wake as he scythed through the defence. In full flight his hand-off gesture was like a royal dismissal to bewildered opponents reduced to look like oxen on an ice-rink. He enjoyed to the full the drama and poetic presence that was part of the most glorious chapter in Irish rugby history. His voice betrays the nerve-tingling excitement as the great moments of the 1940s and 1950s are unreeled before the vivid mind's eye of memory, particularly of his fellow internationals.

'There is a big advantage in being a small country, if that isn't a contradiction in terms, in that it is difficult for good players to slip through the net because of the interpros, the matches between the combined provinces and the rest of Ireland and the final trial. If you were any good at all somebody saw you play somewhere!

'I was not a great tackler. If I had to play rugby as a forward I would never have played the game! Our back row of Jim McCarthy, Bill McKay and Des O'Brien was so strong that I didn't have to bother too much with the normal defensive duties of a fly-half. McCarthy was like greased lightning and an incredible forager and opportunist. I could virtually leave the out-half to our two flankers. I just stood back and took him if he went on the outside.

'I was doubly blessed in that I also had Noel Henderson playing alongside me in the centre. He was a marvellous defender performing many of my defensive duties and I'm not just saying that because he's my brother-in-law!'

The unpredictable often happens in rugby. In 1984 when England played Australia they had to play for 13 minutes with only 14 players, when Steve Mills got injured as his replacement, Steve Brain, couldn't get onto the pitch because the tunnel doors were locked! It was to be his brother-in-law that caused Kyle's greatest surprise in rugby.

'Noel caused a major shock one day at our team meeting. He was a very quiet man and normally was not very loquacious at those sessions. As was his custom Karl Mullen concluded by asking if there was any questions. Noel asked: "What I would like to know captain, is there any way of knowing will the out-half be taking his man for a change?!"

'Noel is the father of four daughters. I met the former Scottish centre Charlie Drummond once who also has a lot of daughters. When I told him about Noel he said: "We're raising good stock for future rugby players." There's a man who takes the long-term view!'

Kyle has particular admiration for his international colleagues who also made their mark at the highest level in other sports. Barney Mullan scored a great try in the decisive Triple Crown match at Ravenhill against Wales in 1948. He was the only player in that side, and the second of only five players, to score in all three games of an Irish Triple Crown victory. He scored 36 points in all for his country and also represented Ireland at clay-pigeon shooting. Des McKee was capped 12 times for Ireland at rugby, including all matches in both 1948 and 1949, scoring tries against England in both seasons. In 1946 he played cricket for Ireland, when as a right-hand batsman, he played in the international first class game versus Scotland in 1946, scoring 16 runs. Kevin Quinn was capped five times for Ireland in the centre between 1947 and 1953. His brother, Brendan, was capped on the wing in 1947. As a right-hand batsman Kevin also played in three cricket internationals for Ireland. Kyle's clearest memory of the Triple Crown winning side is of Jack Daly.

'At the time, we always faced playing the Welsh on their own patch with trepidation. In 1948, though, when we played them in Swansea, Jack sat in the dressing-room punching his fist into his hand saying: "I'm mad to get at them. I'm mad to get at them. I'm mad to get at them." His enthusiasm rubbed off on the rest of us.

'You have to remember that it was such a different set-up then from today. We came down from Belfast on the train in the morning and in the afternoon we went for a training session, using the term loosely, in Trinity College. Johnny O'Meara might throw me a few passes and that would be enough for me. We used an interesting word a lot at the time, "stale", which I never hear now. Basically we believed if we trained too hard we would not perform on the Saturday. It was probably an excuse for us not to do any serious work!

'I always felt that, just as a girl who is born beautiful can only enhance her looks a little bit, you can only achieve a limited amount in rugby by coaching. It's really a question of natural ability. I only dropped a goal once for Ireland. It was from a very difficult angle. If I had thought about it I could never have attempted it. It was just instinctive. A lot of times we were working on a subconscious level. Another time I combined with Jim McCarthy for Jim to score a great try. I got a letter afterwards telling me it was such a textbook score we must have practised it on the training ground. Looking back now it's amazing how few set moves we had worked out, came off'.

When William Webb Ellis gave birth to rugby he had no way of knowing that hotel owners throughout the world would regularly curse his disciples for the trail of havoc left after rugby tours. Kyle has fond memories of the Lions tour to New Zealand in 1950.

'We were gone for six months. Although we had journeyed to France to play an international it was our first real experience of travel. We went out via the Panama canal and home by the Suez canal so it was really a round-the-world trip. We kept fit by running around the ship. Every afternoon we had great discussions about rugby. I learned more about the game in those conversations than I ever had before or since.

'Our champion was Tom Clifford. Apart from the normal luggage Tom brought a massive trunk onto the ship. We were all puzzled about what he could have in it. As cabins were shared players were instructed to only store essential items there, but Tom insisted on bringing in his trunk which immediately caused a lot of grumbles from his room-mates who were complaining about the clutter. They changed their tune the first night, though, when some of us said we were feeling peckish. Tom brought us into his cabin and opened his trunk which was crammed with food which his mother had cooked. So every night we dined royally in Tom's cabin. Someone said that we should all write a letter to Mrs Clifford because she fed us so well on that trip! Tom had a very healthy appetite. To break the monotony on the journey we had all kinds of competitions. One night we had an eating competition. Tom won hands down because he got through the 30 courses that were on the menu!

'We were given two blazers and our jerseys, and two pounds ten shillings a week for expenses. If you adjusted that figure to allow for inflation I can't see chaps like Will Carling and Brian Moore accepting that today! From our point of view the trip was a very enriching experience.'

The Lions lost the Test series three matches to nil with one game drawn. Despite the disappointment Kyle easily won over the hearts and minds of that most discriminating set of critics: the New Zealand rugby community.

The sporting genes in the Kyle family were not restricted to Jack. His sister Betty was the captain of the Irish ladies hockey team and his brother Eric played for Ulster and got a final trial for Ireland.

'It's very difficult for someone in Eric's shoes because you lose your own identity. You are not judged on your own merits but as somebody's brother. It's very hard when you live a life in the shadow of someone else.'

When asked about his most difficult opponent Kyle eventually selects Cliff Morgan.

'I played against him frequently. Cliff was one of the great out-halves. He was brilliant on the Lions tour of South Africa in 1955 and they still talk about his performance on that tour there. The problem playing against Cliff was that I never knew what he would do next. That meant I was unable to concentrate on my own game as much when I played against him.'

After his retirement from the game Kyle's itchy feet led him to work in Indonesia from 1962 to 1964. The ninth of January 1996 marked his 30th anniversary as a surgeon in Chingola, Zambia. He plans finally to retire in his Belfast home. He still returns to Ireland three or four times a year. One of his first tasks, after arranging a golf game with Jim McCarthy and Noel Henderson, is to update himself on the changing rugby vocabulary.

'The last time I was home I was watching *Rugby Special* and I heard someone talking about an "executive high ball". I asked a few people later if they knew what that was. Eventually I learned that it's the new name for the garryowen!

'Rugby now is very different from my day. One of the biggest changes is actually the rugby ball itself. In our day it was a heavy leather ball with a leather lace. On the mud in the Mardyke it was like a big, heavy bar of soap. You couldn't get players kicking goals from the incredible distance that they do now with the new, light ball. Then, players often wore boots with steel toes and kicked with the point of the toe using a straight run towards the ball. Now they kick with the side of the foot. I would have to say, though, that I find it depressing the ritual that takes place before penalties are taken. It seems you can't take a penalty unless you use up a minute and a half. On average there are ten shots at goal in any game which means that 15 minutes are wasted straight away. Of course I appreciate that if you reduce the value of a penalty you will have much more infringement but I do think the laws of the game will have to be changed to allow for a more fluid game.

'There have been changes for the better. When I started playing, a drop goal was worth four points and a try only three. In fact in 1946 we lost an unofficial international 4–3 to France when they scored a drop goal and we got a try.'

Over the years Kyle watched with interest the debate over the vexed question of whether, and to what extent, rugby should turn professional with all the ferocious protestations and the growing bitterness between administrators and players. This antagonism was graphically revealed in Will Carling's description of the RFU Committee as '57 old farts' which caused him to be stripped of the captaincy of the English team. Kyle was surprised at the swiftness at which the potential schism was resolved through the intervention of television moguls like Kerry Packer and Rupert Murdoch.

'In our day the money was not important. Sport was very much a subsidiary part of our life and not done for anything other than enjoyment. You have to remember that soccer players were not paid very much then and Fred Daly only got five hundred pounds for winning the British Open. Now, when rugby unions are taking in millions of pounds, it's understandable that players are looking for a slice of the cake.

'My son, Caeleb, played in the front row and on the flank for Clontarf when he retired at the age of 27 with a neck injury. I told him that he was playing in the wrong position because no one notices you there. More seriously I fear that we could have a two-tier game with a clear division between the show-boys and the workhorses. There are a tremendous amount of unsung heroes in the game, especially in the pack. In the new professional era players in the glamour positions will benefit more because they will be the ones invited to open supermarkets, have their own television shows, write books and so on.

'A significant moment for me came in 1995 in Twickenham when the English crowd, which was always so sporting, booed one of their own players because he was kicking a penalty and not running it. It says something about the way the game is going.'

Throughout his illustrious career Kyle was showered with accolades. Did any of them have a special significance for him?

'The famous poet Louis MacNiece was doing a radio broadcast here in Belfast one evening. He was asked if he could make one wish what would it be. His answer was that he would love to play rugby like Jack Kyle. That's the compliment that meant the most to me.'

13

DONAL LENIHAN

Donal's Doughnuts

I said to the manager: 'This is supposed to be a five-star hotel and there's a bloody hole in the roof.' He turned around and said: 'That's where you can see the five stars from.'

Gordon Brown

During the 1989 Lions tour of Australia the Wednesday team acquired the nickname of 'Donal's Doughnuts' – Doughnuts because they played to 'fill the whole in the middle of the week', and Donal's because they were captained by Donal Lenihan. Lenihan's ready wit was to the fore in a number of occasions on that tour. At one stage Bridgend's Mike Griffiths asked: 'Can I ask a stupid question?'

'Better than anyone I know,' answered Lenihan.

Another time the touring party were driving through Sydney when they passed a couple coming out of a church after being married. Then in all earnestness Jeremy Guscott asked: 'Why do people throw rice at weddings?' Lenihan replied immediately: 'Because rocks hurt.'

Scott Hastings grew impatient when his brother Gavin seemed to prefer playing tennis or going windsurfing with Ieuan Evans rather than with him. Lenihan commented: 'Ieuan's like the brother Gavin never had.'

'What about me?' asked Scott.

'You're the brother he did have,' responded Lenihan.

After defeating Australian Capital Territories 27–11 Lenihan brought the touring party to the Friends of Ireland bar where they were greeted by a priest. After much liquid refreshment it was time for the team to return to their hotel. The priest bade them farewell. Slightly under the influence Andy Robinson told the minister he was wearing his collar back to front.

'I'm a father, Andrew,' said the priest.

'I've got kids myself,' replied Robinson.

'No, I'm the father to hundreds of people in this area,' explained the priest.

'Really. In that case, it's not your collar you should be wearing back to front, it's your bloody trousers!'

In the lobby of the Berkeley Court Hotel Donal Lenihan cuts an imposing figure. He was born very much into a GAA mad family. His Kerry-born father, Gerald, played with the hurling immortals Jack Lynch and Christy Ring but still found time to become an Irish heavyweight international boxer. His heroes were not rugby players but the stars on the 1973 All-Ireland winning Cork side, like Jimmy Barry-Murphy and Billy Morgan.

As was so often the case his rugby career owes a huge amount to his school, CBC, and to the influence of one man, Br Philip O'Reilly, who put a string of internationals through his hands. After captaining his school to Munster Junior and Senior Schools titles he was capped for the Irish Schools and later would follow this up with caps at under-23, 'B', and at full level.

'I never lost a Cup match at school. My parents had never been at a rugby match until I started playing but they got swept away by the fanaticism of the schools final in Musgrave Park. For my first Irish schools match my team-mates included Hugo MacNeill, Paul Dean, Brian McCall, and Philip Matthews. My father told me recently nothing could top his feeling of pride that day seeing me walk out in my Irish jersey. When I went to UCC we had a team of all the talents so I took winning for granted.

'My first full cap was against Australia in 1981 and was really a natural progression from all that went before. Trevor Ringland also made his debut that day. There's always a special friendship between players who won their first caps on the same day. I usually roomed with Moss Keane. He was coming to the end of his career at that stage. Our room was like an alternative medical centre with pollen, garlic tablets and a half-dozen eggs. The mornings of internationals I woke up to see Moss eating three raw eggs. It's not the sort of sight that you want to wake up to! Having said that, Moss was an enormous help to me in the early days. I especially appreciated that he let me make the decisions about the line-out.'

Lenihan was a key member of the Triple Crown-winning sides in 1982 and 1985. He has fond memories of many of the players who soldiered with him in various triumphs.

'The best Irish forward I ever played with was Willie Duggan. He was the Scarlet Pimpernel of Irish rugby because he was so hard to find for training! Having said that, he wouldn't have survived in international rugby so long without training. Willie took his captaincy manual from a different world. His speeches were not comparable with anything I'd ever heard before or since.

'One of my clearest memories of Willie's captaincy is of the morning after the Scotland game in 1984. The papers all had a picture of Duggan with his arm around Tony Ward and speaking to him. It was just before Wardie was taking a penalty. It appeared that Willie was acting the real father figure but knowing him as I do my guess was he was saying: "If you miss this penalty, I'll kick you all the way to Kilkenny!"

'Another of the great characters was Ginger McLoughlin. In 1983 I was chosen to tour with the Lions to New Zealand but because of injury I was unable to make the start of it. Later on both Ginger and I were called out as replacements. Ginger hadn't trained in about two months. We had to travel to London, Los Angeles, Auckland and Christchurch. Both of us were very concerned to get there in the best shape possible and were not drinking at all. There was a lot of supporters on the plane and they were in high spirits. We hit an air pocket and a few of the fans spilled their drink all over us. We smelt like a brewery. Willie John McBride was at the airport to meet us and was not impressed.'

When the Ciaran Fitzgerald era ended Lenihan stepped into the breach and took on the mantle of captaincy: 'I struggled a bit during my first term as captain but was much more comfortable in the role second time around.'

He led Ireland to the inaugural World Cup in 1987. It was not a happy experience for him as he saw his side struggle to make any impression. Ireland's slide accelerated the following season, culminating in a humiliating defeat at Twickenham, when Jimmy Davidson succeeded Mick Doyle. Lenihan attributes the decline, at least in part, to non-playing factors.

'Jimmy Davidson was a very good coach with excellent ideas, who never got the recognition he deserved. The problem was that there was a breakdown in communication between him and some of the players. I don't think he really understood the difference between the personalities of the Munster players and the lads from Ulster.

'I welcomed the news of Fitzie's appointment as coach but I don't think the IRFU did him any favours by appointing him too early in his career. The World Cup in 1987 changed rugby. We were certainly not ready for that change. In 1991 we let a golden opportunity slip through our fingers. Our preparation, though, for that competition was pretty abysmal.'

Indeed for a long time it seemed that Lenihan himself would not participate in the tournament.

'Earlier that year I was told my rugby career was over by the surgeon who operated on me. I missed most of the build-up matches. The team were due to tour Namibia in the summer of 1991. I went for a physical assessment in Thomond Park and Fitzie and the team management were amazed how fit I was, but I had missed out on too many matches and was ruled out of the trip to Namibia. There is a lot of nonsense talked, by players who are dropped, about how badly they want their team to win. In my heart of hearts I wanted Ireland to do badly because it was the only chance I had of getting back into the team.

'One Sunday I was bringing my son to the Tall Ships race in Cork. I heard on the car radio that the Irish management were trying frantically to contact me. Brian Rigney had damaged his knee and they wanted me to fly out immediately. I had to get so many connecting flights I didn't know where I was: London, Frankfurt, Johannesburg and then a four-seater to the middle of the desert. Ciaran Fitzgerald asked me would I be fit to play the following day. I said I would. The one consolation I had was that the match was scheduled for the evening which would give me a chance to get rid of the jet lag. To my horror the match was rescheduled for the afternoon because they were concerned about the state of the floodlights. Before the match I told Terry Kingston, who was captain, not to worry about me if I wasn't participating in the warm-up. I sat in the toilet conserving energy while the others got ready for the game.'

Lenihan acquitted himself well in the game and in the second Test in Namibia, and found himself back on the side for the World Cup campaign. From an Irish point of view the tournament was a story of what might have been.

'The Australian match was the greatest disappointment of my career. We had the match won but we lost it. I remember our bus got stuck in a traffic-jam on the way to the match which meant that we literally ran in off the bus, got togged out and ran onto the pitch. It was a tremendous performance. I think the game was lost when we failed to find touch after the kick-off following Gordon Hamilton's try.

'I genuinely believe we had a 50-50 chance of beating New Zealand in the semi-final in front of our home fans. Our form had been poor up to that match and nobody expected us to do well. Had we won that game I think it would have generated a whole new level of interest in rugby throughout the country. It could have been like the mass hysteria which the Irish soccer team generated during the World Cup in Italy.

'It's funny the things that go through players' minds. I was speaking to Australia's Tim Horan after the match. After the Hamilton try he thought it was all over for them and they would be on the plane home the following morning. He had put a lot of his clothes in the laundry that morning and his big fear was that the clothes wouldn't be ready for the following day! Then Michael Lynagh intervened and took them out of jail with his try.'

Injuries forced Lenihan to depart from the international stage slightly ahead of schedule. 'I knew it was time to retire when the bits and pieces started falling off my body.'

When asked about his most vivid memory of his time as Irish captain Lenihan furnishes a surprising response.

'It was during the World Cup in 1987. Doyler decided he was going to get into shape on the trip because he was two stone overweight. He started to train with the backs and when the lads saw this they stepped up a gear. At the end of the session Doyler was in bits. Later that night we heard that he had been taken to hospital. I will always remember going to see him that evening in hospital in the taxi. I was in the front seat and Syd Millar and Mick Molloy were in the back. At one stage in the conversation Syd said Mick's wife, Lynne, had been on the phone and was very concerned about him and wanted to come down under to see him. Then he said his girlfriend, Mandy, was very worried about him and she too wanted to travel to see him. The Maori taxi-driver turned to me and said with real feeling: "That stuff about holy Catholic Ireland is a load of crap!"

'When we got back from the hospital Brian Spillane asked: "Did he have a girl or a boy?" Some years later, at a dinner, I told this story to a charming woman with an English accent whom I had never met before nor had any idea who she was except that she was very well versed in rugby matters. It turned out to be Doyler's ex-wife, Lynne!'

14

SEAN LYNCH

Called to the Bar

If you carry on niggling me, son, you're going to live up to your name.

Gareth Chilcott to Wales's Dai Young

In 1971 Colin Meads prematurely dismissed the Lions forwards as 'too many sweat bands, not enough sweat.' On a Monday afternoon the Swan Bar in Dublin's York Street is a haven of tranquillity. The owner, Sean Lynch, was one of the men who made Meads eat his words.

One lesson every player has to learn is never to take himself too seriously. A few years ago when *Rugby Special* were doing their review of the year they asked rugby correspondent Stephen Jones to select his man of the year. He went back to England's victory over Australia. The crucial point in the match came when an Australian try was disallowed because of a foot in touch. The TV replay proved it was the correct decision. The linesman who had made the decision that day was Stephen Hildich. He was watching *Rugby Special* at home and got very excited when he heard all the praise he was receiving and as they were preparing to announce man of the year he rushed out to get his wife. Just as she ran in they announced the winner – it was the cameraman who proved Stephen's decision was the right one!

Sean Lynch is not a player to take himself too seriously. Despite his achievements at the very highest level with the Lions his happiest memories are of club successes with St Mary's.

'From my point of view the pinnacle of my career was captaining St Mary's to our first Leinster Cup in 1969. I had the experience of losing two previous finals so it was really sweet for me.'

Success at club level provided the platform Lynch needed to step onto the international stage.

'Denis Hickie and I were capped for the first time against France in 1971 becoming the first current Mary's players to play for Ireland. Jimmy Kelly and George Norton had played for St Mary's and Ireland but were not Mary's players during their international careers. It was a wonderful achievement for the club. When the side was announced there was a great club celebration.'

After just one season at international level Lynch was chosen by the Lions on the historic tour to New Zealand. He was to play a more central role than anybody could have foreseen at the start of the tour. The week before the first Test in Dunedin the Lions had lost their two first-choice props, Ray McLoughlin and Sandy Carmichael, with long-term injuries in the infamous 'battle of Christchurch'. The match confirmed an old adage: 'New Zealand rugby is a colourful game – you get all black and blue.'

Willie John McBride warned his fellow forwards after this bruising encounter: 'You have not seen anything yet. They will throw everything at you, even the kitchen sink.'

Lynchie's prop partner was the squat Scot, Ian McLauchlan, 'Mighty Mouse'. One of his opponents scornfully dismissed him in the words: 'You'll be Mickey Mouse by the time I've finished with you.' Yet it was the Lions who had the last laugh winning 9–3. The crowd's silence after the game bore eloquent testimony to the scale of the shock. From that moment a win in the series was a distinct possibility, though the All Blacks restored parity in the second Test.

The Lions won the third Test 13–3 in Wellington, thanks in no small measure to a vintage display by Barry John. The final Test at Eden Park, Auckland, ended in a 14–14 draw. For Lynch it was do-or-die.

'We were getting very tired at that stage and were anxious to return home, but at the same time we didn't want to squander a 2–1 lead. We were determined to prove that we were the best. Our mood had changed during the tour. When we arrived we probably believed deep down that the All Blacks were invincible. By the finish it was us who thought we were almost invincible.'

Before the match the captain, John Dawes, simply said to the players: 'We have come this far. We're not going to throw it away now.' Dawes looked each player in the eye. Further words were superfluous. Each player knew what they had to do. The joke later among the players was: 'We were so fired up, when the referee ran on to the pitch, three of us tackled him.'

Spurred on like a wounded animal by the ire of a fanatical nation the All Blacks started like a whirlwind, taking the lead after just four minutes courtesy of a soft try from Wayne Cottrell. The tension got to the Lions and they under-performed. However, when they were trailing 14–11, J.P.R. Williams dropped a goal from about 40 yards to tie the match.

Lynch is perpetually grateful to the coach's role in the Lions success and to two coaches who had a big impact on his development into a top class player.

'Carwyn James, the Lions' coach in 1971, was one of the great visionaries of the game. Ronnie Dawson was Ireland's first coach and was very instrumental in bringing Ireland into the modern era. Another great coach I would have to mention is Ned Carmody of St Mary's. He had a lot of insights into the game and was a wonderful psychologist.

'On the non-playing side my greatest memory of the Lions tour is of visiting a vineyard, I think it was run by a religious order. I had red wine, white wine, blue wine and everything that was going. At the end I didn't know where I was or who I was! I wasn't moving very sprightly the next morning.

'We had some great characters in the squad especially Chico Hopkins. He was a comical figure. Willie John McBride was a character in a different way and a fantastic forward. I always say you can build a side around a player like him. Not surprisingly I got on particularly well with the front-row forwards. In effect we formed a front-row club. I learned a great lesson on that tour: that sport builds bridges.'

Personal contests in rugby can generate a lot of fun as well as rivalry. As recently as the 1980s Australia's Andy Slack and New Zealand's Stu Wilson played a game within a game whenever they played against each other even in a high pressure situation like a Test match. Slack carried three Australian coins in his pocket and Wilson three New Zealand coins. At various stages of the game they dropped a coin from their pockets. The winner was the one who collected the most of the other's coins during the match. The loser bought the drinks. That kind of side-show does not happen today.

Lynch too had a strong rivalry with a friend: 'Ray McLoughlin was the toughest opponent I ever came up against. Nobody else ever bothered me too much but Ray made life very difficult. He would be seen as one of the very best worldwide.'

Inevitably when talking of front rows the famous Pontypool front row of Charlie Faulkner, Bobby Windsor and Graham Price, celebrated in song and folklore by Max Boyce, looms large for Lynch. The camaraderie between front-row players is amazing, especially between the Pontypool gang. It is a strange fact of rugby life that people in the same positions on the field tend to pal around together. It was said that Windsor's tactic with novice opponents was to bite them on the ear early in the match and say: 'Behave yourself, son, and nothing will happen to this ear of yours.'

Windsor was one of the game's great raconteurs. One of his favourite stories was about a Welsh Valleys rugby club on tour in America. On coming back from a night on the town, two of the players could not find their rooms. They decided to check for their team-mates by looking through the keyholes. At one stage they came on an astonishing sight. There, in her birthday suit, was a Marilyn Monroe lookalike. Close by was a man who was chanting out with great conviction: 'Your face is so beautiful that I will have it painted in gold. Your breasts are so magnificent that I will have them painted in silver. Your legs are so shapely that I will have them painted in platinum.' Outside, the two Welsh men were getting very aroused and began jostling each other for the right of the keyhole. The man inside hearing the racket shouted out: 'Who the hell is out there?' The two Welshmen replied: 'We're two painters from Pontypool.'

Asked about his opinion of rugby's television coverage Windsor is said to have observed: 'When I was in school we learned a line from Shakespeare's *Hamlet*: "The play's the thing." Today the replay's the thing.'

On the Lions' flight to South Africa in 1974 Windsor was taken ill with food poisoning. He was so ill that he was taken to the back of the plane and told to suck ice-cubes to help him cool down. The team doctor, former Irish international Ken Kennedy, came to take his temperature without knowing about the ice-cubes. When he looked at the thermometer he shouted out: 'Jaysus, Bobby you died 24 hours ago!'

The definitive Sean Lynch story is told by Mick Quinn.

'Lynchie was on the Irish tour to Argentina in 1970. All the players were attending a dinner. A Lord somebody was to be the main dignitary. Before he arrived the players were told that he had Parkinson's disease and to be patient as it would take him a long time to walk to the dinner table. After what seemed a half-hour the Lord eventually made it to the seating position. He was sitting beside Lynchie and said: "Well, Mr Lynch, are you enjoying your tour?" Lynchie replied: "Yes, Mr Parkinson, I am!"'

15

WILLIE JOHN MCBRIDE

The Lion King

It ain't easy, but it sure is simple.

Ronald Reagan

It is inconceivable that a discussion on great Irish forwards should begin without reference to Willie John. The fact that it is unnecessary to use his surname says it all. To say his rugby c.v. is impressive is an understatement: 63 caps, five Lions tours, 17 Lions' Test appearances, captain of the most successful Lions' side of all time. In the 1972–3 season he surpassed the record of Scottish prop-forward Hugh McLeod when he made 43 consecutive appearances in international rugby.

Born one of six children in Toomebridge, County Antrim, he lost his father at four and was brought up by his mother on a small farm. The hardships he experienced give a lie to the perception that rugby in Ireland is only a game for those brought up with a silver spoon.

Gareth Edwards has gone on record to say that Willie John McBride was his sort of captain because of his creed of total commitment, and he would have followed him anywhere. Willie John was wont to say: 'I hate small men.' Each match was rugby's high noon for him. He believed in all or nothing – 'lay down your life or don't come with me.' The phrase 'genial giant' sounds clichéd but it sums him up. On the eve of departing for the Bermuda classic the rugby memories roll off his tongue. He is spoilt for choice when asked about the highlights of his career.

'Beating Australia in the Test in Sydney [11-5] was a great achievement, particularly as we had to strap up three players because of injury to get them onto the field. Our win over Wales in 1970 was also a magic moment. We had an amazing pack of forwards then with world class players like McLoughlin and Slattery. We haven't turned out as good a pack of forwards since. The team was probably at its peak in 1972 but politics probably cost us the Triple Crown. It was great towards the end of my career to lead Ireland to the Championship in 1974.'

Asked about what it was like to play in 'the game' for the Barbarians against the All Blacks in 1973 he laughs.

'When you say I played in it – I was there. I don't think I actually played in it. The match was played at a hundred miles an hour and is unsuitable for a guy like me whose game is not based on mobility. Phil Bennett passed me three times in the one movement. I remember at one point getting the ball and it was hot!'

There was no doubt, though, that his finest hour was the Lions tour in 1974 as an inspirational captain. He coined the famous rallying cry '99' which meant all Lions had to support a colleague in trouble: 'I was a Lion at 21 but losing became a habit. I'd had a baptism of fire in my first Test because I was up against two of the all-time greats in Johan Claassen and Colin Meads. I had to wait nine matches for a win with the Lions.

'The 1974 tour was like all my Christmases at once. Our record was played 22, won 21, drew one, lost none and won the Test series 3–0. Winning became a habit and we liked it. I suppose the sad thing was that there was such controversy about the drawn game, which was the final match. None of us could understand why Fergus Slattery's try was disallowed. The main thing was that we didn't lose the game because of it. If we had it would have taken some of the gloss off the tour. To beat them on their turf was incredible because even now the All Blacks are waiting to achieve the same feat.'

The tour itself was shrouded in controversy.

'You might say we were under house arrest even before we left home. We came under tremendous pressure, spending three days in London where the anti-apartheid movement asked us to pull out of the tour. I met the players and told them: "If you don't want to come, please leave now." There wasn't a sound. It seemed like forever but after a couple of moments I could wait no longer and said: "Okay then, we are all in this together." Once in South Africa, we discovered that the British Government, who were against the tour, had instructed the Embassy to boycott us. The opposition helped weld us together, to mould us into one big family.

'That was the biggest challenge of my life trying to get coalminers from Wales and solicitors from London to mix together. Cracks could have appeared in the squad when we divided into a Test side and a midweek side, but those problems never arose because we kept on winning. We only used 17 players in the four Tests: one change was caused by injury and the other was when we brought Andy Irvine in on the wing. Although he was out of his position [full-back] he was too good a player to leave on the bench. I especially remember after Alan Old broke his leg, Phil Bennett came along to say to me: "Don't worry, I'll play as often as you need me." Those guys had a great attitude to life. They trained hard, played hard but always were a good laugh. When we won the first two Tests we had the Springboks reeling. I think they made ten changes in all for the third Test. That was the big one because it meant that if we won that match we won the series. We trained every day, concentrating on scrummaging, and no quarter was asked or given. Those workouts were much tougher than anything we could have encountered in a match.

'The day before, we travelled on a coach to a little village out of Port Elizabeth and had tea and scones on a very English lawn. We told stories, and laughed and joked a lot. We really managed to relax and the game was put to the back of our minds. As the old man of the party, I was anxious to get to bed early because I needed my rest. But that night it was not easy to sleep. I told the players that evening: "There is no escape. We will take no prisoners!"

'The following day, when I walked into the room where the team had gathered, the air was full of electricity. There were five minutes to board the coach and they stood up. Usually, I would talk about the importance of the game and the reasons for wanting to win. But this time I simply asked: "Men, are we ready?" They looked up. They were ready.

'The first 20 minutes or so were probably the toughest of the whole tour. The pressure on us was terrible. People expected us to win, which can be fatal for any team. We made it hard on ourselves by making mistakes we'd never made before. However, we finally got it together and won 26–9.

'The feeling of greatness in that side was unbelievable. We had the best back row I have ever played with – Fergus Slattery, Gareth Edwards, Phil Bennett and J.P.R. Williams. The real strength of that team, though, was its togetherness, loyalty and bravery. When the tour was finished the players presented me with a lovely, engraved, silver water-jug which read: "To Willie John. It was great to travel with you." That is my most treasured rugby possession. There is a bond between that team that will never die.'

In his final home international McBride scored his first try for his country when Ireland defeated France 25–6. Such was the emotion generated that the crowd ran onto the pitch to celebrate the try. To mark the centenary season of Irish rugby the IRFU arranged a match between Ireland-Scotland and England-Wales in April 1975. It was to be the last time the Ballymena man would lead out a side at the home of Irish rugby. Events took an unexpected turn after the match when he was hijacked by the late Eamon Andrews and whisked away to become the subject of an edition of *This Is Your Life*.

When asked about his most difficult opponent McBride does not hesitate for a second.

'Colin Meads was as hard a man as I ever came across though I also played against his brother Stan who was also a tough nut. Colin [nicknamed Pinetree] was the best, most aggressive, and perhaps the most totally committed player I ever played against. [A small indication of his rugged indestructibility was his remarkable recovery from a horrific car crash, in 1971. His back was in plaster after the accident but he was playing rugby within six months.] There were so many other great players like Gerald Davies, who was the greatest winger I was fortunate to play with.'

On a national level he was a big admirer of Ken Goodall (he was capped 19 times for Ireland between 1967 and 1970 before turning to Rugby League with Workington, scoring three tries. He also toured South Africa with the Lions), an outstanding number eight forward.

A number of Willie John stories have become part of rugby folklore. A story about the 1974 Lions tour shows a different side to McBride's personality. One night, a group of players were disturbed in their hotel in the middle of the night. An undiplomatic war broke out. The tiny hotel manager tried to keep the peace. Two scantily clad players were parading around the corridors and he roared at them to get back into their rooms. Not liking his attitude they told him with all due lack of politeness what to do with himself. The manager's threat to ring the police met with no reaction. At this point along came Willie John. The manager thought his problems were solved when the captain arrived. When McBride seemed to be ignoring the matter the manager repeated his threat to call the police. Willie John called him forward with a tilt of his head. The manager breathed a sigh of relief. His threat had worked. He was in for a big disappointment as McBride bent down to him and whispered: 'How many are you going to get?'

Another story tells how he had been trapped at the bottom of a ruck when a few players kicked him on his head. After the game he was asked did he remember the pounding on his head. He answered: 'I do. I heard it.'

When the Lions won the series in 1974 a magnificent party was staged in the hotel. The festive spirit got a little out of hand and every fire extinguisher and water hose in the hotel was set off. The problem was that nobody thought to turn them off. The result was that the next morning the hotel could have done with the services of Noah's Ark. The touring manager was summoned the next morning to explain the actions of his team. He had gone to bed early and had no idea what had happened until he discovered himself thigh deep in water. He half-walked, half-swam up to Willie John's room and prepared to knock on the door only to discover that the door had been a casualty of the flood. To his astonishment McBride was calmly sitting on his bed, puffing contentedly on his pipe, as it bobbed around on the water. The manager lost control and launched into a vicious tirade. Finally, Willie John replied:

'Alan, can I ask you one question?'

'What?'

'Is there anybody dead?'

He casually dismisses those stories with a chuckle: 'Don't believe all you hear!' He is less than enchanted by all the trends in the coaching of players: 'We played by vision. Today, players have to be led. They watch so many videos. I'm not sure what you can learn from watching videos because every game is so different.'

Listening to Willie John talk it is striking to observe the contrast between his vocabulary and value system to that of the current spate of players. His word is his bond. The idea of a player requiring a contract to play rugby is completely alien to him. There is a powerful undercurrent of sadness in his voice as he talks about the game he loves so well. It stems from an experience of loss, a sense of fragmentation that the old ways are dead or at least on a life-support machine. How would he like to be remembered?

'I'm a very boring person. I've only had the one employer, I've only had the one club and I've only had the one wife. To me loyalty is paramount and I'm worried about the rugby supermarket that is developing where players are moving like commodities on a shelf. I don't like the idea of the cheque book running Irish rugby. You're only as good as your weakest link so you cannot grade players in terms of payment. I'm fearful about some of the noises I've heard in terms of the future direction of rugby. I would like to be remembered as a man of loyalty and as someone who always gave his best.'

16

JIM MCCARTHY

Jim'll Fix It

The state of British sport is mostly serious, but never hopeless.
The state of Irish sport is usually hopeless, but never serious.

Noel Henderson

In George Eliot's *Middlemarch* Dr Casaubon responds to the hope and ardour of his young wife, Dorothea, with a timid, passive, aggressive attitude: 'I don't know what you mean, I'm not listening to you, and anyway I know better.' Casaubon is threatened by Dorothea's energy and idealism. Poor Casaubon would have been totally intimidated by Jim McCarthy. If human drive and energy were electricity he would be a powerhouse.

The Cork-born wing-forward is a product of C.B.C. Cork (winning a Munster Senior Schools Cup medal with the school in 1943). With his club, Dolphin, he won Munster Cup medals in 1944, 1945 and 1948. He was capped 28 times for Ireland between 1948 and 1955, captaining the side four times in 1954 and 1955, and scoring eight international tries. He was also omnipresent in the Irish team which won the International Championship in 1951, and toured Argentina and Chile in 1952 with Ireland.

He is best remembered as a breakaway forward of the highest quality, playing in all four matches in the 1948 Grand Slam year, and for the entire season of 1949. He brought a new dimension to wing-forward play, particularly in relation to helping the out-half breach the opposing half. A flying redhead, he was an invaluable ally to Jack Kyle combining with him to devastating effect. His back-row combination with Old Belvedere's Des O'Brien and Bill McKay in those years is among the finest in Irish rugby history. Where did his interest in rugby begin?

'My father was interested in rugby and sports in general. He was never much of a player himself but the way he talked about his playing career you'd think he was one of the greats. His love of sport was infectious. My sister, Aileen, became an international golfer before she became a Mercy nun. She was a real tomboy. I always felt she should have played rugby for Munster. She would have been the ideal partner for Tom Clifford!'

He attributes Ireland's success in 1948 and 1949 to the fact that so many great players came onto the scene at the same time.

'It's not important to have a good captain when you have a good team because everybody knows exactly what they have to do. Karl Mullen was a great captain but that 1948–9 team had total commitment. We never contemplated losing at any stage. I think attitude is hugely important in rugby. You have to believe you will win before you win.

'The late John C. Daly from Cobh was a terrific player. He was a powerful man and scored the decisive try in Belfast that clinched the Triple Crown in 1948. He turned to Des O'Brien and said: "If Wales don't score now I'll be canonised in Cobh tonight." In fact at the end of the game the fans tore his jersey off his back to keep as a souvenir because Ireland hadn't won the Triple Crown for 49 years. He also went on to play rugby League very successfully. The best passer of the ball I ever saw was John O'Meara. Johnny Hewitt was the second-best out-half in the British Isles during our glory years. He only won four caps for Ireland because he was around at the same time as Jack Kyle, but he would have walked into any other team.

'As any of the older generations of players will tell you the best thing about rugby is the friendships. Last year I was at a dinner to mark the 40th anniversary of one of Dolphin's Munster Cups. Strangely, that team won their six rounds without ever scoring a try. I was making the speech and sitting beside Norman Coleman, a great servant of the club. Since his playing days he's had, I think, three hip replacements and a heart by-pass operation. I began my speech by saying: "I now find I only half-know Norman."'

Ireland's Grand Slam victory in 1948 prompted McCarthy to engage in what the IRFU saw as extravagant behaviour.

'After we won the Triple Crown in Belfast I sent in my expenses to the IRFU. I claimed four pounds and ten shillings but only got four pounds and seven shillings. They deducted three shillings because I had rang my family to tell them we had won the Triple Crown and because I had gone outside the table d'hôte menu. I had ordered two raw eggs to eat the morning of the match. That was part of my ritual. I also took glucose. It probably did me no good physically but psychologically it gave me an extra edge.'

McCarthy toured with the Lions to Australia and New Zealand in 1950.

'It was the last of the six and a half months tours. When you go along on a tour like that it's years later before you really appreciate it. It's amazing how quickly people get used to the star treatment. Welsh coalminers who were reared on anything but the silver spoon quickly assume a new star persona. After a few weeks we were all cribbing about the waitresses.

'Looking back there were some great players on that team. Scotland's Graham Budge was a peculiar case. He had come from nowhere to play in the final Scottish trial, in the four matches in the Five Nations, and then went on the Lions tour and after that was never heard of again. In 1980 I was holidaying in Pebble Beach, in America, and I went to a local rugby tournament. My eye was caught by a headline which read: "Rugby player dies with his boots on." It reported how the previous year a player had dropped dead playing a match on the same ground. It was Graham. He would have been in his fifties then but was still playing rugby when he grabbed the ball and made a run. He dropped dead on the half-way line.

'The other great find of that 1950 Lions tour was Lewis Jones of Wales. He was only in his teens but he looked much older because he was losing his hair like lightning. With his big bandy legs he was the first running full-back. That's the big difference between our time and now. Then, every player's first instinct was not to get tackled. Today, their instinct is to make sure they get tackled with all this talk about recycling the ball. The first people to start this were the All Blacks. It's very effective but not very pretty to watch. It's not so much "win rugby" as no-loss rugby. I'm certain it's not the running game which William Webb Ellis envisaged. For me the only keepers of the true tradition of rugby are France. Why France don't win the home internationals every year is a mystery to me. They do the extraordinary as the ordinary.'

There is one big regret from his playing days.

'We should have won the Triple Crown in 1951. We had the beating of Wales but our penalty kicker, George Norton, was injured and we let the game slip through our fingers. We drew 3–3. They sprung a new kicker, Ben Edwards, who kicked a wonderful penalty and we equalised with a fantastic try from Jack Kyle. We missed the conversion from in front of the posts. Jack's opponent that day was Cliff Morgan, who went

Paddy Reid breaks through the Welsh defence in 1948

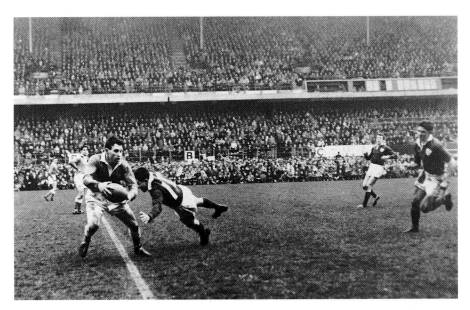

Mick English tackles Cliff Morgan in his debut international in 1958. Noel Murphy and Tony O'Reilly look on

The blessed Trinity: Ireland's greatest ever back row? (left to right) Bill McKay, Des O'Brien and Jim McCarthy

Hope springs eternal: Dick Spring awaits developments

Gone but not forgotten: the late great Shay Deering

Champions! The Irish team which won the championship in 1974 (© Independent Newspapers Ltd)

A star with Bjorn: Mike Gibson with Bjorn Borg

*Brothers in arms: Ollie Campbell and Colin Patterson
in jubilant mood following Ireland's sensational first
Test victory over Australia in 1979*

Melody Maker Mick: Mick Quinn sings for Ireland

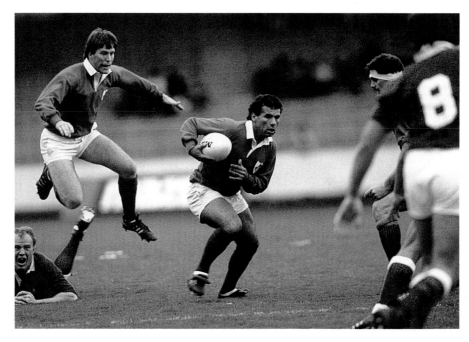

Evasive action: Jinking Tony Ward makes a break (© Inpho, Dublin)

LEFT: The winner takes it all: Jim Glennon receives the Philips manager of the month award from John Coogan

RIGHT: Ciaran Fitzgerald at the line-out (© Inpho, Dublin)

The famous five: five of the all-time great out-halfs, (left to right) Jack Kyle, Eugene Davy, Cliff Morgan, Mike Gibson and Ollie Campbell

Doctor Kyle, I presume? Noel Henderson and Jack Kyle at the 1995 World Cup

on to become one of the greats himself. We won the Championship that year but it should have been the Grand Slam.'

The following year saw McCarthy touring with Ireland to South America.

'It was a total success off the field and a disaster on it. We were the first international team to be beaten by Argentina. When we got there we were told we couldn't play any rugby because Eva Peron had just died. They sent us down to Santiago, Chile, to teach the cadets how to play. After eight days they beat us!

The players didn't take the playing side very seriously. At one stage Paddy Lawler went missing for a few days and nobody had a clue where he was. When he returned, a team meeting was hastily called. The team manager solemnly announced that he had been talking to Dublin, which was a big deal in 1952, and then looked around menacingly and said: "I'm deciding whether or not to send some players home." Paddy stood up straight away and replied: "We've been talking among ourselves and we're deciding whether or not we should send you home!"'

McCarthy became the record try scorer for Ireland for a forward. What was the secret of his success? 'Wherever the ball is you be there. When I was playing for Ireland the best place to be was two feet behind Jackie Kyle.'

A number of players caught McCarthy's eye in the green jersey since his retirement.

'In my position Fergus Slattery was the greatest player in recent times. He was so energetic and chased all over the place. I always felt that Colin Patterson was a great loss to Ireland when he got injured. He had a great ability to score tries which is always a big problem for an opposing side because they don't know what he's going to do next. Of course Ollie Campbell was a superb player and would be a wonderful asset to any team.'

He has some very radical views about the future of Irish rugby.

'I would like to see a one-man management system who would be given total control. If he's not up to the job get rid of him straight away. At the very most a three-man selection system ought to be employed because we have to break beyond the petty politics that goes on and ensure we have the best players available in all positions.'

McCarthy describes his current working status as semi-retirement. He continues to work as an executive with Tony O'Reilly's company, Fitzwilton. His association with O'Reilly goes back a long way.

'Tony came down to take up his first job in Cork and joined us for afternoon tea, which led him to stay a few days, which became two years and in the process became one of the family. When he first came, he would say "your house, Jim, and your children and your wife," but he quickly changed the "yours" to "ours". I had no problem with "our kids" and "our dog" but when he started saying "our" wife I showed him the door!

'I knew the first time I saw him that he would be a success in anything he turned his hand to. He had it all and more. Having said that, I don't envy him. I believe he was never fully exploited on the Irish team. I think he should have been selected at full-back to get the best out of his attacking abilities. There are two sayings which I think apply to Tony: "The bigger the reputation. The smaller the gap," and: "To be good, you've got to be twice as good." Everybody wants to cut the guy with the big reputation down to size.

'I was best man at both his weddings! I only played one season with Tony at international level. When he arrived on the scene he was the darling of the media and could do no wrong. After his first match against France *The Irish Independent* said that I had played poorly and had not protected Tony well enough even though I wasn't playing in the centre! I was dropped for the next match after that report and never played another international. Twenty five years later Tony put me on the board of *The Irish Independent* just to make up for their injustice to me all those years ago!'

17

BARRY McGANN

An Evening with Johan Cruyff

> If you can play as if it means nothing when it means everything, you've got it.
>
> Steve Davis

The anthem for the 1960s' generation was 'Hope I d-die before I get old'. Theirs was the generation which saw an unprecedented departure from previous ages. It was in the 1960s that life as we know it today was shaped and moulded. This was the decade of the Beatles, pirate radio, monster peace-concerts, flower power and Mary Quant. Hope and idealism were the common currency. Nostalgically everything about the time seems good, the concern for peace, the socially concerned songs of Bob Dylan and Joan Baez and the sense of freedom and optimism. Only the 1960s could have produced a character like Barry McGann.

A warm, genial man, he has turned self-deprecation into an art form, especially about his weight. He laughs when I suggest that the epithet for many ex-players who have lost the battle of the bulge could be the same as that of Paddy Drury.

> Here lies the bones of Paddy Drury
> Owing their size to Guinness' brewery.

Although McGann won 25 caps for Ireland between 1969 and 1976 he has an ecumenical background in a sporting sense. His brothers, Sean and Diarmuid, played Gaelic football for Cork.

'I'm the son of a Galway man, a Tipperary mother and being born in Cork I couldn't but be interested in sport! I played everything in Cork: golf, cricket, soccer, Gaelic football and hurling. I grew up at the back of the Mardyke. It was the golden half-mile because it produced so many sports stars, like former Irish soccer international Noel Cantwell and, of course, Tom Kiernan.

'I played soccer for Young Elms. We won the under-15 and under-18 national titles which helped me get a place as inside-forward on the Irish youths side. I was the only Cork player on a side which included Mick Leach and Terry Conroy. We were one of 24 teams for the UEFA finals and finished sixth in the tournament. The highlight for me was when we beat Holland. It was a major achievement since the Dutch side included no less a person than Johan Cruyff!

'Our manager was the late Gerry Doyle. Around the time I was first capped for Ireland I moved to Dublin. Gerry was managing Shelbourne then and persuaded me to play for them. They had some tremendous players at the time, like Ben Hannigan and Eric Barber. What I most remember is the slagging I used to get whenever I went back to play in Cork. One time we were playing Cork Celtic. As I ran onto the pitch I heard a voice saying on the terraces: "Who's that fellah?"

"That's McGann the rugby player."

"Oh, wouldn't you know it by his stomach"!'

An even more damning indictment of McGann's bulk was

subsequently provided by Tony O'Reilly's quip: 'Twice around Barry McGann and you qualify as a bona fide traveller!'

The links between Shelbourne and the Irish rugby team extend further than McGann. Paul McNaughton was capped 15 times in the centre for Ireland in the late 1970s and early 1980s. He was also a noted soccer player scoring 21 League of Ireland goals for Shelbourne. He also played senior gaelic football for Wicklow, thus earning the distinction of playing at the highest level in Dublin's three main sporting theatres: Gaelic football at Croke Park, rugby at Lansdowne Road and soccer at Dalymount.

At Presentation College McGann's rugby education began.

'I started playing with the junior side at 12 and had three seasons as a junior player and two as a senior captaining the winning Munster Schools' Senior Cup side in 1966. After I left school I went straight on to the Cork Constitution team. I'll never forget what Noel "Noisy" Murphy said to me when I started off: "You just play the ball and we'll look after you."'

Noisy did his job well because within three years McGann was making his international debut.

'I was a sub for the final trial. Mike Gibson was playing at out-half for the Probables and Johnny Moroney for the Possibles. Gibson fractured his jaw in the game and Moroney moved over to the Probables and I came off the bench and onto the Possibles. It was obvious that Gibson would miss the opening game of the season but when the team was picked Moroney was picked on the wing and I was selected at out-half.

'The tradition was that the team was announced on Sunday morning. I heard about it on the half one news on the car radio. I was travelling to Donnybrook where Lansdowne was to play Bective. The first indication I had that I had entered a new phase of my career was that as soon as I got out of the car a journalist rushed up to me for my first interview. The match was cancelled because of the weather and we adjourned to the bar. I was the last one to leave – around midnight. I did get down to hard work after the game. My first international season was my best.'

McGann grabbed his opportunity with both hands and feet, contributing a drop goal in Ireland's 17–9 victory, their first victory over the French in 11 years. The big question was 'would McGann hold his place?' because surely he could not hope to displace Mike Gibson when he recovered from injury. A solution was found by bringing Gibson back into the centre. McGann laughs at the memory: 'I gave Mike Gibson a whole new career as a centre.'

England were despatched 17–15 in Dublin and McGann scored his first international try that season when Ireland defeated Scotland 16–0. The Triple Crown was now on. The Cardiff Arms Park showdown is best remembered for arguably the most controversial punch in the history of international rugby when Noel Murphy was sensationally floored by the 'Bargoed beanpole', Brian Price. After ten minutes the Welsh forward broke from the ruck to do his Cassius Clay impersonation. Murphy, in his final international (after winning 41 caps and touring twice with the Lions) was left sprawling on the ground. Ireland lost 24–11. McGann remembers the game clearly.

'It was a very physical match. The press made a lot of the fact that Prince Charles was attending his first match as Prince of Wales and right in front of him Brian Price knocked out Noisy. People now will not appreciate just how sensational the incident was at the time. There was not a culture of sending players off then the way there is now so Price continued on his merry way for the rest of the game. That was really the beginning of the great Welsh team with Gareth Edwards to the fore.'

There were a number of matches which evoke a warm glow on McGann's face.

'Beating France in Paris was a great thrill. I especially remember Ray McLoughlin's try. He was in the wrong place at the wrong time and fell over the line with the ball! Playing against the All Blacks was also a magic moment. We drew with them, 10–10, in 1973. Tom Grace got a try in the last moment in the right corner. I missed out on rugby fame because I officially missed the conversion that would have won the game for Ireland. The kick was so high that it was difficult to see which side of the post the ball went but, to this day, I'm convinced that the ball did not in fact go wide. Earlier that week the All Blacks had got out of jail against Munster in Musgrave Park with a penalty in injury time when we drew 3–3. Another chance of being part of history snatched away from me. Not a lot of people know this but I was part of the Munster squad that defeated the All Blacks in 1978. Every rugby fan knows the name of the Munster team but no one knows the name of the subs. I was sub to Wardie.'

A decline in form deprived McGann of participating in Ireland's victory in the 1974 International Championship.

'I got Mick Quinn his ten caps for Ireland because I was his only competition and I wasn't up to much at the time!'

The arrival of Tony Ward effectively marked the curtain call for McGann's representative career.

'Wardie was a class player who had everything. Few Irish players ever excited a crowd they way he could. He was just a breath of fresh air. I know to an outsider he took my place on the Munster team and his arrival ended my international career but I had nothing except admiration for him. Around the time he exploded onto the scene I was having serious injury problems. I broke my leg and then had trouble with arthritis in my knee so even if he hadn't arrived my international career would have finished.'

Ward and McGann seem to have formed a mutual admiration society. Ward, himself a former League of Ireland soccer player, was a big fan of his rival for the Munster shirt.

'Irrespective of whether we met at a Munster training session or on the occasion of our games against Cork Constitution, Barry always sought to give me advice. It could be said that his sense of comradeship rebounded on him in the sense that I took his place on the Munster side, but I will always be grateful for his remarkable philosophy of sport. When it came to tactical kicking Barry was without peer, though he was not the fastest in the world. The main memories I have of him go back to my own schooldays in St Mary's and Fr Kennedy telling us that when you got within ten or fifteen yards of the opposing line it was sacrilege to kick the ball away. Then I watched Barry playing for Ireland and saw the amount of tries he would set up from that position with his little grubber kicks for Alan "Dixie" Duggan to run on to.

'Barry had great physical presence and was a wonderful team player. He could kick from the proverbial sixpence. I remember playing for Munster against Ulster in Thomond Park in 1976 and Johnny McDonnell, who was playing at centre for us, had to leave the field. McGann came on with ten minutes to go and almost as soon as he came on I passed to him and straight away he thumped an almighty ball into the air and it came down with snow on it – so whether it was out-half, centre or prop-forward he was going to kick.'

McGann does not allow himself to have regrets about his career.

'I don't allow myself to give into the "if only" syndrome but I would have loved to have toured with the Lions. I was on stand-by for the 1971 tour to South Africa. They didn't bring a second out-half because they had a number of utility backs who could slot in at number ten. Barry John was the first choice.'

How does he react to the perception that he never properly fulfilled his potential because he was not dedicated enough?

'Rugby was never more than a recreational activity for me. Having said that I didn't lack application. I trained hard when I needed to but I enjoyed the social side. My business career was also important so rugby was never the only thing in my life.'

What's the secret of being a good out-half?

'That's a big question but I think it boils down to taking the right options. There are some out-halfs who have all the skills but they're not good at adapting to varying circumstances. A guy who can take the right option eight out of ten times is top class. If I was asked to show perfection from an out-half I would go back to Ollie Campbell during Ireland's Triple Crown win of 1982. That season Ollie seemed to take the right option ten out of ten times especially for the classic try he set up for Moss Finn.'

As president of Lansdowne he is concerned about the future of the game with the introduction of professionalism.

'There are a lot of big questions to be answered about where the game in Ireland is going. What part will the schools or universities play in this new era? Could the whole fabric of club rugby as we know it be lost as the best players are tempted away? The whole scene is fraught with pitfalls. My big worry is that the changes have come from top-down instead of the bottom-up.

'The rugby scene was very different in my time. There were no real stars until Tony Ward came onto the scene. I missed out on the beauty contest! I do recall, though, that at one stage the Ladies' Column in *The Evening Press* referred to me as "our chubby hero". My own mother was delighted with the final line in the feature: "Every mother should have one." Now because of Sky Sport and so on rugby stars are treated almost the same way as Madonna!'

Asked about his outstanding memory from his Irish days McGann pauses only briefly.

'It was towards the final days of my international career. I was a sub for Mick Quinn at the time. Syd Millar was the coach then. I had the reputation of being a very laid-back player but I was serious when I needed to be. Because of work I was late for a training session although genuinely I got there as quick as I could. The training session at Anglesea Road was in full swing when I got there. I went over and apologised to Syd for being late and asked him what he wanted me to do. I had a strong feeling he didn't believe I had made much of an effort to be there but he told me to warm up. Instinctively I rubbed my hands together and blew on them and said: "Okay, coach, I'm ready." Moss Keane was in stitches but I'll never forget the bemused look on Syd's face. I think that incident probably cost me ten caps!'

18

Hugo MacNeill

Supermac

It seems a neat game, but do they really bite ears off?

Elizabeth Taylor

Capped 37 times for Ireland, Hugo MacNeill scored eight international tries, a record for a full-back making him perhaps Ireland's greatest attacking full-back of all time. More recently he has been acclaimed, with Trevor Ringland, as the brains behind the Peace International between Ireland and the Barbarians in the wake of the Canary Wharf bombing and the breakdown of the IRA ceasefire. A schoolboy wonder, he captained the Leinster and Irish Schools' sides. Having won his first full cap against France in 1981 he was one of only six players to play in all six matches of the 1982 and 1985 Triple Crown victories and won three Test caps on the 1983 Lions tour of New Zealand. What is his happiest rugby memory?

'Probably the highlights of my career were winning two Senior Cups and a Junior Cup with Blackrock College, particularly with a running side. There is no doubt that the low point was when we lost the Leinster Cup to De La Salle Churchtown when I was captain. Obviously it was fantastic as a young person to be part of the Triple Crown win in 1982. In retrospect what was most fascinating about the whole experience was the diversity of personalities that made up that side. To me Moss Keane is not only a giant of rugby but a giant of humanity. Contrary to the image of him as a rugger bugger he's incredibly intelligent, very sensitive and acutely aware of other people. He's always looking out for the quiet person and was very encouraging to me when I came on the scene. Players like Moss were able to celebrate difference. I noticed a big contrast when I went on the Lions tour in 1983. Some non-Irish players looked down a bit on others because of the job they did. Some others thought you were a bit snobby if you were going to college in Oxford.

'Players like Willie Duggan operate on two levels. They have a public persona of being hard men but underneath they have great awareness of people. I remember going for a walk with Willie before the Wales match in 1982 and still being a bit in awe of him. It wasn't exactly: "Well, Mr Duggan, how will we do?" but it was close enough to it. He told me that he fancied us and had bet that we would win the Triple Crown. That gave me confidence. In 1985, following his retirement, our relationship was more like that between two equals. I promised to get him tickets for the Scotland match. I was sharing a room with Brian Spillane and the phone rang. I answered with the words: "The Spillane–MacNeill suite." Immediately I heard Willie respond: "You might as well be sleeping together you spend so much time together on the pitch!"

'I got my own back on him the night before the match. I went out for a walk and when I came back I saw Willie, all dressed up, with a number of business friends. He called me over and I said: "Willie, it's a great thrill for me to see you here."

"Why's that, Hugo?"

"Well, in all the years I've known you it's the first time I've seen you in the team hotel the night before a match!"'

In the early years MacNeill had a unique way of releasing the tension before home matches.

'I was studying Anglo-Irish literature at Trinity College at the time. On the Thursday before international matches we gathered together in the Shelbourne hotel. We always had some time off on the Friday morning. I took a break from the build-up by popping down to Trinity and sitting in on Brendan Kennelly's class on Yeats which I really enjoyed.'

After his sojourn in Trinity, MacNeill won two Oxford Blues, captaining them in the Varsity match. Despite his stay abroad Hugo maintained close contact with his colleagues on the Irish side.

'In my time at Oxford I invited Ollie Campbell over to speak at one of our dinners. What did he do but tell a story against me? He said an American tourist had come up to me in Oxford and said: "Scuse me, where is the library at?"

'I allegedly made no effort to conceal the contempt in my voice when I answered, "This is England. Here we speak the Queen's English. We do not end a sentence with a preposition."

'"OK," said the tourist, "Where is the library at, asshole?"

'I did get my back on him though. Ollie's biggest problem is that he can't say no when people ask him to do them a favour. I rang him up one night and put on an accent and told him I was Mick Fitzgerald from Irish Marketing Ltd and was organising a beauty competition for nurses, and that I wanted him to be one of the judges, knowing full well that he would hate that kind of thing. He sighed and sighed, struggling to come up with a plausible excuse. Eventually he asked me what date the contest was. When I gave him the date he said: "Oh, that's an awful shame. I'm really sorry but I have another function on that night. It's such a pity because I always wanted to judge a beauty contest."

"That's no problem Ollie." I replied. "You see one of the prizes we are going to offer is a night out with Ollie Campbell. We'll pay for everything and it'll be first class all the way."

"Gosh, I'm afraid I'm going to have a lot of commitments around that time. I won't have many nights free."

"But that's the beauty of this Ollie; we'll arrange it for any night that suits you!"

'The panic was getting ever more noticeable in his voice and I could visualise him writhing in his chair as he tried to find a way to back out of it. Eventually he said he was backing away from that type of thing. Then I asked him if there were any of his colleagues who would be willing to do that kind of thing. He blurted out my name immediately and provided my phone number faster than you could say Tony Ward!'

Towards the end of January 1981, 44 Irish rugby players were written to by the IRFU requesting that they indicate if they would be available for the Irish short tour of South Africa in May–June. The letters went out amidst a welter of controversy as political, clerical and media people objected to the notion of Ireland having sporting contact with South Africa. A number of players declined the invitation. Perhaps the bravest decision not to travel of all was that of MacNeill who was just establishing his international place at the time. It took remarkable moral courage for an emerging star to turn down his first overseas tour with his country. Hugo did manage to extract some fun out of the touring situation.

'Around about this time there was a lot of money being offered under the table for players to play in exhibition games in South Africa. One of the ways I sometimes wound up my colleagues in the Irish team was to ring them up, put on a South African accent and offer them £25,000 to play in such a match. It was always interesting to see who showed great interest but I'm not going to name names!'

The following year saw MacNeill playing an integral part in Ireland's

Triple Crown win. His admiration for his colleagues on that Irish side knows no bounds. The team that defeated Scotland in the deciding match was: H. MacNeill, M. Finn, M. Kiernan, P. Dean, K. Crossan, O. Campbell, R. McGrath, P. Orr, C. Fitzgerald (capt.), G. McLoughlin, D. Lenihan, M. Keane, F. Slattery, W. Duggan, J. O'Driscoll.

Having been a virtual novice in 1982 MacNeill was one of the more senior players when Ireland regained the Triple Crown in 1985.

'That year there was a great uncertainty and apprehension before the Scotland game. We had no recognised place kicker and had such a young side. After our win there was so much excitement and freshness that no one could sit down. I had come through the schools and universities with these guys and I really enjoyed the buzz.'

What caused Ireland's star to wane so dramatically the following season?

'We won the Triple Crown playing good rugby but I think we got complacent the following season. If you look back at our matches in 1985 we could have lost all of those matches. We had a lot of good fortune. In 1986 we were not going to surprise people playing more of the same. We needed to advance our game but we didn't.'

Ireland's form in the post-Mick Doyle era slumped dramatically, culminating in a humiliating 35–3 defeat at Twickenham in 1988. At least the match generated one of the most celebrated stories in recent Irish rugby folklore. MacNeill went AWOL during the game. Although Ireland went in with a 3–0 lead at half-time they were slaughtered in the second half. When the second half started Hugo was not there and nobody knew where he was. The joke after the game was that he went in to make a phone call. By the time he came back onto the pitch they had run in for two tries! MacNeill was involved in a similar situation in a match against France. What was the explanation for these incidents?

'It's the usual story of making a mountain out of a molehill. What happened in both cases was that I picked up head injuries in the first half and had to go off with Mick Molloy for treatment. In the French match I returned with my head strapped so I could never understand the mystery.'

Now based in London Hugo is well able to tell stories against himself.

'I was down in Cork with Moss Finn, Donal Lenihan, Michael Kiernan and we were having lunch with five or six rugby fans. In any other place in Ireland sports fans would have passed the time by picking their greatest ever Irish team. Not so in Cork. They picked the worst ever Irish team! I kept my head down as they discussed the merits of three of my predecessors for the position expecting to have my name mentioned at any minute. After they made their choice for full-back I remarked with relief: "I suppose I can relax now." Quick as a flash someone said: "Hang on boy we haven't picked the subs yet!"

'Another time I was at Malahide with Ollie Campbell, at a festival or something. It was not long after the Triple Crown and we had a very high profile then. At one point I was conscious of a group of girls looking at us. I heard murmurs of: "Yes it is." "No it isn't." Shortly afterwards I felt someone tap on me on the shoulder. It was a young lady who asked me if I was Hugo MacNeill, the Irish rugby player. When I said I was she turned around and went back to her friends. I heard her whisper: "Jaysus, I've never been so disappointed in all my life. He's nowhere near as good-looking in real life as he is on television!"'

19

PHILIP MATTHEWS

Observe the Sons of Ulster Marching On

> Forward play is like a funeral. You have to get in front, with the family; not behind with the friends.
>
> Michael Benazet

Rugby players sometimes suffer from 'Orson Welles syndrome'. Like the famous star of the screen, their crowning moment of glory came at the very start of their careers. Nothing that followed could match it. Philip Matthews fell into that category. Matthews was a truly world-class player before his illness. He was a great reader of the game and one of the few players in Irish rugby who could drive players back in a tackle because of his great upper body strength. He was also one of a handful of Irish forwards who could actually sidestep whereas many of his peers seemed content when they got the ball just to drive into their opponent.

He was born in Gloucester and had his first introduction to rugby at lunchtime at school when he was eight years of age. He left his mark on proceedings by scoring a try – at the wrong end! Soccer was in his family tree because his father, Mike, had a trial with Stoke City. In 1969 his English father and Irish mother took the family to Newtownards at a time when the Troubles were breaking out in Northern Ireland.

Matthews was educated at Regent House Grammar School. There he would come into contact with two people, one a teacher, Dave McMaster, the other a student, Nigel Carr, who would play a prominent part in his life. The fruits of McMaster's success as a coach were plain to be seen in the fact that Matthews played on the Irish schoolboys' side for two seasons, captaining the team in his second year against an Australian side that included the Ella brothers and Tony Melrose. Curiously, though, Carr was never capped at schoolboy level.

'Nigel was a year ahead of me at school. He was one of the outstanding players of his era yet he never played for the Irish schools' side. Politics had a big bearing on the selection of those teams. As a child watching people like Gareth Edwards on the Lions tour in 1974, I had always dreamed of playing with the Lions. I remember before I left school Dave McMaster saying both Nigel and I would play for the Lions within ten years. In my early days Dave used a fire and brimstone technique with me so I was pretty chuffed with that sentiment, though I didn't take it too seriously.

'Nigel and I had so many parallels in our career it was unreal. We shared the same house in university. Both of us did our PhDs in science. We went on to play together for Queens, Ards, Ulster and Ireland. He is very intelligent and has a quiet wit which makes him great company. Nigel looked for a long time as if he was always going to be the bridesmaid, never the bride, until he got his first cap. I thought he should have been capped much earlier. Okay, so people will say you couldn't have dropped Fergus Slattery and Ireland were winning for most of that time, but in my view Slats was not playing his best rugby then and on form I feel Nigel should have been selected much earlier. In my view he was one of the most important pieces in Mick Doyle's jigsaw in 1985. It was he who brought continuity into the game. He was one of the best I played with or against.

'I will never forget hearing the news of the horrific bombing in 1987 that gave him the injury that ended his career. We were having a squad session and Syd Millar broke the news to us. I remember our anxiety for him and also for Philip Rainey and David Irwin. It was such a personal tragedy for him and his loss to the team was incalculable. The squad was devastated and I believe it did have a negative impact on our psychological preparation for the World Cup. It's very hard to focus on rugby when something like that happens.'

From Queens, Matthews progressed to playing for Ulster and made his international debut against Australia in 1984. How did he hear about his selection?

'I was taking a tutorial of undergraduates in Queens and I knew the team was due to be announced. I felt I deserved to be selected but it's one thing to feel that you ought to be picked and another to have the selectors think the same way. I rang the sports department at *The Ulster Newsletter* and asked was the Irish team chosen yet? They replied: "Who wants to know?" When I told them they said congratulations so I knew I was in. Willie Anderson was also chosen for his first cap. Both of us were invited to the local radio station. We got there at more or less the same time and gave each other a hug. He's the greatest character I've ever met. I don't think people in Ireland realise just how big a profile he has in the international rugby community. He's on a par with people like Campese.

'The nearest Irish rugby has produced to him since his retirement is Gary Halpin. Gary's a panic. He spent a few years in America on an athletics sponsorship and came back with an awful lot of Americana. It's tremendous for team spirit to have such a naturally funny guy. The Triple Crown side had a good mixture of personalities. Brian Spillane was so laid-back he nearly fell over!

'I have a clear memory of the crowd's roar as I ran onto Lansdowne Road for my debut. It was louder than it ever seemed afterwards. I'll never forget the hair standing on the back of my head, the leg draining and the tongue-drying emotion. It was the speed of the game that I found hardest to adjust to.'

That day was to prove the most significant in Matthews' life because at the post-match reception he met Lisa Flynn, daughter of former great Kevin Flynn – the woman who would become his wife. Love stories begin in Irish rugby! Matthews cringes at the memory.

'I was in a bit of a drunken haze at the time. I remember I was also introduced to Kevin that night and I doubt if he was very impressed. I'm pretty sure that he didn't want his daughter falling for a drunken yob! I asked Lisa to be my guest at the dinner after our next home international against England. I almost forgot about it but the rest of the lads reminded me and told me that as a former chairman of selectors it would not be a good idea for my international future to let his daughter down!'

That season also saw Ireland drawing 15–15 with France in a very bad-tempered affair. Early in the match Brian Spillane got a kick in the head and was replaced by Brian McCall. Matthews sustained a shoulder injury but the only option on the subs bench was the prop Mick Fitzpatrick, so Matthews continued almost to the bitter end so as not to upset the balance of the side even though his shoulder was giving him a lot of pain. 'The adrenalin kept me going.' There is a definite 'if only' echo to his voice as he recalls his Triple Crown experience.

'To be honest the magic of the whole thing largely passed me by. I regret it didn't happen later in my career when I would have appreciated it much more. My attitude in those games was: "We beat them. Let's get off before the crowd came on." After we won the Triple Crown I went back to Belfast. The average man on the street there was not too pushed but I know the guys down in Cork and Limerick were being fêted like heroes.

'We had a nice bonus after that with a tour to Japan. It was a fabulous place to travel. We were not really seriously challenged on the playing field. It is such a hospitable nation. Every reception we went to we got some kind of gift. It was the closest I've ever been to being like one of the Beatles. After one time we played a match we were mobbed by school girls in the same way they mob Sumo wrestlers.

'I missed all the games the following year because of injury. We had a more mature team in 1987 and should have won the Triple Crown. The World Cup was a big disappointment. We weren't mentally prepared for the Welsh game. My clearest memory of that match was getting stamped on by Paul Moriarty. Doyler's illness should have been a rallying force but it wasn't.'

Doyle was succeeded by Matthews's great friend, Jimmy Davidson, but his reign ended in failure.

'Jim is one of the few Irish-produced coaches. Very few people can coach players from one to 15 but he could. It was a shame his period as coach didn't reap greater rewards. In the end it wasn't working. If he had the team he wanted, playing the style he wanted, I think he would have been a success but because he wasn't a selector he didn't have that freedom. The compromise he was forced into did nobody any favours. There was also a personality problem of sorts. Some of the non-Ulster players never seemed to click with him and that made a difficult situation almost impossible.'

Matthews found himself Irish captain but in some respects it was a poisoned chalice.

'I looked on the captaincy as a burden. I wanted to make sure that I could be there for the rest of the lads. Perhaps my own game suffered in the process.'

As a result of his selection as Irish captain Matthews became a hot favourite to captain the 1989 Lions tour to New Zealand, but it was not to be.

'Missing out on the Lions tour was the biggest disappointment of my career. All the hype in the media for the year before was saying that not only was I a certainty for selection but I would also be captain. When Ronnie Dawson rang to tell me I would not be travelling it was a real bombshell.'

Matthews's form was seriously affected by health problems.

'I developed a viral illness. The problem started when I got the flu and went back to training too early. I realised I had a problem at one squad session when I was doing a light warm-up; I went on my knees, grasping for breath. Simple things like calling a line-out exhausted me. Looking back now I should have taken three or four months off to get fully fit. I was trying to train like a professional athlete, five nights a week, eleven months of the year. Ollie Campbell and Fergus Slattery both got viral infections. Players sometimes push themselves too hard and the body reacts accordingly.'

Matthews also found himself at the centre of attention when he started appearing in a television advertisement for an agricultural product manufactured by his employers. There were some murmurings that he might have been in breach of the IRFU's amateur ethos.

'I never got into hot water about it. To be honest I was hoping I would and that there would be a media storm, as there had been about Tony Ward, because it would have brought more publicity for the firm and the product. I eventually told the IRFU that I hadn't got a penny from it and that it was part of my job.'

In the build-up to the World Cup in 1991, Matthews, Des Fitzgerald and Brendan Mullin formed a triumvirate which negotiated with the IRFU over the way players were to be remunerated for their efforts.

'The IRFU wanted us to sign a participation agreement where we would sign over all rights about the use of our photographs and so on, to them. In effect we were being asked to give them a blank cheque. They wanted to squeeze everything out of our commercial appeal but to give us nothing in return. It was a bitter pill for them to swallow but we said no. I heard that at one stage Naas Botha had led his team-mates in a mini-revolt against his club officials. A short while before they were due to go out on the pitch for a crucial match they said they would not play until they got a better deal. The club gave in to their demands.

'In 1991 it went down to the wire as to whether the Irish players took part in the World Cup or not. A deal was only worked out at the eleventh hour after some frenetic contacts with Ronnie Dawson. In fact at the time of the inaugural dinner of the tournament we were still meeting Ken Reid to negotiate an agreement. It was probably the first evidence of player power in Irish rugby because we got a deal that was to our satisfaction. We put ourselves under pressure in a way but that made us more determined. In the end I think we could and should have done even better. We lost to Australia because we didn't slow down the game after Gordon Hamilton's try.'

The following year would be Matthews' last in the Irish jersey. Work and family commitments contributed largely to his decision. Playing for Wanderers he sustained an injury on the back of his knee. Incredibly he was diagnosed as suffering from gout even though he had the most unlikely profile for it.

'I came back onto the Irish side too soon. The advice I got was that I would be fine and the team needed me. I didn't perform to my potential because I wasn't fit. The season was a bit of a disaster. My enduring memory of that season is of Ralph Keyes being booed by the Irish fans in Lansdowne Road after missing a number of kickable penalties. Emotionally I was very down after that. It was possibly the lowest point for me in rugby.'

20

MICK MOLLOY

Healing Hands

A forward's usefulness to his side varies as to the square of his distance from the ball.

Clarrie Gibbons

Dr Mick Molloy is almost unique among former Irish rugby internationals. He was raised in Cornamona, County Galway, as a native Irish speaker. He was capped 27 times over an 11-year period, between 1966 and 1976, most of them in partnership with Willie John McBride, and scored two international tries. On the Friday evening before a home international he is a whirlwind of activity in the lobby of the Berkeley Court hotel passing around bandages and various bottles to members of the Irish squad.

In many respects it is difficult to imagine this soft-spoken, gentle man frenetically foraging in the scrum. His rugby career only began when he went to Garbally College in Ballinasloe.

'At Garbally I came under the influence of a wonderful coach and educationalist Fr Ryle. He was a brilliant judge of character and potential. He coached both athletics and rugby and got athletes to play rugby and vice versa. Apart from rugby I also represented the school in the high jump, the discus and the javelin. In my final year at school I was sports captain.

'Fr Ryle was amazing. At one stage he persuaded Harold Connolly, an Irish-American who was then the world champion hammer thrower, to come to the school to give us a demonstration. Another time he persuaded no less a player than Cliff Morgan to give us a coaching lesson. Such was his desire to learn that he was constantly seeking new ideas. He got permission from his bishop to attend the 1960 Olympics but the bishop attached a condition to the trip: Fr Ryle was forbidden from watching the women swimming in case his morals were corrupted!

'Of course the big hero in my first year was Ray McLoughlin, though because he was a few years ahead of me in school it wasn't until we played together for Ireland that I got to know him. He has had a huge influence in the development of Irish rugby. He was way ahead of his time as a captain. He is a great organiser and has a brilliant mind. Although he is best known in professional circles for his business activities Ray got a first class honours degree in chemical engineering. He applied scientific principles to his time as captain. One of the things that is most often forgotten is that Ray coached the forwards during part of Tom Kiernan's reign but he did it in a low profile way and kept well out of the limelight.

'After I left Garbally I went to UCG and wanted to play Gaelic football. I turned up for the first training session of the year and saw that there were 22 inter-county players available for selection. UCG had some of the giants of Gaelic football at the time, like Enda Colleran and Martin Newell who was one of the best players I ever saw. He was so dedicated and fit and was a marvellous athlete, though he was unbelievably inaccurate in front of the goals!

'I decided if I was going to make any impact on the sporting world in college it would have to be at rugby. The implications of that decision were very serious then because it meant that I was jeopardising my chances of playing Gaelic football in the light of the infamous "ban" [imposed by the GAA which prohibited people who played so-called "foreign games" from playing Gaelic games].'

After making his mark with UCG and Connacht he was chosen to make his debut in that most intimidating of venues, Paris, in 1966. In the final trial the Probables had won 30–3 and were selected *en bloc*. As was the norm the match ended in an Irish defeat.

'There were a number of players who were a big help to me, Ray McLoughlin, Noel Murphy, Willie John McBride and Mick Doyle. Doyler was a very knowledgeable player. I got a lot of conflicting advice on what to do with my first ball but my Gaelic football experiences helped me no end. I caught the ball cleanly, marked it and kicked it well.

'We had a great team in the late 1960s. Yet we never won a Triple Crown because we lacked a top class penalty kicker. There is absolutely no doubt in my mind that if we had the good fortune to have Ollie Campbell on our side at the time we would have won at least one.'

Historically, in the West of Ireland the shadow of emigration lurked like a vulture hovering over its prey. It was the traditional Irish solution to economic problems. It churned out an assembly line of bodies for the boat to England and America. There were many scenes of families travelling *en bloc* to the train station. Everyone wore their Sunday best. The mother was blind with tears. The father's eyes were dry but his heart was breaking. Men did not betray emotion. It would have been seen as a sign of weakness. The young people leaving leaned out of the window choking with sadness as they saw their parents for perhaps the last time. Younger brothers and sisters raced after the train shouting words of parting. Sometimes white handkerchiefs were produced and waved until the train went out of sight. Those handkerchiefs gave a ritual, almost sacramental solemnity to the goodbyes. Their presence was a symbol of defeat, a damning indictment of an economy unable to provide for its brightest and most talented. Like thousands of Connacht people before him, Molloy moved to London, which necessitated a new club: London Irish.

'London Irish were a funny team to play with in many respects. Firstly, the turnover of players was so high. Ken Kennedy and myself were the only two players who played with them for ten years. Secondly, the socio-economic status of some of our supporters was drawn from the very upper crust of English society. It was not unusual to see MPs and people of that ilk arriving in chauffeur-driven cars, and the parties afterwards were out of this world. At one point the man who changed the scores on the scoreboard was a member of the House of Lords! Thirdly, we had a number of celebrities among our regular supporters: Richard Harris, Dave Allen and Spike Milligan were frequent visitors.'

Molloy also played rugby at county level for Surrey. He plays down the suggestion that Connacht players, especially those who continued to play for Connacht clubs at the time, found it very hard to get their place on the team.

'I knew that I would have to work very hard to hold my place. I was very careful about my diet. In fact my problem was putting on weight! Willie John was always at least two stones heavier than me. I trained on my own and did a lot of work with weights which gave me the strength I needed. I'm amazed that even now very few of the modern players do weight training. My strength was in the loose and my mobility. I used to run five or ten miles a day which, in retrospect, was useless to me.

'The highlight of my career was when we beat Australia 11–5 in 1967 in Sydney. We were the first international team to win in Australia. A disappointment for me that year was that I lost out on the opportunity to play the All Blacks when our proposed international had to be cancelled because of an outbreak of foot-and-mouth disease.

'The disadvantage for me was that I found it hard to get time off work for rugby. I had to do a lot of night duty and when I toured Australia in 1967 and Argentina in 1970 all my holidays went for those years on the tours. The Argentinian tour in particular was great fun. As we were Irish and largely Catholic there was a great reception for us. What amazed me the most is that we met people who were no more than third-generation Irish and yet they were speaking in Roscommon and Galway accents. At one stage I thought I was back in the West of Ireland!'

The Argentinian tour spawned a major controversy in Brazil. The Irish squad were ordered off the plane, allegedly because they were drunk, but that was a clumsy effort to conceal the fact that the airline had overbooked.

Having had a professional relationship with many ex-players he is understandably reticent about commenting about them, though after much persuasion he does list the players he admired most.

'I greatly admired my predecessor on the Irish team, Bill Mulcahy, a great and very tough player and of course Willie John. Then there was Tony O'Reilly who had it all, though this caused some to be jealous of him: a great player, good looks, charm and brains. Ronnie Dawson was a great rugby brain and way ahead of his time as a coach. The two international players I admired most were the French pair, Spanghero and Duaga.'

He returned to work and live in Ireland in 1979 and immediately became part of the backroom team with the Irish squad and was also a Munster selector.

'I have been involved now for 18 years as medical officer which has given me a great joy. The downside is that it is very time-consuming. I'm very lucky I'm married to a rugby fan! The highlight for me was obviously the Triple Crown victories in 1982 and 1985 and the enduring memory has to be those marvellous kicks from Ollie Campbell. The interesting thing is that while obviously training sessions have changed they haven't changed too much. The one thing that is gone now is the four- or five-mile runs. I also coached UCC in my early years back home where I had the pleasure of seeing people like Donal Lenihan flower into players of international class.'

For Molloy rugby was part of his education for life.

'As in anything the greatest thing you learn is that a team is as strong as its weakest link. The other thing I discovered was that it was the very quiet players who needed to be watched most closely. The guys who do all the aggressive talking seldom follow it through on the pitch but the lads that say nothing are the ones that could throw a punch at you.'

21

JOHNNY MOLONEY

Johnny B. Goode

The women sit, getting colder and colder, on a seat getting harder
and harder, watching oafs getting muddier and muddier.
Virginia Graham on a rugby match

From his office in Sandyford Industrial Estate former Irish scrum-half Johnny Moloney has a panoramic view of the Dublin mountains. The years have been kind to him. He is just a half a stone heavier now than in his playing days. A very single-minded player, in a schoolboy match he was charging through for a try when a despairing dive by his marker robbed him of his shorts. True to form he raced through for the try in his underpants before worrying about getting new togs!

Moloney was a most underrated player even though he won 27 caps for Ireland. He was the ultimate third wing-forward. With his athletic build, his workrate around the field and ability to read the game his impact was phenomenal. His peers rate him as one of the best all-round tactical scrum-halfs they played with. Like most Irish players he developed his interest in rugby at school.

'St Mary's was a wonderful rugby kindergarten. After I left school I made it on to the Mary's club side and was lucky enough to win Leinster Cup medals with them in 1969 and 1971, which helped me get on the international side in 1972 against France.

'On Ireland's tour to Argentina Mick Molloy was a great help to me. As a senior he took me under his wing and helped me with my training. I have to confess that I did not expect a big second-row forward to have such fine skills. He was a great passer and kicker.

'The joy of being selected for Ireland was heightened for me because Tom Grace was also picked on the team. Our careers overlapped a lot. Gracer really had a great will to win. I remember in a match for Ireland against England he was up against David Duckham who came into the match with a great reputation. The first time he got the ball Gracer ran into him and knocked Duckham clean over. Every time Duckham touched the ball that day he dropped it. It was one of the best examples of a player psyching out an opponent I have ever seen. Duckham wasn't at the races that day and Gracer came out a clear winner.

'I can't remember much about the build-up to my first cap. I'm naturally a very calm person but that quality was accentuated that week. I recall that there was a wonderful dinner after the match. The French subs were in great singing voice.

'I was one of five new caps with Tom Grace on the right wing, Wallace McMaster on the left, Con Feighery in the second row and Stewart McKinney at wing-forward. I always think of that side as a team of three fives. The five new caps, five senior stars, that is, Tom Kiernan, Kevin Flynn, Mike Gibson, Willie John McBride, Ray McLoughlin and five rising stars Slats, Ken Kennedy, Barry McGann and my two club mates Denis Hickie and Sean Lynch. It was an ideal blend.

'For me the most strange thing was the way different players prepared on the day of the match. I would be one of many who would be up early and psyching myself up before the game, but I was fascinated on the tour to Argentina when I roomed with Barry McGann to see him comfortably sleeping in bed until noon.'

With typical modesty Moloney makes no mention of the fact that he scored the first of his four international tries on his debut. In the process he became the first player to score a four-point try for Ireland helping his country to a 14-9 win at Colombes – the last time Ireland won a full international on French soil. Moloney's memories are almost all happy ones.

'The one regret I suppose was that we didn't win a Triple Crown. I think were it not for "the Troubles" we would have won it in 1972 when Scotland and Wales refused to travel to play us, because we won both our away matches to France and England and the Welsh were a coming side rather than the dominant force they were later in the decade. Having said that, winning the International Championship in 1974 was great and being selected on the Lions tour to South Africa was fantastic.

'There was an incredible bond on that tour from day one. No one could identify any single factor for this. There were no cliques on the team. It was the fabled "all for one and one for all". The only "particular friendship" I recall that developed was between Dick Milliken [a great Irish centre whose career was tragically cut short by injury] and Ian McGeechan. Willie John McBride was a wonderful captain. It was not that he was a great tactical thinker but because he commanded such respect from all the players.

'In a strange way I remember the singing almost as much as the matches. I think it was the beginning of *Flower of Scotland* becoming the theme song for the Lions. I recall before one of the matches we arrived at the ground halfway through the song. Nobody even thought about moving until the song was over. It created great passion on the bus and that was carried on to the pitch. The highlight of the tour was when we won the third Test. Essentially our job was done and after that we were able to relax.

'I suppose the great character on the tour was the Welsh prop-forward Bobby Windsor. He had some great exchanges with waiters on the tour. One went as follows:

Windsor: "I want one egg boiled for exactly 26 seconds and I want another one boiled for 25 minutes 14 seconds. And I want three slices of toast which are pale gold on one side and burned pure black on the other."

Waiter: "But sir, that's simply not possible. We can't go to all the trouble to fill an order like that."

Windsor: "Oh yes you can, sonny boy. That's exactly what you dished up to me yesterday!"

'Another time we were all tucking into a big meal of steaks and so on Bobby was feeling a bit under the weather and just asked for an omelette. The waiter said: "What kind of omelette would you like sir?" Bobby just looked up at him and barked: "A f***ing egg omelette!"'

The highlight of Moloney's career was being chosen to lead his country.

'I have much stronger memories of being made captain of Ireland than of my first cap. I was not selected for the final trial that season. John Robbie and Colin Patterson were the two scrum-halfs. I came on at half-time but did not have a great game. The convention at the time was that the team for the first international of the season was announced the evening of the trial. All the players in contention for selection gathered that evening. To be honest, in light of my performance in the trial I was certain I would not be selected. Reluctantly I went along just to observe the properties. I was stunned to discover not only had I been selected but that I was made captain!'

In 1979 Colin Patterson made the scrum-half position his own and Moloney's international career appeared to be ending, not with a bang but with a whimper. Rugby tours are notorious for their unpredictability. The Irish tour to Australia in 1979 was no exception. More accurately, unpredictability was the order of the day. Moloney went on the tour as a cover scrum-half for the incumbent Patterson but won a shock call-up as wing three-quarter for the Tests after the frailties in the Irish three-quarter line were savagely exposed in some of the warm-up matches. Having won 23 caps as scrum-half he went on to win four caps on the wing. That tour of Australia provided one particularly amusing memory for Moloney: 'I was sharing a room with Terry Kennedy at one stage. Rodney O'Donnell was rooming with Mike Gibson. I can't think of a greater contrast of personalities unless you put Tony O'Reilly rooming with Moss Keane! Mike was very dedicated, prepared meticulously and normally went to bed by ten. Rodney was very laid-back and an early night for him would be midnight. He dropped into our room for a chat one night and later we were joined by Paul McNaughton.

'Paul asked Rodney who was he rooming with. When he answered him Paul pretended to be very sympathetic which made Rodney a tiny bit uncomfortable because Paul had shared with Gibbo the week before. He told him that when he went back into the room he would discover that the sheets and blankets on his bed would be folded neatly, half-way back, the light would be left on in the bathroom and the bathroom door would be left slightly ajar. Then when he went into bed he would be asleep about half an hour when Gibbo would jump on top of him in the bed. Rodney was very sceptical but a couple of hours later when he went back to his room and saw just as Paul described: the light on in the toilet, the bathroom door slightly ajar and the covers folded back on the bed. The next morning he came down for his breakfast like a zombie. He told us he hadn't slept a wink all night because he was waiting for Gibbo to jump on top of him!'

Not surprisingly Moloney's international career was very important to him but his commitment to his club was huge and left him with many happy memories.

'We toured Russia in 1977 but I have no recollection of where the invitation came from. I was captain of the touring side and I was recently reminded by some of my colleagues on the trip that I was a very strict one. There was a lavish dinner in our honour the night before one of the matches with all kinds of delicious food on the menu, but I insisted that our players have the healthiest diet. What was worse, from their point of view, I wouldn't let them near any drink before the match.

'I did let them relax after the games. One of our colleagues, J.B. Sweeney, was less than impressed with the reception the Russians had provided us with and the news that the bar was closing ridiculously early. He was in the FCA and was well up on military matters. He went for a walk over to the American Embassy and got talking to one of the soldiers outside. The result was that he got an invitation into the "mess" in the Embassy. Word trickled back to the rest of us and we joined him. That became our regular social outlet and at one stage we were invited there for breakfast.

'It was a strange environment at the time because we had two Russian police going everywhere with us who were keeping tabs on everything we did. One of them was Nikitia who spoke perfect English but with an American twang and the other was an older man, with no English, who was calling the shots. At no stage could we escape the feeling that "big brother" was watching us.

'We did a lot of fundraising before the trip and it really cost us nothing to travel out. It was the pre-Glasnost, pre-Perestroika era and everybody out there was mad for Western goods, especially jeans. We had all our team blazers and jumpers and O'Neills' playing gear so we were able to sell off our jeans for about £75 in today's money. But our master-stroke was to convince the Russians that O'Neills was the Irish for Adidas! That tour cost us virtually nothing as a result of our blackmarket activities. It was ironic that in the Embassy mess we could buy European beer with the local currency but in the hotel we could only buy the local brew, which tasted horrible, and that with American dollars. We were flushed with Russian currency following the sale of our "wally" jeans supplied by J.B. and Terry Kennedy.'

One figure looms large in Moloney's comic reminiscences of his days with Ireland.

'We were playing England away. Stewart McKinney went through the pages of *Mayfair* magazine and saw the number of an escort service. He rang it up and booked a lady of the night for Mick Quinn. I had to play my part by keeping Quinny in his room and slipping out just before she was due to arrive. I only know this from hearsay, you understand, but she was wearing a raincoat with nothing on underneath but suspenders and some very skimpy underwear. Quinny had to pay her £25 just to get her out of the room. After she left he came out the corridor and everyone in the squad was looking out from their rooms laughing at him. It was the only time I ever saw him lost for words!

'Quinny would sometimes involve me as his partner-in-crime. He had this trick he played on every player gaining his first cap. A lot of players, before their debuts, start to feel that they are a bit sluggish and not at their best. Quinny would pretend to be very sympathetic and tell them he had the solution. He would inform them in the strictest confidence that the top players always took a freezing cold bath to give them an edge in a big match. The only reason why this was not generally known was that it was a trade secret.

'The biggest casualty in all of this was Freddie McLennan. We put him in a cold bath and added buckets of ice. We told him he had to wait in there for 20 minutes, otherwise it was no good. He was squealing like a pig. When his time was up he couldn't move and had ice on his legs. The rest of the lads were all waiting for him outside. Quinny got away with murder.'

Moloney unwittingly found himself embroiled in controversy after his playing career ended. He was invited to assist Ciaran Fitzgerald during his tenure as Irish team coach. When the fortunes of the Irish team took a sharp downward spiral he discovered at second hand that he was 'surplus to requirements'. Moloney's normal easy-going manner changes perceptibly when asked about this incident. He assumes the mantle of a diplomat and chooses his words with great care.

'Let's just say there are ethics which should govern this type of situation and sadly they were not adhered to in my case. I had no problem with being dropped from the Irish backroom set-up but the way it was handled . . . could have been a lot more sensitive. The proper protocol was not observed.'

22

BILL MULCAHY

Hair Today, Gone Tomorrow

The Holy Writ of Gloucester Rugby Club demands: first, that the
forwards shall win the ball, second, that the forwards shall keep
the ball, and third, the backs shall buy the beer.

Doug Ibbotson

One of the most curious features of Irish rugby is that everyone refers
to former Irish captain, Bill Mulcahy, as 'Wiggs' yet hardly anybody
seems to know the origin of his nickname. So was Mulcahy 'follicly-
challenged' as a young man and had he recourse to a hairpiece?

'I deny that categorically! In fact what happened is that as a boy I did
a lot of doodling in my copy books. One of them was a wig-wam and my
school friends decided that should be my nickname. Over the years that
became abbreviated to Wiggs.'

A doctor attached to the medical centre at Aer Lingus, Mulcahy was
born in Rathkeale, Co. Limerick. He won Leinster Cup medals with
Bective Rangers and a Munster Cup medal with Bohemians in 1962. A
product of St Munchin's College in Limerick, there he learned the
subtleties of the game, especially those carried on between broadly
speaking consenting adults in the privacy of the scrum. He was capped
on 35 occasions for Ireland between 1958 and 1965, captaining the team
eight times between 1962 and 1964. His wife is a cousin of the noted
golfer John O'Leary. He is also noted for his quick wit. Once, when
asked by Tony O'Reilly how he would like the ball thrown into the line-
out, he replied: 'Low and crooked!' Of all the people interviewed for this
book he was easily the most difficult to persuade because of his inherent
modesty.

He made his international debut in 1958 in an historic match as part of the first ever Irish team to defeat a touring side, when Ireland beat Australia 9–6 at Lansdowne Road, thanks to a late try from Noel Henderson. The team in full on that day was: P.J. Berkery (London Irish), A.J.F. O'Reilly (Old Belvedere), N.J. Henderson (NIFC, capt.), D. Hewitt (Queen's University), A.C. Pedlow (CIYMS), J.W. Kyle (NIFC), J.A. O'Meara (Dolphin), B.G.M. Wood (Garryowen), A.R. Dawson (Wanderers), P.J. O'Donoghue (Bective Rangers), J.A. Donaldson (Collegians), W.A. Mulcahy (UCD), N.A. Murphy (Cork Con.), J.R. Kavanagh (Wanderers), J.B. Stevenson (Instonians).

Understandably it was a big thrill for the debutant.

'It was a wonderful feeling to be on the Irish team. The previous season I had played on the Probables side in the final trial but had been overlooked. That season I was only on the Possibles but was selected. Your debut is always a tense affair. You've got a burning passion to do well but you run on to the field fearing that you will be a one-cap wonder rather than embarking on an illustrious international career. For me the thrill was magnified because I ended up playing with my childhood hero, Jack Kyle. As a boy I was glued to the radio listening to all his matches. He was such a charismatic figure, modest, unassuming, generous, affable and a wonderful colleague.

'The classic story told about Jack concerns John O'Meara's first cap when he was to partner Jack at half-back. He was naturally a bit apprehensive about partnering the unquestioned best player in the world and was debating how he would address Jack. Should he call him Dr Kyle or Mr Kyle? John travelled up in the *Cork Examiner* van and walked meekly into the team hotel. Immediately he walked in the door the first person to greet him was Jack who said: "Congratulations, Johnny. Delighted to see you here. Where would you like me to stand on the pitch?" Who else would have shown such modesty? Apart from Jack I was lucky to play with some other great players, like Willie John. Another player I had a lot of time for was Gerry Culliton, a very honest player and a great worker.'

He was one of ten Irish players to make the Lions tour to New Zealand and Australia in 1959. The side was captained by Ronnie Dawson. The eight other Irish players were Gordon Wood, Syd Millar, Noel Murphy, Tony O'Reilly, David Hewitt, Niall Brophy and Mick English, with Andy Mulligan making the trip as a replacement to cover for injured players.

'It was a tremendous experience although I had to put off my finals. I had to sell this idea to my late mother, who was a widow and she had more than a few misgivings about me putting my career on hold for the sake of rugby. We had some wonderful entertainers. O'Reilly and Mulligan had us in stitches specially with their simulation of the Queen's Christmas Day speech. Another great character was Mick English.'

Lions tours are a mixture of serious rugby and fun. One effort to break the monotony in a rugby tour is a court session where players are judged by their peers and given an appropriate punishment for their transgressions. On the 1993 tour Judge Paul Rendall sentenced Scott Hastings to listen to two hours of Richard Clayderman tapes on his personal stereo after being found guilty of having his hair cut in a style that was 'an affront to what little hair Graham Dawe had left'. Nicknames are another way of keeping up the levity. On the 1980 Lions tour Bill Beaumont's backside was jokingly known as 'the outboard motor'.

Under the leadership of Ronnie Dawson, the fifth Irish player to captain a touring side, the 1959 Lions set an all-time record of 842 points and, in the process, ran in 165 tries. Mulcahy was one of six Irish players, with Tom Kiernan, Niall Brophy, David Hewitt, Syd Millar and Bill McBride, selected on the Lions tour to South Africa in 1962. Mulcahy's loss to the Lions after only nine games when he was severely injured in a match against New South Wales, badly affected the strength of the scrum and was a significant contributory factor to the Lions' ultimate failure. When fit he had been the perfect partner for the great Welsh lock, Rhys Williams.

While playing for the Lions was a great honour for Mulcahy it did not compare with playing for Ireland. Ian McLauchlan, 'Mighty Mouse', was at the centre of a revealing incident on the 1974 tour. He asked Stewart McKinney which was the greater honour: to play for Ireland or the Lions. Stewart thought for 10 seconds before saying Ireland. Mighty Mouse slapped him on the face: 'Did I say the wrong thing?' asked McKinney.

'No, you gave the right answer.'

'Then why did you slap me?'

'Because it took you 10 seconds to find it.' replied McLauchlan.

Mulcahy was also honoured with the Irish captaincy.

'When I became captain my big worry was that I would not be up to the job. The captain's role was very different then than it is now because we had no coach nor back-up team so there was a lot of additional responsibilities. We had no squad sessions. Now everything is organised on a more professional basis.

'I was not an instant success at the job, to put it mildly. We went to

Twickenham with nine new caps and got hammered 16–0. I think the sweetest moment of my career was going back to Twickers two years later and getting revenge in the best way possible by defeating them 18–5, especially because of Pat Casey's famous try under the posts. It was great that Kevin Flynn also got two tries that day. He was a wonderful player who was unlucky with injuries. It's probably true to say we hadn't a great side at the time but we had some great players. I especially remember Jerry Walsh's great commitment and I can still see him coming back from an international with two black eyes. As captain it's important to work out your own style in terms of your own personality.'

Different personalities employ a wide variety of strategies to motivate teams. Phil Bennett psyched up his team against England. 'Look what these f***ers have done to Wales. They've taken our coal, our water, our steel, they buy our houses and they only live in them a fortnight every 12 months. What have they given us – absolutely nothing. We've been exploited, raped, controlled and punished by the English – and that's who you are playing this afternoon.' Wales won handsomely. In 1984 England coach Dick Greenwood's speech to his team before their match against Australia at Twickenham was simply two words: 'England expects.' England lost 19–3.

Since his retirement Mulcahy has been very involved in Skerries rugby club. His sons, Sean and Billy, have been on the fringes of the Irish squad. At international level the opponents Mulcahy admired most include South Africa's Avril Malan and New Zealand's Colin Meads. He is not totally happy with the way the game is evolving though he is sensitive to the need to reward players. He has watched the increasing mental and psychological pressures on players due in part to the more intrusive demands of the media and the escalating pressures of paying spectators. There is also an increased requirement for peak physical fitness.

'The game has become much more physical with players working out in gyms. I feel that the guys of my era would feel that the fun has gone out of the game. We would feel that whatever about the money we had the best years. The friends we made in rugby are friends for life. Players don't mix as well as they used to. Some of the social side is diminishing.'

In February 1996 a leading doctor disclosed that the greatest demand for the 'morning after' pill in Dublin is on the Mondays following home rugby internationals. Rugby receptions have tended to be boisterous. In 1890, after the official dinner for the Ireland and Wales match, because of the high spirits of the players the police stopped the party and summonsed the players to attend Dublin District Court the following Monday morning. Mulcahy laughs at the memory of one incident when he got into the spirit of things.

'After one of our trips to Paris I was feeling very, very good at the reception thanks to a large amount of wine. At one stage I went out to the toilet and returned to the top table. I was chatting away in my amazingly dreadful French before I realised that I had got my directions totally wrong and instead of attending the rugby reception I was at a wedding!

23

BRENDAN MULLIN

The Broker

Fear is the great scourge of modern rugby.

Cliff Morgan

The picture in Brendan Mullin's office, in Davy's Stockbrokers, joins three generations of Irish rugby greats: Eugene Davy (capped 34 times for Ireland in the 1920s and 1930s, captaining the side in the 1932-3 season. In 1930 he scored three tries in the space of 20 minutes against Scotland at Murrayfield), Tony O'Reilly and Brendan Mullin.

Mullin was born in Israel because of his father's work with the United Nations. There his sporting passion was soccer. It was not until second year at post-primary school that he came to live in Ireland. He was an outstanding schoolboy talent. Blackrock has provided three of them in recent times – Hugo MacNeill, Mullin and Neil Francis.

Mullin played in a variety of positions on the wing, full-back and out-half.

He also excelled at running and quickly established himself as a champion sprinter. At the suggestion of his coach, he turned to the 110 metres hurdles when he was 16. He was drawn to the discipline because it called for both speed and technique. Although he was told at one stage he could not succeed at the highest level at both rugby and athletics he went on to represent Ireland in both codes at senior level, breaking the 30-year-old Irish 110 metres record in 1986. Like Michael Kiernan he was an athlete in the strictest sense of the word. That is one reason why they complemented each other so well and put pressure on the opposition. He won a record six Irish Schools' caps in 1981 and 1982, captaining the side three times. After school he played with Trinity College.

'We had a great back line with Paul Clinch, Johnny Sexton and Fergus Dunlea. I progressed on to playing with Leinster in 1983. We had a wonderful side at the time and from my point of view it was great to play with so many household names. Although he was in the twilight of his career, Mick Quinn was playing wonderful rugby at the time and we became great friends. He is responsible, though, for spreading some mistruths about me. Contrary to his oft-repeated assertions he did not introduce me to my wife! [Mullin is the brother-in-law of former Irish flanker Derek McGrath, a promising player whose career was sadly curtailed by injury.] It's not true either that I said: "On his day Mick Quinn is the best player in the world. Unfortunately his day is always a Monday!"

'One of my great regrets, though, was that I never got the opportunity to play with Ollie Campbell, because he was such a fantastic player and I think it would have been a great education to play with him.'

Leinster were coached at the time by Mick Doyle. For the only time in our interview he declines to comment when asked his opinion about Doyler. Mullin also played two Blues with Oxford.

'I had two great years at Oxford from both academic and sporting perspectives. It was a very cosmopolitan place. We beat Cambridge in my first year in the Varsity match and lost the second. The games were very intense which prevented us from having classic matches. In my second year David Kirk [who captained the All Blacks to the inaugural World Cup] played for us. He had a great presence and was a great character who made a big impression on everybody. I understand he is now involved in politics in New Zealand. I would be very surprised if he didn't go all the way.'

He made his full debut against Australia in 1984, though he was not part of the original selection. An injury to Keith Crossan saw Michael Kiernan moving from the centre to the wing and Mullin stepped into

Kiernan's place. How did he hear about his call-up to the international side?

'Mick Cuddy, who was an Irish selector then, rang my mother at home. I was in the middle of a lecture in Trinity at the time and I was shocked when my friend, Mick Cooke, called me out of the hall. It was a major breach of etiquette to disturb the rest of the class. It was years later before I got around to explaining the circumstances to my lecturer at the time.'

Ireland lost 16–9. The 1980s saw a remarkable sequence of Irish results: whitewashed in 1981, Triple Crown and international champions the following year, joint champions in 1983, whitewashed in 1984, Triple Crown and international champions in 1985, and whitewashed in 1986. For the Five Nations, Crossan returned on the wing and Kiernan was brought back to the centre but it was Moss Finn, not Mullin, who lost out in 1985. Mullin was an ever-present in Ireland's Triple Crown side scoring a try in the crunch match against England after he blocked down an attempted relieving kick from the English full-back.

'Morale was low after Ireland were whitewashed in the 1984 International Championships. Then "Dad's Army" was discarded and we came up with essentially a new and very young side. We played with a youthful innocence in 1985, almost arrogance. The whole season was fantastic. The Scottish match set us up well for the other games. We were losing with a minute to go but Trevor Ringland scored a try after a thrilling back movement and we won 18–15. The manner of our victory was almost as pleasing as the win itself because we played some sparkling rugby.

'For me there is no better place to play rugby than Cardiff Arms Park. It just has no equal. We hadn't won there since 1967 going into that match but we beat them 21 points to 9, with great tries from Keith Crossan and Trevor Ringland. I remember there was some discussion before the match about what we would do when the crowd started singing at us to intimidate us. Brian Spillane said: "We'll sing back at them!" In some of the pictures showing the arm-linked scene you can see Brian singing at the crowd. Don't ask me what, though! In fact Cardiff Arms Park has been very good to me. My record there with Ireland is four wins, one draw and no defeats.

'The English game was a pretty torrid affair but we came out on top 13–10 with Michael Kiernan's late drop goal. That was the day Michael probably proved that he was a kicker of the highest class. We went into that campaign without a recognised place kicker which was a big change for Ireland after the era of Ollie Campbell and Tony Ward. It was considered a big gamble but it certainly paid off. I've a soft spot for that game because I scored my first international try in that match. The following season we were whitewashed. I think our opponents had spotted the weaknesses in our side, for example we had problems in the scrum and they exploited them to the full. We didn't get the bounce of the ball that season and could have won a couple of games.'

How good a captain was Ciaran Fitzgerald?

'In rugby, more than in any other team game, the captain has a vital role to play. In other codes the captain can be a figurehead and get away with it but in rugby he has a key job to do. Off the field he must work on the psychological preparation of the team and then on the field he must be a superb motivator to get the best out of his players. I don't respond to shouting and roaring. Michael Bradley, too, was that kind of quiet personality so we needed a more low key approach but Ciaran Fitzgerald understood that. That doesn't mean we were any less passionate about playing for Ireland.

'What marked Ciaran out from everyone else was his ability to work so well with the different personalities in the team, handle their idiosyncrasies as individuals and collectively fire them with a burning will to win when they stepped on the field of play. Never was the dictum "all for one and one for all" better displayed as far as the Irish team was concerned than when Ciaran was captain.

'He was a great man for the big occasion, who revelled in the atmosphere when the Championship or Triple Crown was at stake. I believe that leaders are born and not made. Of course you can develop your leadership qualities but, to be a great captain, you must be born with innate qualities and Fitzie had them. If he was as bad as his detractors claimed Ireland, under his leadership, would not have achieved so much.'

Ireland's subsequent poor run of form is reflected in one of the jokes of the time. In 1990 Nelson Mandela was freed from his years in captivity. The first thing he allegedly said after he was released was: 'Have Ireland won a match since I was thrown into that bloody place?'

In 1989 Mullin was selected for the Lions tour of Australia, winning one Test place, and he was the leading try scorer on the tour, with six tries. 'Playing for the Lions was very special for me. It is the next step up after playing for your country.' That same year he was voted Irish Rugby writers Player of the Year. He also toured Japan in 1985 and Namibia in 1991 as well as the World Cup to Australia and New Zealand in 1987 and South Africa in 1995.

'The 1987 World Cup was a big disappointment to be honest with you. It was badly organised. The hotels and training grounds were sub-standard.'

Dissatisfaction with facilities is an occupational hazard for rugby tourists. The story is told that on the Lions tour to New Zealand in 1993 the secretary of the touring party, Bob Weighill, asked for an extra pat of butter to accompany his bread roll. He took umbrage when he was told this would not be possible. 'Do you know who I am?'

'No sir'. The waiter listened impassively as Mr Weighill listed his auspicious catalogue of titles. Then he softly replied: 'And do you know who I am?'

'No.'

'I'm in charge of the butter.'

The 1987 World Cup also saw an Irish fiasco when, before the opening game against Wales, the IRFU insisted that the national anthem ought not be played. *The Rose of Tralee* was chosen as a replacement. Mullin's memories of the 1991 tournament are only slightly happier.

'The second World Cup didn't seem to be real because we were based in Ireland. Our preparations were dreadful especially when we lost warm-up matches to club sides which really saps away confidence and morale. We played poorly in the tournament but came right in the quarter-final against Australia, only to lose in the final match. I firmly believe that if we had beaten them we would have gone on to beat New Zealand at home in Lansdowne Road.'

The following year Mullin decided to retire from his international career but in the summer of 1994 he was persuaded to make himself available for selection for the Irish team again.

'I was mentally tired in 1992 and work pressures were such that I felt I couldn't give rugby the commitment I needed to maintain my standard. I continued to play in a very good Blackrock side that, in a few years, went from playing in Division Two to a team that came close to winning the All-Ireland League. Meanwhile the Irish international side seemed to be having problems in the backs. I was approached to make myself available for the Irish side. It was a difficult decision to come back on a number of levels. For a start you are subjected to more severe scrutiny and greater criticism when you make a comeback. I worked harder to get myself into shape and I was glad I came back because I got the opportunity to captain my country. It was also a wonderful experience to compete in the World Cup in South Africa. They had the infrastructure in place which really made it an enjoyable occasion for everyone. We had a great team spirit, though we didn't do ourselves justice in the final match.'

Having won 54 international caps Mullin has been at the heart of the recent negotiations about the contracts for the Irish squad. Where does rugby go from here?

'The future is unclear for rugby. I think there have been a number of positive developments. Professionalism was inevitable because the game had become professional in all but name. I think in the future we will see players having shorter careers because it will not be possible to combine a career and international rugby and obviously players will want to secure their long-term futures.'

24

CON MURPHY

Murphy's Law

'Every old man I see reminds me of my father' was one of the lines from Patrick Kavanagh that was almost literally beaten into me during my school days. Con Murphy reminds me of my grandfather. He cuts a small figure and is not what I expect a former international full-back to be. His mantelpiece is adorned with his 1992 Digital R.W.I. Hall of Fame award.

He has an unnerving habit of looking deep into your eyes and then into some unseen mystical place. At first I found it a bit disconcerting to be constantly addressed as 'child of grace' or 'child' but eventually I too became infected with his childlike enthusiasm. He was reluctant to be interviewed because he did not think his memory was adequate. Somewhat to my surprise the conversation did not initially focus on rugby. I discovered a man capable of the most subtle investigation of aspects of the human condition which philosophy and theology have customarily claimed as their proper territory. I felt I had come face to face with what scholastics call 'the ground of being'. Rugby talk came initially as a trickle then, as he cast away his inhibitions, swelled into a flood.

When Ireland played France at Lansdowne Road on Saturday, 25 January 1947, they had 14 new caps in the side. Lansdowne full-back, Con Murphy, was the only capped player, having won three caps against England, Scotland and Wales in 1939 and was the only Irish international to survive the postwar era. He also played for Leinster before and after World War Two, as well as in four of Ireland's unofficial internationals in 1946 and four times against the British Army in 1943–5. Fittingly Murphy's international swansong was in Ireland's record 22–0 defeat of England at Lansdowne Road. In an evaluation of Murphy's career it is difficult to avoid the cliché 'small in stature but giant in performance'.

It was at soccer, though, where Murphy first made his mark. He played for Bohemians and was a junior soccer international. However, the most tense matches he ever played in, even the Triple Crown decider, was in the altar boys' league. He laughs at the memory. 'Some of the lads who were supposed to be altar boys had whiskers on them!'

He jumps from his chair with the excitement of a boy playing his first match to provide a demonstration of the way he practised his skills with a paper ball. John Aldridge would have been proud of the way he can still swivel. 'It's all about balance,' he says.

Attending CUS school his rugby passion was born, particularly when he came under the tutelage of Ernie Crawford. Crawford won 30 caps for Ireland, 15 as captain, as a full-back between 1920 and 1927, and was a noted tackler and handler. His enduring legacy to rugby today was the invention of the word 'alickadoo', saying to a colleague who decided to read an oriental book rather than join in a game of poker, 'You and your bloody Ali Khadu!' His son-in-law, Jim Ritchie, captained Ireland on his first cap in 1956.

'Crawford taught me to tackle properly. When you look at players today very few of them can tackle properly.'

He is back on his feet demonstrating the skill of tackling. Murphy's international debut came against England at Lansdowne Road in 1939. Ireland won 5–0 courtesy of a try from Harry McKibbin which was converted by Sinclair Irwin. There followed a 12–3 victory over Scotland. That match featured an unusual event. Back-row forward Mike Sayers marked a Scottish drop-out and then dropped a goal from the mark. The Triple Crown was decided in wet weather at Ravenhill. The match provided the nadir of Murphy's international career. He relives the moment and a haunted look darkens his face.

'I can still see the ball coming down from the heavens as if it was yesterday. I missed the catch because of the slippy ball. They got a scrum and scored a try. That is the biggest regret of my rugby career because the Triple Crown literally slipped through my fingers. You don't get chances like that too often.'

Ireland lost 7–0 to Wales. One spectator in the crowd that day was Jack Kyle.

'The war interrupted a great career for Con. He was a magnificent player. I vividly remember watching him play for Ireland and wondering if I would ever get the chance to wear the green jersey like him. At that time, of course, we had no television so we learned about players like him on the radio. There was such excitement listening to the radio. Now when I'm in Zambia I tune in on the World Service to the radio. You can see the game in your imagination.'

Now in his 80s, Murphy's memory is not what it used to be and he has a particular problem with names, but he discovers a new lease of life when he takes me to the hall to see me out. I stop to admire his impressive collection of photographs. This is the key which unlocks a tidal wave of memories of his playing days. His face lights up like a Christmas tree. He is like a child in a sweet shop, especially when talking about one famous player.

Second-row forward Blair Mayne won only six caps for Ireland in the 1930s. With his massive frame, gained from years of lifting weights, his finest hour was the Lions tour of South Africa, in 1938, in which he played 20 tour matches – though curiously he was the only member of the party not to score on the tour. He also became Irish Universities Boxing Champion. He was awarded three bars on the D.S.O. and was made Légion d'honneur for his sterling service during World War Two in North Africa.

Craving excitement he had enlisted in the British army in 1940 and found himself deployed in the desert in North Africa under General Auchinleck and, later, General Bernard Montgomery in what was known as the Eighth Army. The opposition was formidable because the Germans were masterminded by 'The Desert Fox' Field Marshall Erwin Rommel and his African Korps wreaked havoc on the British forces before the decisive battle of El Alamein on 23 October 1942. At one point Mayne had come very close to capturing Rommel. The incident subsequently was the basis of a lengthy conversation with Con Murphy.

'I asked him what he would have done if he caught Rommel. He told me without blinking an eyelid: "I would have slit his throat." The way he said it I don't think he was joking.'

Mayne was tragically killed in a car accident in 1955 at the age of 40. He cuts an imposing figure in the photograph.

'Because I was so small the opposition often tried to intimidate me and sometimes tried to take me out of the game. Whenever anyone "did me damage" Mayne would come and pick me up and say: "Are you okay little man? I'll sort him out for you." The first chance he got he took revenge for the assault on me and I was left alone for the rest of the game.'

Other names roll off his tongue, like Sam Walker who was Ireland's second captain of the Lions on their 1938 tour of South Africa. History was made in the last match of the Test series when all eight Irishmen in the panel played on the winning Lions' team. Later a BBC commentator, Walker died suddenly in 1972.

Murphy has special affection too for Charles Vesey Boyle. He won nine international caps for Ireland between 1935 and 1939, scoring one international try, and would have won more but for the intervention of World War Two. He won the Distinguished Flying Cross in the war. Later his son, Peter, became the youngest ever President of the Leinster Branch of the IRFU.

Next on his list is Bob Alexander, an exciting flanker, noted for his dribbling, who won 11 international rugby caps for Ireland between 1936 and 1939. He also played 14 times, including all three Test matches on the Lions tour, scoring more tries than any other forward on the tour – six. He also played cricket for Ireland, when as a right-hand batsman and bowler, he took 29 runs in a Test match in 1932. While serving as a captain in the Royal Enniskillen Fusiliers in Burma, at the age of 33, he was killed in action. His international rugby team-mate, George Morgan, won 19 caps for Ireland and toured with the Lions to South Africa in 1938. He too represented Ireland at cricket. The year 1937 saw another of Alexander's colleagues, international athlete Charles J.P. Reidy, winning his only cap for Ireland.

Finally Murphy recalls the winner of the 1987 Digital R.W.I. Hall of Fame award, Mark Sugden – the master of the dummy. Sugden has become part of Irish rugby legend particularly after he sold four dummies on the way to his winning try in 1929, the first time Ireland beat England at Twickenham

'His dummies were so brilliant that you'd think you had the ball in your hands yourself. It was all in the way he used his eyes.'

The biggest influence, albeit indirectly, on Sugden's career was Harry Thrift who won 18 caps for Ireland in the opening decade of this century. He captained Ireland once, in 1908, against England because that day Ireland had seven players from Trinity in the side, the greatest twentieth-century representation in the international team. He was also an international class sprinter. When Sugden was playing out-half for Trinity, Thrift came up to him and said: 'Sugden, you're the worst fly-half I've ever seen. Why don't you take up snooker?'

Sugden switched to scrum-half and the rest is history. He formed a lethal combination with the Simon Geoghegan of the 1920s, Dr Denis Cussen. A natural crowd-pleaser, Cussen won 15 caps on the wing for Ireland, scoring five tries. He also represented Ireland in the 100 metres in the 1928 Olympics in Amsterdam and was the first Irishman to break ten seconds in the distance. He subsequently became official medical officer to the British Olympic team. Sugden also played cricket for Trinity where he lined out alongside Samuel Beckett.

Until very recent times Murphy ran the line for Lansdowne. Recent Lansdowne teams also feature prominently in the collection. He has special admiration for Philip Danaher whom he describes as an 'outstanding full-back but he should have stuck in that position because he could have been one of the very best'. Danaher is one of an élite group of Irishmen who have played in three positions on the Irish international team: full-back, wing (as substitute) and centre. He is also part of another select group: those who have played senior championship football – playing for Limerick against Kerry in the Munster final in 1991.

Murphy is bitterly disappointed by the changing face of Irish rugby.

'Amateurism in rugby is dead. Whenever I go down to the club now all the players are interested in talking about is money. It's not the game I love any more. I can see rugby becoming a game for only the rich clubs. My big fear is that club rugby as we know it will die.'

Ibsen's hero, Peer Gynt, asks: 'If I am what I have and if what I have is lost, who then am I?' Observing in his twilight years that, because of his property-structured existence, he has failed to be himself, that he is unfinished, incomplete. Murphy feels that down the line rugby through its entanglement with business might find itself in a similar predicament.

The rugby future is not what it used to be.

25

DES O'BRIEN

The Leader of the Pack

I have lived in important places
in times when great events were decided.

Patrick Kavanagh

Uniquely among former Irish rugby internationals, Des O'Brien's biggest sporting regret is that he never tried to qualify for the Wimbledon tennis championships. But then again O'Brien is not your typical rugby international. Apart from playing 20 times for Ireland he also competed 14 times at international level for his native country at squash, as well as representing Wales at hockey, and being a reserve on the Welsh tennis team. A noteworthy feature of Irish rugby is the number of internationals who also excelled in other sports. Frank Stoker, a relative of Bram Stoker the creator of *Dracula*, has a unique place in sporting history. He was capped five times at rugby for Ireland between 1886, won the Wimbledon Mens' Doubles title in 1890 and 1893 with Dr Joshua Pim and was runner-up in 1891 – thus making him the first rugby international to win a senior Wimbledon title. In 1888 his brother, Ernest, was twice capped for Ireland.

A renaissance man, after his retirement O'Brien did a Masters degree in architectural history and speaks about rugby in a break from rehearsals from his performance in a Gilbert and Sullivan production. The Edinburgh-based ex-Guinness employee commutes regularly to Ireland. A meticulous man, he is steeped in the tradition of rugby and its various personalities. He considers that he played his best rugby with Old Belvedere, where he starred on the first two of their consecutive Leinster Cups in the 1940s. He subsequently lined out for Wasps and

London Irish and was leader of the pack when Ireland won the Grand Slam in 1948.

'We were the undisputed kings of wheeling the scrum. In an England game we wheeled the scrum from our own line to their half. Another time we wheeled our opponent's scrum seven times. Every time there was a scrum you could see the fear in the opposition's eyes. Half of our training was spent practising dribbling. When the laws changed shortly after that the tradition of wheeling the scrums waned dramatically and the art of dribbling died completely. I really feel half of the game died with it.

'I found the secret of leading an Irish pack was to keep them under tight control from the start, otherwise they went off like a cavalry charge, and died away in the last 15 minutes of each half. We had a very tight set scrum that only timed the shove when the ball left the scrum-half's hand. We gave a stone a man away to the 1951 Springboks and yet we could shift them back two feet at every scrum. In those days the hooker had to fight for the ball and two feet was all he needed.

'In the five years I played for Ireland nobody had a wife or a motor car. We either walked or cycled. This gave us a natural fitness which players don't have today. I know this might sound like boasting but I think we were the fittest back row that ever played for Ireland. Jim McCarthy in particular had exceptional fitness. Our other colleague in the back row, Bill McKay, was 400 yards sprinting champion and a boxing champion. The three of us played together 14 times for Ireland and only lost three times.

'The only adjective that fairly describes Jack Kyle is genius. One of our favourite tactics was to deliberately starve him of the ball for 20 minutes and lull the opposition into a false sense of security. Then we fed him and they were destroyed. He was also in a class of his own when it came to kicking for touch. George Norton was probably the first Irishman to exhaustively practice place kicks. In his case practice certainly made perfect. I was lucky enough to play with some great characters, like Barney Mullan who scored the first try in our Grand Slam run. He was a very colourful personality and a powerful, stocky runner. Another was John Smith, the prop from Queen's University. I remember listening to him being interviewed for the radio. He was asked on what side he played in the scrum. In his best Northern accent he replied: "Sometimes I play on the right side, sometimes I play on the left side – but not right and left at the same time!"

'J.C. Daly was an extraordinary character. Before the war he only played with the thirds for London Irish. As he departed for combat he said: "When I come back I'll be picked for Ireland." He was stationed in Italy during the War and had to carry heavy wireless equipment on his back. As a result his upper body strength was incredible. Before internationals he did double somersaults to confirm his fitness. Having scored the winning try to give us the Grand Slam in 1948 he was nearly killed by spectators at the final whistle. His jersey was stripped off his back and people were wearing pieces of it on their lapels for weeks afterwards. Jack was whisked off from the train station in Dublin the next day by a girl in a sports car whom he had never met but who was sporting a piece of his jersey on her blouse. He stayed with her for a week and lost his job when he went back to London!'

Strangely O'Brien's most satisfying victory did not come in either of the Triple Crown years.

'I think the match that pleased me most was when we beat Scotland 6–5 [O'Brien himself scored the try, with Noel Henderson adding a drop goal] at Murrayfield in 1951. We lost George Norton after 15 minutes so we had to play with only 14 players for 65 minutes. By the same token the biggest disappointment of my rugby career came that same year when we only drew with Wales. That cost us the Grand Slam. It was sickening because we had the beating of them but without the injured Norton we missed easy kicks.'

On the plus side the match spawned a friendship which endures to this day between O'Brien and the great Cliff Morgan who was making his debut for Wales.

'Before the match I sent a telegram to Cliff, which I know he still has, which read: "Congratulations, Cliff. I hope you'll be insured!" He was a bit green in his first international. During the match he dived into the ruck and he was getting himself kicked to bits. I shouted in at him: "For Christ's sake, Cliff, get out of there fast. Do you want to get yourself killed?" After that he never made the same mistake again.'

O'Brien marvels at the perks players have today.

'We wore our own club socks when we played for Ireland. The clubs liked that as did we. Wales wore letters on their backs instead of numbers at the time. Team dinners after internationals were held in Mills' restaurant in Merrion Row – just the team and half a dozen officials. Speeches were brief as we all wanted to get to the three big dances being held from ten until three in the Gresham, the Metropole and the Shelbourne. We would be guests of all three. The night before a Dublin game we would usually take the opposition team to the Gaiety Theatre. We had to pay for our own tickets! You were only given one jersey a season, no matter how many games you played. You could be dropped if you pinched a jersey after a game!

'In my first two years the players were not allowed any tickets even to buy! Before the Scotland game in Dublin in 1949 Karl Mullen was offered two tickets to buy for his parents. The team decided no tickets, no game and there was quite a scene in the Shelbourne on the Friday night – Karl got his tickets and after that the IRFU agreed, with reluctance, to let us buy two tickets each. Big deal!

'I was on the first team to take a plane to a match when we went to France. Our touring party amounted to 68, of whom 40 were alickadoos!'

It is both amusing and illuminating to read the correspondence O'Brien received from the IRFU down through the years. The letter which informed him of his selection to play against South Africa in 1951 provides a fascinating insight into rugby sociology on many levels. Note the addition of the phrase 'no room booked'. As O'Brien's mother lived in Dublin he was expected to take lodgings with her. After the 1949 'players' revolution', internationals were entitled to two tickets each but were given only two days to pay for them, which was incredibly difficult for a player like O'Brien, based outside Ireland, given the state of communications in 1951.

D.J.O'Brien, Esq., "Ffynnon Delio" Pendoylan, Nr. Cowbridge. GLAM.
Date 2nd December, 1951.

Dear Sir,
I have pleasure in advising that you have been selected to play for:–
Ireland v South Africa
At Lansdowne Road
On 8/12/51. at 2.30 p.m.
and shall be glad to receive your EARLY acceptance.
Headquarters Shelbourne Hotel
where programme of final arrangements will be issued.
Your jersey will be supplied, and must be returned immediately at the conclusion of the game, otherwise a charge of 25/– will be made.
The Irish Rugby Union provides transportation and pays Hotel Expenses. (Gratuities, telegrams, 'phone calls, etc., etc., being of a personal nature, MUST NOT be chargeable on the I.R.F.U.) Should you, however, incur any other legitimate expenses, please furnish particulars on attached Form to Hon. Treasurer.
Please bring your Dinner Jacket.
As a member of the team or travelling substitute, you are entitled to two East Stand tickets which will be sent to you on receipt of £1: 10s –d. received within two days.

Each travelling player or substitute to provide himself with training togs, clean white knicks, towel and soap and see that his boots are in good playable condition. Own socks.
Yours truly
RUPERT W. JEFFARES, Secretary.

Kindly travel to arrive in Dublin in time for training at College Park, Friday 7/12/51 at 3.30 p.m. No room booked.
Congrats again Des. Will you please Captain the side and arrange (when training in College Park) for Team Meeting Shelbourne Friday evening 5 p.m.

Irish Rugby Football Union

Ireland v.
(Date of Match)
Expenses of
Train and Boat Fare .....   £   :   :
Hotel Expenses (Bill enclosed)   :   :
Miscellaneous (details below)   :   :
            Total,   £   :   :
            _____

    Signed,.....................................

The following year some curious medical information was sought off him prior to the tour to Argentina, in 1952. Note the reference to 'mental derangement'.

D.J. O'Brien, Esq.,   30th May, 1952

IRISH RUGBY UNION TOURING TEAM.

Argentina 1952.

Dear Desmond,

    In connection with the above, the following should be forwarded to me as soon as possible.
    (1) Unexpired passport (Irish or British).
    (2) Medical certificate (on headed quarto size paper) which, while certifying the general state of good health of the holder, specifies that "the holder does not suffer from

trachoma, any infectious or contagious disease or mental derangement". This certificate must be authenticated by whoever carries out this work in the British Ministry of Health.

(3) Certificate of vaccination against smallpox (enclosed herewith for careful and detailed completion). This certificate must be authenticated by whoever carries out this work in the British Ministry of Health.

(4) Three passport photographs, these are required in addition to any that may be necessary for passport purposes.

(5) P/O 14/2d. to cover cost of visa.

It is essential that you should be vaccinated at once and that those not holding valid passports should obtain same with the least possible delay and remit them to me together with the other necessary documents.

Yours sincerely,
Billy James, Secretary.

O'Brien's thoughtful personality is the antithesis of the fabled 'rugger bugger'. But he was not alone in this respect on the playing fields.

'One of the images a lot of people have of rugby players is that they are ignorant buffoons. On that Grand Slam side Noel Henderson, Jack Kyle and myself had a great interest in poetry. It broke the tedium of many a train journey for us. Jack was particularly interested in the the poetry of Yeats and he's also a great Patrick Kavanagh fan. We swapped poems and read poetry to each other. We even wrote our own poems. Mind you if our rugby was the same standard as our poetry we would never have won the Grand Slam!

'When I was with London Irish a regular spectator at our games was the great poet Louis MacNiece. I often tried to talk to him in the bar afterwards about poetry with no success. He always said: "I came here to watch rugby not to talk about poetry."'

O'Brien had the daunting task of succeeding Karl Mullen as Irish captain. The captaincy provided him with one of his happiest memories of playing for Ireland.

'Looking back it was all a lot of fun! Before an international the president of Ireland, Sean T. O'Kelly, the first Irish president to attend a rugby international, was being introduced to the teams. He was a man who was, let's say, small in stature. The match was being played in October so the grass was long. As captain I was introduced to him first. He said: "God Bless you Des. I hope you have a good game." Then I heard a booming voice in the crowd: "Hey, Des, would you ever get the grass cut so we'd bloody well be able to see the president!"'

26

PHIL O'CALLAGHAN

Top of the Props

Kick ahead, Ireland, kick ahead. Any bloody head.

Ray Gravell

Prop forwards get a hard time in rugby, particularly from backs. The standing joke is: 'Prop forwards don't get Valentine cards for religious reasons – God made them ugly!'

Like Moss Keane, Phil O'Callaghan was one of the great characters of the game. He toured three times with Irish parties, to Australia in 1967, to Argentina in 1970 and to New Zealand and Fiji in 1976. Apart from his fire on the pitch he was also noted for his quick wit. The most oft quoted story about him is the story of the day a referee penalised him and said: 'You're boring [the term used to describe the way a prop-forward drives in at an illegal angle into an opposing prop-forward] O'Callaghan.' Philo's instinctive retort was: 'Well, you're not so entertaining yourself, ref.' The referee penalised him a further ten yards.

During another match O'Callaghan put out his shoulder. The former Irish captain and leading gynaecologist Karl Mullen attended him. Dr Mullen said: 'I'll put it back but I warn you it will be painful.' He did and it was. According to the story Philo was screaming his head off with the pain. The doctor turned to him and said: 'You should be ashamed of yourself. I was with a 16-year-old girl this morning in the Rotunda as she gave birth and there was not even a word of complaint from her.' Philo replied: 'I wonder what she bloody well would have said if you tried putting the f***ing thing back in.'

The Dolphin player was capped 21 times for Ireland over a ten-year period between 1967 and 1976, although he won no caps from 1971 through to 1975. He really established his credentials when Ireland went to Australia for a six-match tour in 1967. The omens for the Test match were not favourable. The previous week Ireland had lost 21–9 to New South Wales on the same Sydney venue. However, tries from Jerry Walsh and Pat McGrath and a conversion and drop goal from Tom Kiernan gave Ireland an 11–5 win.

'One of the highlights of my career was when we became the first team from the Northern Hemisphere to beat Australia, in 1967. We had a magnificent team brilliantly led by Tom Kiernan. After winning on the Saturday we had a great celebration and we all went to Mass on the Sunday evening. Although it was the *evening* after the night before, one of our lads feel asleep. During the most solemn point of the Mass he suddenly shouted out from his slumber: "Hallelujah."

'We stopped off in Hawaii. At one stage we were standing at the side of a swimming pool. I had my back to the deep end and was pushed in by a now popular, or infamous, journalist. I was not able to swim and went under. The guys thought I was faking it when I didn't surface. I owe a great debt of gratitude to Terry Moore who dived in and lifted me out of the water long enough to give me the air I needed before I went down again. The late, great Jerry Walsh found the pole for cleaning the pool and extended it to me and I eventually hauled myself out of the pool. I asked Jerry later why he had not dived in. He said: "Why ruin the tour by having both of us drown?"'

O'Callaghan was one of 23 players selected on a depleted Irish squad (deprived of the services of Mike Gibson, Ken Kennedy, Fergus Slattery and Roger Young) to tour Argentina in 1970. The challenge facing the Irish was compounded by the fact that the tour was in August which meant that the visitors were ring rusty after a three-month lay-off, whereas the home sides were competing since the previous April. Moreover, Argentina were still bullish in the wake of recent victories over Scotland and Wales. Ireland lost three of their seven matches including both Tests, 8–3 and 6–3 respectively. They also lost 17–0 to an Argentine 'C' side. To add to Ireland's problems O'Callaghan was sent off in the first Test.

'The guy who was sent off with me had been put off four times that season. From information we received later we learned that getting me sent off was a pre-planned move. Both Tests were played in a second division soccer ground. Each time we got into their 25 a penalty was given against us. Whenever they got into our 25 they were given a penalty.

'At one stage we went to Bocca Juniors' stadium for the World Club Championship final between the Dutch and the Argentinian champions.

There is a history of crowd trouble at such venues. One of our lads was whistling on the way into the stadium. For this "crime" he was thrown into jail for 24 hours! It was a magnificent venue and a very intimidating atmosphere. It was the first time I saw fires in the stadium. The home supporters turned against their own side because they were so dissatisfied with the performance.'

O'Callaghan had the image of being a 'hard man'. Was this a fair perception?

'You have to meet fire with fire. There were times when front rows faced you like a bull facing a bullfighter. The French especially used a combination of the prop and the hooker to try and soften you up. Once you showed you could not be bullied you were fine. I was tough and hard but fair.'

O'Callaghan's disappointment about that incident pales into insignificance when compared with the pain he experienced during the darkest chapter of his career. Time may heal all but his scars are still discernible.

'The biggest disappointment of my career came in 1970 when I was dropped from the Irish team at a time when I was the number one contender for the Lions' position. I can say with my hand on my heart that I was playing my best rugby in the years I was off the Irish team.'

Despite the vagaries of the Irish selectors, rugby's prodigal son would return, though. In 1976 after Ireland suffered a record defeat, 26–3, at the hands of the French in Paris, O'Callaghan was restored in the front row.

'My happiest memory in rugby was being recalled to the Irish team for the Test match against New Zealand in 1976 having spent six years in the international wilderness. I knew back in 1970 that the next Irish tour was six years away and made a bet, of two pints, in a pub in Cork that I would make that trip to New Zealand. I got great pleasure from claiming that bet six years on. We had a lot of hard games on the tour. We were unfortunate to be beaten in the Test. Although we lost we never let the head down and did Ireland proud. That side were great ambassadors for their country.

'We had great characters in the squad, none more so than Brendan Foley. He is a thorough gentleman and great fun to be with. At one stage on that tour he came down to the foyer of the hotel which had a big fountain. He went in to the middle of it to do some fishing. He didn't catch anything! After that he was known as "Foley never caught a fish".'

That tour concluded with a match against Fiji which is an intimidating venue to play in. Ireland defeated their hosts 8–0. There were heavy areas of the pitch, so much so that frogs were jumping on the playing surface during the match.

'Normally there are shouts of joy after an Irish team is announced. The Fiji game was no exception. However, so humid was the climate that this time all the hurrahs came from the players not selected. I was one of them! It was much more interesting looking out on the most beautiful ocean in the world than watching the match. The Fijians were lovely people but there was a bit of an incident after the game between one of our players and one of theirs. When asked about the resolution of the incident my colleague in all earnestness said: "I gave him a black eye!"'

Ireland's experiences were not unique. When England played Fiji a few years ago the English players were very intimidated by the crowd and the sea of black faces. Will Carling is said to have remarked: 'Jesus Christ – we'll be lucky to get out of here alive.' Jeremy Guscott immediately stepped in and said: 'Speak for yourself.'

O'Callaghan is a huge admirer of the many players who soldiered with him in the Irish jersey, including Tom Kiernan, Mike Gibson, Willie John McBride, Mick Molloy, Jerry Walsh, Ken Goodall, Alan Duggan, Ken Kennedy, Noel Murphy and Barry McGann. Among their number was Barry Bresnihan who was capped 25 times in the centre for Ireland between 1966 and 1971, scoring five international tries. He went on two Lions tours, to Australia and New Zealand in 1966 and to South Africa in 1968, where he played three Test matches. On the 1966 tour he wrote himself into the history books by becoming the first replacement in representative rugby. He is brother-in-law of Con Feighery who was capped three times in the pack for Ireland in 1972. Con's brother, Tom, a prop forward, was also capped for Ireland.

Special praise is reserved for one man. 'The best wing-forward I've ever seen was Shay Deering. He was such a wholehearted, committed player and one of the greatest characters I've ever met on or off the field.'

One of his strongest memories is of an incident involving Barry McGann.

'The night before an Irish squad session McGann, Shay Deering and I and a couple of others had frequented a few pubs. In fact we were even thrown out of one of them! The squad session the next day started with some laps around the pitch. Shortly after we started off I heard Barry shout at me: "Cal, don't leave me." I dropped back with him and we were lapped once or twice. The cruel irony of the situation was that after the session he was selected and I was dropped!'

A number of players prefer the tight-head prop position as it allows them to have both shoulders in contact with the opposition, while at loose-head they have only one. For all his international career O'Callaghan played at tight-head but in his latter days, with Dolphin, he switched to loose-head. 'I enjoyed playing at loose-head and was sorry I hadn't played there earlier in my career.'

Many of his happiest memories are of his playing days with Dolphin.

'The most difficult opponent I've ever faced at any grade was Tom Carroll of Garryowen and Munster. He was small in stature and huge in heart. Most props come out with their guns blazing for the first few minutes and then settle down but Tom was like that from the first minute to the 80th. Jim Dennehy of Highfield was my next most formidable opponent. I loved the challenge of playing against them both.

'I was fortunate to play for a great Dolphin side, though we never won anything. My clearest memory of those times is of a match played on a bitterly cold November day. I was lifting one of our forwards, Eoghan Moriarty in the line-out. He shouted down at me: "Philo, let me down. My hands are frozen."

'The Old Wesley and Leinster player Bobby Macken joined us for a season. The following year he went back to Dublin. When we next played against each other I was standing on the wing, as usual, when he came charging towards me but to my surprise he tapped the ball into touch. I asked him: "Are you afraid of me, Bobby?"

"No, but I'm afraid of running into your mouth!" he replied.'

After retirement O'Callaghan played in the proliferation of 'Golden Oldies' tournaments but although he initially enjoyed it he found the excessive emphasis on winning a bit distasteful. He echoes a recurring theme with many former internationals.

'I feel in rugby today we're missing out by putting too much importance on winning and not enough on making friends. I made many friends in rugby throughout the world. If I ever needed them I'm sure I could ring them up and they would be there for me. Those deep bonds are not there today. Players come in, take part in the match and go off and do their own thing. The social side is not near as strong as it used to be. This trend worries me because I'm afraid in years to come the game will be much the poorer for it.'

27

JOHN O'DRISCOLL

John O'Desperate

The Irish do not gladly tolerate common sense.

Irish rugby fan

No Irish international, apart from Johnny Moloney, is more inappropriately nicknamed than John O'Driscoll. 'John O'Desperate' is the consummate gentleman. The morning after Ireland's 30–17 victory over Wales, the Exiles' coach is in ebullient form particularly in the wake of an excellent debut from one of his charges, Simon Mason. How did this Manchester-born doctor, who is a leading dermatologist, end up winning 26 caps for Ireland?

'My father, Florence, a GP from Skibbereen, played rugby at Roscrea and we got our passion for rugby from him. My brother, Barry, is 13 years older than me. As a boy I spent the weekends travelling to see him play. After he was capped for Ireland my burning ambition was to emulate his achievement.'

When Ireland drew with France in their opening fixture of 1971, Tom Kiernan broke a bone in his leg and he was replaced at full-back by Barry O'Driscoll, who went on to retain his position for the entire season.

'Even though he could have played for Leinster or Munster, Barry opted for Connacht largely because of the influence of their coach, Joe Costello. Our grandfather was a Connacht man. When I went to medical school in London I joined London Irish where Mick Molloy was a great influence on me. I think the best thing that ever happened to me was to declare for Connacht. In my years with them I never felt like an outsider. When I played my first game for the province they

148

hadn't won an interprovincial match for 12 years and I played with them for five years before we won a game.

'We were rarely heavily beaten because we played with such enthusiasm. We had some great players, like the McLoughlin brothers and Glaswegians' Mick Casserly, who was one of the unluckiest players I know because he never played for Ireland. Our coach, Tony Browne, epitomised the Connacht attitude as did Irish selector P.J. O'Dwyer. There was never any backbiting nor recriminations. I consider it a great education into the ethos of the game. Nowadays you don't have any tolerance for failure. Just look at what happened to Jack Charlton when Ireland lost a few matches.'

Although he played in a final trial in 1976–7 he had to wait for another year before being selected for Ireland. The following season he fractured his cheekbone, in October, which caused him to miss the interprovincials. Although his injury was not completely healed he was selected for his second final trial.

'The selectors were basically experimenting with a number of different number eights playing in different positions. I was chosen at number eight and had a special mask made for protection. It was one of those days everything went right for me. I won my first cap against Scotland in 1978 but got knocked out during the game. When I came around the first thing I heard was a great cheer. My replacement, Stewart McKinney, had scored a try. That meant no more caps for me that season.'

The Irish side that day was: Tony Ensor, Tom Grace, Paul McNaughton, Alistair McKibbin, Freddie McLennan, Tony Ward, John Moloney (captain), Phil Orr, Pat Whelan, Mick Fitzpatrick, Moss Keane, Donal Spring, John O'Driscoll, Willie Duggan, Fergus Slattery.

Four weeks later it was off to France. The Irish were handicapped by the presence of just one specialist second row when Emmet O'Rafferty, due to make his international debut, was forced by a cruel twist of fate to withdraw four hours before the kick-off having sustained a calf muscle injury in training the previous day. Harry Steele was called into the second row and O'Driscoll was contacted in London to act as a cover player. O'Rafferty never played for Ireland.

The Australian tour in 1979 marked the rehabilitation of O'Driscoll's international career, though, like Willie Duggan, he was not chosen on the original touring party. Both made the trip down under by the back door when Mike Gibson, the younger, and Donal Spring were forced to cry off the touring party because of injury.

'The pundits were expecting Australia to hammer us, especially as the previous year they had destroyed the mighty Welsh. The Irish selectors took an incredibly brave decision in selecting Ollie Campbell at out-half. The Test results proved their decision was the correct one. In terms of our Triple Crown victory in 1982 Ollie's presence in the side was crucial.'

With Rodney O'Donnell, Colin Patterson, Ollie Campbell and Shannon's Colm Tucker, O'Driscoll was chosen on the Lions tour to South Africa in 1980. Tucker was an interesting selection because he was unable to command a regular place on the Irish team. Tony Ward, Phil Orr and John Robbie subsequently joined the squad as replacements. O'Driscoll played in all four Tests.

He has particular memories of Rodney O'Donnell on that tour. Rodney's middle name could have been 'superstition'. He had a huge fear of anything connected with the number 13. On tour not only did he refuse to stay in a room numbered 13, or 213, or a room on the 13th floor but he would not even stay in a room in which the numbers added up to 13, like 274.

He had an interesting theory about the psychology of the rugby ball. When an opponent had kicked a goal against his team he felt much better if the ball came down in such a way that he was able to throw it back over the crossbar, his theory being that the next time, the ball was either unsure where to go, or would lose the habit of travelling in the right direction.

When he believed in something there could be no deviation. He always insisted on being the last man on the team bus and would patiently wait for everyone to assemble onto the bus regardless of the climatic conditions. He refused to walk over a line. On a stone pavement he would make the most bizarre movements to avoid treading on a line. Such an event could only trigger tragedies of apocalyptic proportions. With all this practice some of his fellow players said he could have been world champion at hopscotch!

Yet another ritual was preparing to tog out before games. He had to put on his togs in such a way that the material did not touch his skin on the way up. Should such a calamity occur he would begin the whole process again – and if necessary again and again until he got it exactly right. The second part of this operation was that he would never button up his togs until he was running onto the field.

He was preoccupied with exactitudes to the point that he went around every room adjusting pictures so that they hung straight on the walls. This tendency was dramatically illustrated on Ireland's tour to Australia in 1979. In the middle of Noel Murphy's team talk he jumped up to the astonishment of all present to adjust the position of the telephone.

One of his most famous idiosyncrasies was his desire to get into bed each night without touching the bottom sheet. The task had to be executed with military like precision. If he failed the first time he tried, he kept trying, until he got it exactly right. Only then did he allow himself to relax.

'Like Rodney, Willie Duggan had to be the last one on the field. The big question was what would happen when they both played together? The rest of us all ran onto the pitch. We waited and we waited but no sign of either. Eventually Willie came running out. He was very determined to be last but Rodney was going to be last.

'I roomed with Rodney during the Lions tour which was an unforgettable experience. He had a ritual for everything, including going to bed. He had to leave his shoes a certain way and so on. The whole saga lasted at least 20 minutes. To wind him up once he got into bed I would adjust the picture in the room so that it wasn't hanging straight. It was unthinkable for Rodney to even contemplate going to sleep in such an environment so he had to get up straight away and settle it. Of course when he was up he couldn't just jump back into bed but had to go through his entire ritual again. He did get his own back on me though. I couldn't sleep with any light on in the room so he always parted the curtains.'

A Friday the 13th fell on that tour. Ollie Campbell and John Robbie rose at 6.30 a.m. that morning and, with taping, made lines right across the lobby outside O'Donnell's room and pasted the number 13 all over the lobby and the elevator. As a result Rodney was afraid to leave the room for the entire day!

Tragedy struck against Griquland West in the penultimate game of the tour when the Lions won 23–19 and O'Donnell sustained a serious injury tackling the massive Danny Gerber. Although he walked off the field, when he was examined in hospital it was discovered that he had dislocated his neck between the sixth and seventh vertebrae and that he had come within a fraction of an inch of being paralysed for life. Prompt intervention by O'Driscoll on the pitch prevented more severe repercussions. To compound the problems, when the ambulance finally arrived the driver got lost on the way back to the hospital, depriving the Irish player of the quickest possible care.

By this time O'Driscoll, Willie Duggan and Fergus Slattery had firmly established themselves as the most effective Irish back-row combination since the days of the 1948 Grand Slam side.

'Fergus and Willie played hard on and off the pitch. The difference was that whereas Fergus never seemed to show any ill-effects the next day, Willie did! It was an accepted fact that Willie was last for every exercise in training. Our recurring nightmare was that Duggan would beat one of us into second last place! This would suggest that we were totally unfit and almost certainly lead to our demise on the Irish team.

'In June 1983 I went with "Slats" to Barcelona to play an exhibition game, against a French selection, with the Wolfhounds. The match was to be played at midday. The evening before the game Fergus was looking for somebody to go out with him for a night on the town. In the circumstances nobody wanted to take up his invitation knowing the tough conditions awaiting them the next day but eventually he recruited the replacement prop-forward. The next morning the two lads returned from their adventures as the French team were heading out to train! Fergus was not a bit phased. On the bus to the game Phil Orr was taken ill and to his horror the "partying" sub had to take his place. Slats played like a man inspired but I've never, ever seen anyone suffer on the pitch like his partner!'

After a disappointing season in 1981 when Ireland were whitewashed, the Triple Crown unexpectedly came on the horizon when Ireland played Scotland in 1982.

'I loved the adrenalin rush I got when I played for Ireland. I always found the tension helped me to perform. That Scottish game was an exception. Although we had done brilliantly against Wales and England the communal tension in the dressing-room that day was striking. I felt it was very unhelpful to the entire team. The one exception was Ollie Campbell whose kicking, even by his own high standards, was fantastic that day. He settled us down.'

After Ireland won the Championship in 1983, O'Driscoll was selected to tour New Zealand with the Lions in the company of his Irish colleagues Trevor Ringland, Michael Kiernan, David Irwin, Ollie Campbell and Donal Lenihan. Although he played in two Tests it was not the experience he hoped for.

'I was injured in the first match and didn't play for three weeks. You need to be playing on a tour like that. We were not as evenly balanced as we had been in 1980. The press were very unfair to Ciaran Fitzgerald which didn't help. By the standards of the time the criticism of him was way over the top. Nowadays that kind of sustained media assault has become commonplace.

'After the highs of 1982 and 1983 the following season was a disaster as we were whitewashed. The balance between success and failure is relatively fine. Ollie was injured which disturbed our rhythm a lot. We lost confidence when we started losing. I was ill for the '84–'85 international season and never regained my place. Even though I was a few years younger than them I was regarded as the same vintage as Willie Duggan and Fergus Slattery and as part of "Dad's army". In fact I continued to play for Connacht for a number of years and hoped to make it back onto the Irish side, but it was not to be. I never actually retired.'

When Jonathan Davies switched from rugby League to Rugby Union he was asked what was the main difference between the two codes. He said in rugby League you pay your taxes. O'Driscoll welcomes the fact that the new era of professionalism has at least ended the 'shamateurism' of previous years but is troubled about aspects of the future of the game.

'American sport is all about money. I hope rugby will not go down that route. My chief worry is that we could have a situation where there isn't room for players who don't want to make a career out of rugby to play at the highest level. Rugby is not a safe career because of the risk of injuries. It is tough but it should be possible for players with careers to train twice a day. That will change, though, if clubs demand their players for weekend matches and international squad sessions have to be held on weekdays. I think rugby people have to be careful about playing too many matches, not only because of the physical aspect but because of the psychological preparation required. I see problems down the road for English players in this respect because the club structure is so strong. I'm particularly worried about the future of the small clubs who have given so much to the game down through the years. That is why the interprovincial structure is so important to provide a platform for players from such clubs to show their wares.'

Like so many of his colleagues O'Driscoll has a treasure trove of memories from his playing days. One goes back to South Africa in 1980.

'The only unpardonable sin on a Lions tour is to miss training. No matter how awful you feel or how low your morale is you simply must get out to the training field at the appointed hour. Sunday was a day for total relaxation. To pass the afternoon Ray Gravell and I played a card game with a difference. The penalty if you lost a hand was to take a drink – a mixture of spirits and orange juice. When I lost I noticed that Ray was adding in extra spirits to my drink. I thought I was being very clever by saying nothing and adding in a lot of extra juice. What I didn't know was that Gravell had absolutely laced the orange juice with spirits! The next morning I had the mother of all hangovers and had to miss training.'

28

Tony O'Reilly

The Life of O'Reilly

I ran much faster than those who run without thinking.

Pele

There are good public speakers, there are great public speakers and there's Tony O'Reilly. Watching him in action it is difficult not to feel overwhelmed by the sheer weight of his personality. Every word is carefully chosen, every pause and gesture are carefully orchestrated. The atmosphere is electric, like a revivalist meeting with a touch of fanaticism. The crowd wait for him to come up to the podium like a presidential candidate. As he speaks all eyes are on him, seemingly transfixed. It appears that if he had asked them to try walking on water they would have been happy to do so. His little asides are priceless gems; intimate, wry, and chatty by turns, but always drawing his captive audience into moments of shared experience.

Coached at Belvedere College by the legendary Karl Mullen he played his first match when he was six years of age. His mother asked the priest what he thought of the small players on show. The Jesuit, who had no idea who she was, answered: 'The red fellow's the best.' She glowed with pride. The red fellow was her son. Such was his impact that when he played in an Under-nines match, with the team leading by 30–6 at half-time, the coach told him to give the opposition a chance and pass the ball more. The young O'Reilly answered: 'Ah, Father, you're only wasting your time. If I pass it they'll knock it on, or drop it.'

As a schoolboy he also excelled at soccer playing for Home Farm but he turned his back on the game on foot because of an assault. During a match he made a bone-crunching tackle on an opponent. The boy's mother rushed onto the pitch and attacked O'Reilly with her umbrella. The future Lions sensation remarked: 'Rugby is fair enough – you only have your opponent to deal with. Soccer you can keep, if it involves having to deal with your opponent and his mother.'

Belvedere also provided a nursery for O'Reilly's entrepreneurial skills. When he was seven he was the only boy in his class to make holy communion. To mark the occasion a priest gave him an orange – an enormous luxury during the war years. Like most of his friends, O'Reilly had never seen an orange. O'Reilly subsequently claimed: 'After I ate the centre I sold the peel for one penny per piece, thereby showing a propensity for commercial deception which has not left me since.'

In the 1953–4 season O'Reilly captained Belvedere to the Leinster Cup final only to see his side lose 11–3. For once it was O'Reilly's grace in defeat rather than his powers on the field that caught the eye. Twenty-five years later, O'Reilly's sportsmanship on that occasion reaped a handsome dividend. When he was president of Heinz, the company ran into a potentially catastrophic problem over a US Federal Drugs Administration test of its tomato ketchup. While there was no threat to health, and the test was unreliable, if the FDA sustained the result Heinz would have to recall all its ketchup in the shops, at a cost of £35 million as well as a hammer blow to its reputation. In the end Heinz's fate lay in the hands of the president of the Del Monte Company who had the casting vote on the adjudicating committee. O'Reilly went to make his case personally to the man in charge. He was taken aback to be told: 'Mr O'Reilly, in my parish in San Bernardino is a parish priest called Father McCarthy. He was a scholastic when you were playing in the super-bowl many years ago in Ireland. He said you lost a game but you showed considerable style under pressure. He's a good friend of mine and he says you were a sportsman and a good fellow – I will take his word. The Del Monte Company will vote with Heinz on this.'

Such is O'Reilly's flair with words it is difficult to imagine that he was once out-quipped – but miracles do happen. England beat Ireland 20–0. As he walked off the pitch O'Reilly turned to Tom Reid and said '20–0! That was dreadful!'

Reid responded: 'Sure, weren't we lucky to get the nil!'

Such is O'Reilly's penchant for witty quips that he is sometimes mistakenly credited with any classic rugby comment, such as: 'I thought it was chicken!' when an English official remarked at a post-match dinner that the soup was tepid. In fact the player responsible for this remark was the Scottish lock Alister Campbell.

O'Reilly is very much the Roy of the Rovers of Irish rugby. Having first been capped against France as an 18-year-old in 1955, he was the undisputed star of the Lions tour to South Africa in the same year. The Lions were captained and managed by Irishmen, Robin Thompson and Jack Siggins respectively. The squad featured five Irish players: Thompson, Tom Reid, and Robin Roe in the forwards and O'Reilly and Cecil Pedlow among the backs. O'Reilly scored no less than 16 tries, a record number, and emerged as top scorer. In doing so he followed in a great Irish tradition dating back to Larry Bulger. He was capped eight times as a winger between 1896 and 1898. He played four Test matches for the Lions in the 1896 tour of South Africa, and was the first Irish player to score a try for the Lions. His older brother, Michael, was also capped for Ireland. Both represented Ireland in athletics.

O'Reilly's quick wit was again evident on the tour. Asked as to what he had been doing looking the other way as Springbok goalkicking ace Van der Schyff took the kick, which would have given South Africa victory over the Lions in the first Test of the 1955 series, he replied: 'I was in direct communion with the Vatican.' Van der Schyff missed and the tourists won 23–22.

In 1959 O'Reilly went even better on the Lions tour to New Zealand and Australia, amassing a staggering 22 tries. It is probably a testimony to his importance to the team that he played in more matches than any other player, 24 in all. However, this time it was another Irish player, David Hewitt, who was top scorer with 106 points.

Among the Irish players chosen on that Lions tour with O'Reilly was the late Gordon Wood. He was capped 29 times for Ireland between 1954 and 1961 at loose-head prop, scoring one international try and forming a formidable front row in the late '50s and early '60s with Syd Millar and Ronnie Dawson. Thirty-five years later Ireland's tour to Australia would see the emergence of a new star – his son, Keith, who earned rave reviews for his performances as hooker.

O'Reilly's achievements on the field do not seem to square with his own assessment of his playing style: 'I suppose you could say I was a slightly furtive player. I hung back waiting for the game to show itself to me rather than show myself to the game.'

One of the many tributes paid to A.J.F. O'Reilly down through the years was: 'Never have you satisfied so many women in the one day.' Despite O'Reilly's erstwhile reputation as something of a ladies' man this is not what it seems. The source was Irene Johnson rejoicing at his generous donation towards the running of the 1994 Women's Hockey World Cup.

O'Reilly could have been a film star. The late Noel Purcell recommended him to Al Corfino, the casting director of the film *Ben Hur*, for the role that was eventually played by Charlton Heston. O'Reilly's physique made him ideal for the scenes in the galleys. Purcell arranged for a meeting between the director and O'Reilly but the rugby player never showed up. The story of O'Reilly's possible role in the film made headlines in places as far away as South Africa.

In 1963 following Ireland's 24–5 defeat at the hands of the French, O'Reilly was dropped for the only time in his career. Although the news came as a shock O'Reilly had arguably never consistently reproduced his Lions' form in the green jersey. It seemed after 28 caps his international career was over. Seven years later, in an ill-judged move, the Irish selectors persuaded him to come out of retirement to play against England at Twickenham in place of the injured Billy Brown, for his 29th cap. To put it at its kindest, O'Reilly, now firmly established as a commercial giant because of his work in business, was anything but a lean, mean machine at that time. His shape prompted Willie John McBride to remark: 'Well, Tony, in my view your best attacking move tomorrow might be to shake your jowls at them.'

Ireland lost 9-3 and O'Reilly gave an undistinguished performance. In the final moments he dived boldly into the heart of the English pack. As he regained consciousness he heard an Irish voice shouting: 'And while you're at it, why don't ya kick his f***ing chauffeur too!' The Heinz slogan is: 'Beanz Meanz Heinz.' After the match a wag was heard to say: 'I never realised Heinz means has-beens!'

29

PHIL ORR

Here Orr There

The front row is an immensely technical place where brain and brawn collide; it is one which has fascinated me since I played with a prop whose shorts caught fire during a game as a consequence of carrying a light for his half-time fag.

Bill Lothian

Phil Orr's rugby allegiances have often been questioned: 'My father was from Newtownards. He played for Ards and later Palmerstown when he moved to Dublin. People have said I'm a "half-Ulster player".'

His brother, David, played for both Munster and Leinster juniors. At High School, Rathgar Orr's rugby career was born where he played Senior Cup for three years. He also played for two years with Leinster schoolboys. Trinity College, where he obtained a first class honours degree in Maths, was his next rugby nursery. Dick Spring was secretary and captain of the club at the time. In 1973 he was a sub on the Leinster team and graduated to the team the following year. He played for the Irish universities against the All Blacks in 1974 to mark the IRFU's centenary year.

'Their coach said to Roly Meates: "It was like playing against schoolboys." The other memory I have of the game is of Dick Spring sprinting 50 yards to "sort out" one of the All Blacks after he overstepped the mark.'

In 1976 he made his international debut in Paris as Ireland lost by a then record 26–3 coming in as a late replacement for Paddy Agnew.

'It was a very strange experience for me. I don't think people appreciate the culture shock Paris is for you, especially the first time. If

I was in charge of things I would be inclined not to bring over the Irish team until the Friday, not on the Thursday, as is the norm. The food is so unfamiliar and the language gap brings its own problems. Then as you are driving through Paris guys are looking at the shop windows and it's very hard to keep the focus that is needed. I feel we need a better psychological preparation for the French matches.

'My clearest memory of the whole weekend was breakfast the morning of the match. I was rooming with Stewart McKinney and he ordered breakfast in bed for both of us, scrambled eggs and toast. We were waiting for ages and ages but with no sign of any service. Stewart went out in the corridor and saw a few waiters walking up and down with trays of food. He simply grabbed one from a very surprised waiter and exchanged pleasantries and brought in the tray. I remember very little about the actual game except that it went very quickly and I was black and blue all over. I learned to react quicker after that and to look after myself better.

'One thing I never could understand, though, was the hassle that some players would put themselves through the morning of a match. We all only got two tickets each at the time but there were lads who would be getting themselves in a rash worrying about tickets for family and friends. That's no way to prepare for a big match.

'The adrenalin is really flowing before an international so it's crucial to keep your mind right. For home internationals we always stayed in the Shelbourne. On the night before a match and on the day of the game the lobby was a hive of activity. New players were told not to hang around because they would get too caught up in the occasion and their performance would suffer. In the early years I followed that advice fairly religiously but at the end of my career I would deliberately go down to the foyer just to get the adrenalin flowing.

'One thing that always bugged me on those occasions was that on a rugby weekend Dublin goes rugby mad. On the Friday afternoon, evening, night and Saturday morning everybody was going to some reception or party. It seemed that the only people not drinking was us!'

Orr was one of only three Irish players, with Willie Duggan and Mike Gibson, to be selected on the Lions tour to New Zealand in 1977. When Geoff Wheel withdrew from the tour Moss Keane stepped in for him.

'The biggest shock for me about the Lions tour was the British Press. We would get on the team bus and there would be two busloads of journalists watching everything we did. All of these guys are looking for a different angle and would dish up any dirt they could find or even a whiff of trouble. The pressure that puts you under is immense. I think that British sport is being destroyed by its journalists.

'I enjoyed the Irish and Leinster tours more than the Lions tours. The 1977 Lions tour lasted three and half months, which is too long. One of the things I learned is that the Irish will talk to everybody. The non-Irish Lions won't. The Lions are not very popular in Australia and New Zealand because basically they hate the British, though they like the Irish. I particularly enjoyed Ireland's tour to Japan because it was such a different culture. I was lucky to play for a great Leinster side in the late 1970s and early 1980s. We never expected to lose and we could always shift into a higher gear whenever we were threatened in any way.

'One of the clearest memories I have is of touring Romania with Leinster in 1980. It was like entering a time warp. Most of the time we were starving because there wasn't enough food, largely because it all went up to Moscow. There was nothing in the shops except bare shelves. If you wanted an orange, for example, you had to order it the day before. One incident stands out for me. We stopped for a meal of sorts in a half-way house. As we got off the bus what struck me most was that there wasn't the sound of a bird to be heard. I learned later that DDT had killed all the insects and the birds had migrated.'

The belief at the time was that one in every four people in Romania was an informer for the Securitate. It subsequently emerged that this was a lie deliberately put about by the Securitate to keep everyone in line lest they were talking to someone who would report them back for subversion or, perish the thought, making a joke about the dictator, Nicolai Ceaucescu. Orr had other experiences where rugby and politics converged.

'We also made a tour to Venice with Leinster. It was a pretty bizarre event. I remember we travelled to the match by boat. We were on one side and our opponents were on the other. The boat brought both teams back together and the meal didn't start until a quarter past midnight. The Mayor of Venice invited the officials and a few of the players for a reception in Venice's equivalent of the Mansion House. I was one of a few players who went to the reception. We were all dressed up in our official blazers. As we went into this very impressive building we noticed there was a sheet covering a table. We were all a bit taken aback when the Mayor, who was a communist, strolled out in the most casual of clothes, a grandad shirt and jeans as far as I can remember. Then the sheet was taken off the table and we saw that our reception was in fact a few bottles of minerals. My colleagues were less than impressed but I thought it was absolutely hilarious.'

The high point of Orr's international career were the Triple Crown victories of 1982 and 1985. The low point came in 1986.

'I lost my place for the Welsh match to Paul Kennedy of London Irish, I think more because of the final trial than because of the drubbing we got from France in our opening match of the campaign. I was up against Dessie Fitzgerald on one side of the scrum and Jim McCoy was up against Paul Kennedy. Jim was pretty secure in his place and I don't think Paul thought he had any real chance of getting into the side, so they weren't trying too hard but Dessie was mad keen to get picked and was wired to the moon that day so I didn't give the "commanding performance" I would have liked.

'It would be a lie to say I was not very disappointed to be dropped. It made me even more determined to get onto the side. The hardest part of the experience for me was taking my place in the queue at the turnstiles to get into Lansdowne Road for the Welsh match. I played a club game for Wesley that morning and the lads were slagging me on the way to the match asking me if I would be able to find Lansdowne Road on my own because I was so used to travelling there on the team bus.'

In the final match of the 1986 season, Orr regained his place for the home game to Scotland, which Ireland lost by the narrowest of margins. The occasion was all the more memorable because he had the honour of leading the team onto the field. This event left an interesting legacy which hangs proudly today in Orr's home. Some of the Irish players penned a tribute to him and organised a singing telegram for him. He suspects Hugo MacNeill was the author. Hugo was one of Ireland's finest full-backs but on this evidence he is no Seamus Heaney or Bruce Springsteen! The best line of this neatly typed, lengthy ode which Orr has had framed for posterity is: 'The greatest prop among the Celts!' However, it is the short handwritten message at the side which catches the eye: 'The next 50 is the toughest. Sam Torrance.'

The celebrated golfer happened to be a guest in the Shelbourne Hotel that evening and was readily persuaded to join the festivities.

'The next season the inaugural World Cup was taking place and I wanted to be part of it so I trained that bit harder. To be honest the tour was a great disappointment. The travel arrangements and the hotels were of a poor standard. I remember in Wellington it got to the stage where I would bring a book down to our meals because we would have to wait so long for food.'

Asked about the players he admired most, Orr comes up with his equivalent of the magnificent seven.

'My debut coincided with Phil O'Callaghan's reincarnation on the Irish side and I got on very well with him from day one. He was a great character but very committed to the cause. There were other wonderful personalities around at that time who I admired greatly, like Mossie Keane, Willie Duggan, Fergus Slattery and John O'Driscoll. They were all well able to enjoy themselves but on a one-to-one basis they were very serious. Another common link between them was incredible commitment. With my mathematical mind I was very impressed with Mike Gibson's methodical build-up to the game. The only word to describe it was professional.

'I know the backs will disagree with this but I credit the forwards with our Triple Crown victory in 1982. There were a lot of jokes about "Dad's army" because the pack were supposed to be so old, which is not quite true. I was one of those "rugby Dads" but I did not think of myself as old. People are always surprised to hear that both John Robbie and Ollie Campbell were capped before me. It was said that it was harder to get off the Irish forward line than it was to get on it but we did the business that year. Having said that, I want to acknowledge that we would not have won the Triple Crown were it not for Ollie Campbell. From that tour in Australia in 1979 I was a huge admirer of his kicking abilities. He was the difference between glory and disappointment.'

With 58 caps including 49 consecutively (one short of the Scottish international Sandy Carmichael's record of 50 caps) he became the world's most capped prop-forward. Will his record survive?

'The wear and tear is such that I don't think any prop-forward will be able to keep going for 12 years at the highest international level as I did. What is different now with the World Cup and so on is that there are more internationals, so players are picking up caps now much faster than they used to.'

Even when he departed the Irish scene he still had time for a last hurrah on the international stage.

'After the inaugural World Cup I retired from international rugby but later that year I was invited to play for a World XV in Japan as part of the All Blacks tour. I met the English players at the airport in London. I learned that I was leading the pack but that we had two loose-head props, the English international Paul Rendall and I, but no tight-head prop. Worse still we learned that they had selected a Japanese prop who was also a loose-head. I told Paul that I had the solution to this problem. I was the oldest so I would play loose-head.

'Worse was to follow when we got there. They had Japanese players as hooker and as a scrum-half who couldn't speak a word of English

162

between them. These are the two most important positions on the field in terms of making the calls on the pitch and giving instructions. It made absolutely no sense to have non-English speakers in those key positions in a team of essentially English speakers! We learned the Japanese for "one", "three" and "five" and limited ourselves to three calls. To confuse the opposition I came up with the idea of using Japanese brand names so that our call would be "Honda One" in Japanese and so on. Then it was brought to my attention that one of the Japanese players worked for Honda and didn't like the company name being used in this way. So that ended my masterplan!

'We all knew the All Blacks were in a mean mood. They had defeated Japan 106–4 in the Test game. The mistake the Japanese made was scoring a try. If they hadn't had the cheek to score a try I reckon the All Blacks would have let them off with a 50-points defeat. I can't remember much about the match except that we were murdered in the first-half at tight-head prop. All I could say by way of tactical insight at half-time was: "We're going to retreat carefully!"

'I do remember that after the game the players said we wanted to be brought to the Japanese Disneyland. The All Blacks had arranged to go in advance and agreed to take us on their team bus. The problem was that the organisers hadn't got clearance for us. When we arrived we went inside first but the Blacks were refused entry. They weren't used to this type of treatment and there were ructions about it!'

Orr is still heavily involved in Old Wesley and was club president for its centenary year. Indeed such was his affection for the club that once when he played for Leinster against Italy he did a rugby impression of a 'Klinsmann dive' and rolled around in agony four minutes from time so that his club-mate, Mick Jackman, could win his first cap for Leinster. Observers were a bit puzzled about Jackman's psychic powers because he was warming up well before Philly got his 'injury'. So now his playing days are over what is his happiest rugby memory?

'My second most memorable moment was beating Wales in Cardiff in 1985 and the most memorable was going back there two years later and beating them a second time!'

30

COLIN PATTERSON

The Trying Game

> Did you say in the water or on the water?
>
> Aussie journalist questions the management
> statement that David Campese was jogging in
> water in order to ease a groin strain.

Colin Patterson, 'Patty', is a gifted storyteller talking in a way that is delightfully descriptive and wickedly insightful of human foibles. An accomplished mimic, his impression of Noel Murphy is devastating. While studying law at Bristol, he played for English and British Universities. With his fast fingers and his ability to switch the options he won 11 caps for Ireland before 1980, scoring five international tries. His career was tragically ended by injury when he went on the Lions tour of South Africa in 1980. It happened in the penultimate game, after having played in three Test matches. One of his teachers had a huge influence on his sporting career – though not in the way he intended.

'I went to a non-soccer school and in my first year played both hockey and rugby. After that we had to choose between rugby and hockey. A teacher put a lot of pressure on me to choose hockey but true to my personality I chose rugby because of that.

'When I broke into the Ulster side Mike Gibson was a big inspiration to me because of his dedication. In fact when Ollie Campbell came into the Irish squad Gibson and Ollie would stay on the pitch on their own for extra training. They didn't drink so they had nothing else to do! An Ulster selector, Joss Lapsley, saved me about three or four seasons: he taught me so much about the game and knew how to deal with my abrasive character. He had a photographic memory but would never speak to me the evening after a match but left it to the following Monday or Tuesday. He broke down the key moments of the game and asked me why I had chosen the options I took and I explained why I hadn't seen better alternatives. His answer to this was usually: "Yeah, you didn't look." Through his help I learned to read the game much better and became more tactically aware.'

Patterson made his international debut against the All Blacks in 1978.

'I heard about it a week before the match. I was so nervous I must have thought about ringing up ten times and telling them that I was unable to play. After the team-talk and once we got on the team bus, with the garda escort, I started to relax and really enjoy the occasion.

'One of my clearest memories of winning my first cap is of a piece written about me in a local newspaper. The journalist in question had rung my mother a few times but had been unable to contact me. Yet when I opened the paper I saw a big piece full of quotes from me. I tackled the journalist about this afterwards. He said: "It's the sort of thing you would have said!" Throughout my career the amount of quotes attributed to me written by journalists who I had never even met defies belief. I didn't have that problem with *The Irish Times*. In their case the difficulty was that I never should have been picked for Ireland in the first place. I was described as Ireland's sixth choice.'

Patterson immediately struck up an instant rapport with his half-back partner, Tony Ward, on and off the field. It was said that they went together like ham and eggs, and that Patterson could find Ward in a darkened room. The scrum-half was heard to proclaim that Ward was not the first person he would want to meet in those circumstances!

'As a boy, soccer was my first love. My late father was a director of Glentoran. My dream was to play at centre-forward and wear the number nine shirt. As a boy, Tony's dream was to wear the number ten shirt for the Irish soccer team. We both ended up wearing the right numbered shirts but in rugby instead of soccer. We first played together for the Ireland B side against Scotland who had a half-back combination of Roy Laidlaw and John Rutherford but we came out well on top and won 7–3, Tony kicking a penalty and I scored a try. We clicked immediately on and off the field.

'I later went on *The Late, Late Show* with Tony when he was the golden boy of Irish rugby and landed him in big trouble. Wardie was involved in a serious relationship at the time and Gay Byrne asked him if he had a girlfriend. I quipped immediately: "One in every town." Tony had a lot of explaining to do to his young lady after that! He was also asked if he had thought about defecting to Rugby League. When Tony rejected the idea out of hand Gay turned to me and said: "Tony is looking down on Rugby League Colin, how about you?"

"When you are only five feet five inches you can't afford to look down on anything," I replied.

'The personality difference between Tony and me was also evident on that visit. We were both asked what we would like to drink. I said two Irish coffees please which was not what they normally provided and would take a bit of trouble on their part. Immediately Tony intervened and said:

"Oh, no. Don't go to any trouble for us."

"Okay, Tony, I'll drink yours as well," I answered and we both got our Irish coffees.

'I loved winding Tony up. Of course he gave me the ideal opportunity after the publication of his page-three style pose in his swimming trunks before the Scottish game in 1979. I pinned up the photo on the wall and kept gushing to him about his fantastic bum and how no woman could possibly resist him. People kept asking me why he was dropped. There were all kinds of speculation including the ridiculous notion that Wardie was caught in bed with one of the selectors' wives. Tony is not like that. I think that the essential difference between Tony and Ollie was that Tony, like myself, was an inside runner whereas Ollie was an outside runner. As both were superb kickers I feel it made for a better balance to have an inside and outside runner playing at half-backs.'

Patterson observed the sensational decision to drop Campbell for Ward from close quarters on Ireland's tour to Australia in 1979.

'The Tuesday before the first Test we were playing Queensland but Tony and I had been told we would not be playing. I saw the other scrum-half, Johnny Moloney, that morning and he was fit and well so I could relax. I ordered a big fillet steak and egg for my meal. Shortly afterwards Noel Murphy came to me and told me I was playing. I told him to get lost and not to be kidding me because I had seen Moloney that morning and he was fine. Then Noisy said: "Johnny's on the wing." My steak started wobbling in my stomach but I would have to play. Myself and Ollie played well in what was effectively a Test match and we won. After the match there were a lot of barbecues. We were watching them from out our window and started singing *Waltzing Matilda*. The Aussies began throwing beer cans at us but we had the last laugh because many of the cans were half-full so we grabbed the cans, drank the beer and threw the cans back at them!

'After the storm about Wardie being dropped off the team the Australian press rubbished our chances of winning the first Test. One headline read: 'Ireland to be Paddywhacked into Rugby Oblivion.' We beat them 27–12! If ever a victory was sweet this was it. The place went berserk. I have a picture at home taken in the dressing-room which shows Ollie and I together grinning from ear to ear. It was such a turn-up for the books. The only comparable story I can think of such a misjudgement came at the turn of this century. Two men, Mr Marks and Mr Smith, were talking. Mr Marks outlined his plans for a new shop and asked Mr Smith to be his partner. Mr Smith replied: "Nah. It'll never work." Mr Marks found a new partner – Mr Spencer. The result is history!'

After Ireland's success in Australia they were confidently expected to take the Triple Crown the next season. With his tongue firmly in his cheek Patty offers an unusual explanation for Ireland's failure to so do.

'We should have won the Triple Crown in 1980. I blame Ollie Campbell! Although we defeated Scotland and Wales we lost to England. At one stage Jim Glennon was bursting through and we had the overlap with Ollie on one side and me on the other. I was certain I was going to score a try but the ball went to Campbell and not me and he fluffed it. It's time he was de-canonised!'

With his small stature Patterson was an obvious target for intimidation on the rugby pitch.

'I prided myself on my ability to take punishment. The tougher it got the better I liked it. Whenever I got crushed by somebody I got up immediately and said to him: "Good tackle soldier," which really annoyed them. At internationals there were a number of efforts to verbally intimidate me. I never let that sort of bullshit get to me. The best example of this was when we played Wales in 1980. Where Stuart Lane wasn't going to stuff the ball up my anatomy I can't say. I eventually turned around and said to him: "Stuart, you don't mean that." It was my last home game for Ireland so the BBC gave me the video of the match. When I watched it I saw again Stuart bursting into laughter and saying: "You're a cheeky wee bollocks." The more a player tried to intimidate me the more I wound him up by waving at him in the lineout and so on. Apart from the fact that it helped me to win the psychological war it's the only fun us small fellahs get!'

In 1980 tragedy swooped like a hawk flying down from the sky, a fearsome beast, ferocious as it ripped and shred and tore, attacking all it saw when Patterson's career was prematurely ended on the Lions tour to South Africa. It was one of those moments, those breaths of time, when sadness and joy share the narrow path of life. Patty was at the height of his powers when all was taken from him in an accidental clash.

'It all began with an innocuous incident. I was screaming in agony the pain was so intense. My situation was not helped by the fact that the referee tried to play amateur doctor with me and started poking around with my leg. I was stretchered off but they are so fanatical about their rugby out there that two fans rushed on. One took my discarded boot and the other my sock and he asked me if I would give him my shorts.'

For all of that, Patterson has many happy memories of his time with the Lions.

'It was a real education touring with the Welsh. That was the era when you paid for your own telephone calls home. They had three great tricks devised never to pay for a telephone. Plan A was to charm the hotel receptionist into giving them the secret code they could use to make calls without having them charged to them. Plan B was to distract the receptionist and for one of them to sneak in behind the desk and steal all their telephone bills. Plan C was when a journalist asked for an interview they traded it for a phone call.

'Best of all though was when we went into the Adidas factory. We were allowed to pick a bag of our choice and stuff it with gear. Most of us selected the most stylish bags and filled them with gear. All the Welsh guys, without exception, took the biggest bags in the shop and walked out with half of the gear in the factory! In 1983 when Trevor Ringland was chosen to tour with the Lions to New Zealand the advice I gave him was: "Be sure and stay close to the Welsh when they visit the Adidas factory!"

'One night they did a classic wind-up on the English player Mike Slemen who was the leading try scorer on the tour. All of them gathered into the one room and rang him up pretending to be from the BBC World Service, with a suitably posh accent. They fed him a lot of compliments and he started blowing his own trumpet and claimed that he probably was one of the best players on the tour. Eventually the Welsh lads could take no more and shouted: "Slemen, you're a useless f***er." The Englishman was mortified that he had been caught out so badly.

'I believe we would have won the Test series had Fergus Slattery been chosen as captain. When I came onto the Irish scene I watched in awe as he did what he did. I would have run through a brick wall if he asked me because I know he would have done the same for the team. I think we would have been better off with an Irish captain rather than an Irish coach because Noel Murphy was brilliant at motivating the Irish lads [one of his instructions to the squad during a training session was: "Spread out in a bunch"] but not so good with the Welsh who require a different type of motivation. We had very light backs on the tour and needed quick ball. When I said this to the forwards, Jeff Squire told me: "You'll get the ball when we've finished with it." We should have been playing a rucking game but instead our forwards favoured mauling. In the Test matches we also had two blind-side forwards in the back row which didn't give us the balance we needed.'

The wrecked medial ligaments from his injury caused Patterson to revise his career plans. Had he not got that injury he had arranged to go out and play in Australia for a season. In fact he already had his ticket bought.

Patterson was a rugby ecumenist, singing the National Anthem with gusto before matches even though he was not from Nationalist stock.

'Wardie taught me the first six or seven lines of the anthem and then I discovered that I could sing it to the tune of *The Sash*. I sang the first half of *The Soldier's Song* and the second half of *The Sash* just to give it a political balance!'

He has great admiration for the characters in the game.

'Scotland's Jim Renwick is a fabulous character. When the English came up to play, the Scottish coach gave a rabble-rousing speech about all the damage the Sassenach did down through history when they crossed the English border: raping their women, pillaging their homes, destroying their property and stealing their children. Despite his history lesson England hammered them. When Jim got back into the dressing-room he said: "Damn and blast. My wife is going to be raped again tonight!"

'Freddie McLennan is another great personality. Once, when we played England, Freddie and John Carleton were having a real jousting match. At one stage John sent Freddie crashing to the ground in a tackle. As he was going back to his position Freddie shouted at him: "John, John. Is my hair all right?" If you watch the video of the game you'll see John cracking up with laughter and Freddie straightening his hair.'

31

MICK QUINN

The Mighty Quinn

Old rugby players never die – they simply have their balls taken away.

Anon

'Mine has been an eventful career.' This is Mick Quinn's summation of his life in rugby which brought him ten caps for Ireland at out-half. Although he is not one of the giants of Irish rugby in the same way as Jack Kyle, he is certainly a giant of the after-dinner speech on the rugby circuit. Yet his rugby career might have perished before it started.

'I played soccer with the well-known soccer nursery Rangers and was offered a trial with Everton. For a few minutes I dreamt of being the new George Best but my mother intervened and told me I was going to boarding school and not to Everton. I really developed my interest in rugby at Newbridge College. In my final year we won the Schools Cup for the first time in 40 years. We had lost 31–0 to Blackrock College in a friendly at home, early in the season, but we beat them 19–5 in the final on St Patrick's Day. It was an incredible buzz. After that game my great mentor, Fr Heffernan, told me to aim high and I would end up playing for Ireland.

'After I left school I joined Lansdowne. I remember going to a training session for the first time and meeting former international Con Murphy when I went inside. He told me just to join in but didn't look very impressed or interested. I knew I had made my mark when the session was over and he rushed over and said: "What did you say your name was?" In my first year I played for the third team. My full-back was no less a person than former Irish international Mick English.

Lansdowne had some great players at the time like 'the red rocket', Vinny Becker. It was a shame that he played for Ireland on the wrong wing so that the Irish public never saw him at his best. He was faster than Jonah Lomu. The next season I was on the first team and playing for Ireland when I was only 20.

'I don't remember much about the build-up for my debut except that I fell asleep during Willie John McBride's team-talk! Ray McLoughlin told me that I was a cheeky bugger. Willie John was a wonderful captain because he had such a great presence. I remember when I came onto the international scene first I addressed him as "Mr McBride".

'It was pay-for-play with a difference. I had to pay for my jersey. We beat France 6–4 for my first cap. The player who scored their try was killed by lightning some time later. The great J.P. Romeau missed the conversion. As it was my first cap there was no way I was going to part with my jersey but I really wanted Romeau's. I went back into the dressing-room and asked Ray McLoughlin for his number one jersey. You have to remember that he is a very successful businessman, heading up the James Crean Company – so he's not short of a few bob. He sold me his jersey for £10. I rushed out and swopped jerseys with Romeau. I was thrilled with myself when I returned but suddenly the French man came into our dressing-room. With his dreadful English and my awful French communication was a problem but it didn't take me long to see that the problem was that he wanted a number ten jersey. I used sign language and said to him: "Zero fello offo!"'

Quinn was an ever present in Ireland's Championship success in 1974. That season provided him with his finest hour.

'My best game for Ireland was unquestionably against England in Twickenham in 1974. Although the final score, 26–21, was deceptively close we hockeyed them that day – scoring four tries. It was such a wonderful feeling after the game to know that I had played to my very best and the team had performed to its best. I have an unbeaten record against England and Wales – not many Irish internationals can say that. Okay, so I only played against them once!

'I enjoyed every minute of my international career. I don't think I ever played a bad game for Ireland which is a good feeling to have. The great thing about rugby is the friendship even with your rivals for the Irish jersey. I get on great with Tony Ward even though he was the main impediment to my international career. In his biography, *The Good, The Bad and the Rugby*, he jokes that if it wasn't for Ollie Campbell he would have got 40 caps. When I read that I rang him up and said if it wasn't for him, Mike Gibson, Barry McGann, Ollie and Paul Dean, I would have won 80 caps!

'Wardie's great champion was Ned Van Esbeck of *The Irish Times*. Whenever I kicked a great penalty it was just a great penalty but when Wardie kicked one it was "a wonder strike from the master craftsman". Whenever I was kicking exceptionally well I would shout up at Ned and ask him whether or not Wardie could have bettered that.

'There was a time I got one up on Ollie. I am good friends with Chris De Burgh and was with him in Rome for the World Cup quarter-final in 1990 when Ireland lost to Italy. It was incredible to see the way all the Italians mobbed Chris before the game but we went into the middle of the crowd just as ordinary fans. I saw some of the U2 guys up in the stands with their bodyguards away from the riff-raff but Chris wasn't like that. After the match Jack Charlton and the players went on the team bus but the Irish fans were still in the stadium yelling for Jack. I ran out and asked him to come back out on the pitch which he did. I walked out behind him and when I looked up there was Ollie in the stands. So I waved at him knowing full well he would be wondering to himself how that so-and-so Quinn managed to get on the pitch with Jack Charlton!

'One of the highlights of my career was winning the three-in-a-row of Leinster Cups in 1981 with Lansdowne. We beat Old Belvedere in the final and it was nice to put one over on Ollie on the pitch. After the match the team bus was bringing us on to the victory celebrations. I suggested to the boys we should "lob a moon" or display our bums out the window to the people of Dublin. This proposal was enthusiastically agreed to. When we were on display I turned around and saw there was a car travelling alongside the bus. To my horror the occupants were my father, mother and sister. My mother told me afterwards that she had recognised my bum because it hadn't changed since the time she used to change my nappies! I told her I found that hard to believe.

'When we were on tour with Ireland in Fiji in 1976 the team bus took us on a day trip. John Robbie suggested we lob a moon which we did. Suddenly we heard an anguished scream. It was John shouting: "My God, I've lobbed my wallet." It had fallen out the window and Christmas had come early for some lucky local.

'Of course there was Moss Keane. Whenever we played for Ireland on the Saturday, Moss and I would still turn up for the match with Lansdowne on the Sunday, even though we wouldn't be in the best of shape. For Moss, though, it would be a case of the morning after the night before. You don't get that kind of dedication to the club as much today.'

After the high of the Championship victory in 1974 Quinn was quickly brought down to earth.

'The one great disappointment of my career was when I was a standby for the Lions tour to South Africa. The English fly-half Alan Old got injured near the end of the tour. I got a call at home from one of the Lions management team, Albert Ager, who told me to get ready for the trip to South Africa. An hour later I had my bags packed and at the hall door. Then another call came from Ager, a name I will never forget, telling me that in fact I would not be travelling and asking me, did I mind? What a question to ask! Of course I lied and said no but it was devastating. It turned out that after he had called me, someone else rang Mike Gibson, who had declined the invitation to tour initially.

'It would have been a great honour not just for me personally but for my family if I had toured with the Lions. My father was not a sporting man but he was very proud that I played for Ireland. He seldom drank but when he did he really drank. Once he was having a few drinks with John Joe Whyte of *The Irish Times*. He told John Joe that I had acquired my ability from him and that he himself played for Monaghan in the 1928 All-Ireland Gaelic football final – not even knowing at that stage if Monaghan had played in the final that year! The next day my father's story appeared verbatim in *The Times* – John Joe hadn't realised he was being wound up and didn't bother to check out the facts.'

Quinn, though, did get the chance to tour with Ireland. His worst moment in rugby came on one tour.

'On the New Zealand tour in 1976 we were losing 15–3 to Canterbury. I was sub. From my point of view everything was going great. When you are a sub you don't really want things to be going well for the team because if it does, how else are you going to get your place back? Larry Moloney broke his arm so Tony Ensor replaced him. Wallace McMaster got injured and with a sinking in my heart I realised I would have to play on the wing. It was my first time ever to play in that position. I was petrified and I can tell you I wished I was wearing brown shorts!

'As I walked on one of their players Alex "Griz" Wyllie came over to me and said: "You've come a long way to die, son." When I was in Newbridge, Fr Heffernan had always drilled in to me the belief that you should never let anybody intimidate you. At that stage I made the biggest mistake of my life. I said: "Listen pal if my dog had a face like yours I would shave his arse and get him to walk backwards." Every chance he got after that he clobbered me. Even when the ball was somewhere else he kept coming at me. When I said, "the ball is over there", he answered: "I couldn't give a f*** where the ball is. I'm going to kill you."

'On that tour Jimmy Davidson was called into the Irish side as a replacement. He was so happy to be selected that he jumped for joy when he got on the team bus for the first time. He jumped so high that he smashed his head against the roof and needed six stitches.

'For his first game on the tour we were worried about things getting out of hand on the pitch. At one stage there was a mêlée in the ruck and Pa Whelan mistakenly stamped Davidson on the head. Initially the lads thought one of the New Zealand guys had done it and there was bedlam for two minutes. When order was restored, the first thing we heard was Davidson shouting: "You f***ing idiot, Whelan." After the game he needed plenty of stitches.

'At one stage Willie John McBride and I were invited to South Africa to play for a World XV against the Springboks. I was interviewed on South African TV and asked what I thought of the main contenders for the number ten shirt with the Springboks, and if any out-half had impressed me. I mentioned that I had been taken by this new kid called Naas Botha who I had seen play on television. The next day I was training when this fellah came over to me and I recognised him as Botha. He wanted to thank me for my compliments.

'Naas was a hugely controversial figure in South Africa. They either loved him or hated him. We got on very well and I subsequently invited him to come over and get some experience in Lansdowne. I thought nothing more about it until some months later I got a phone call at home. It was Naas. He said he would like to take up my offer of hospitality. I told him that he would be welcome and asked him when would he be travelling over. Then he told me: "Well, Mr Quinn, I'm ringing you from a place called O'Connell Street in Dublin!" He brought his brother, Darius, with him who since became a Dutch Reformed Minister. He used to organise prayer meetings in my house!'

Perhaps Quinn's most enduring legacy to the rugby landscape is the number of players he has given nicknames to.

'I called former international scrum-half, Tony Doyle, "Gandhi" because there was more meat in a cheese sandwich. I called the Wesley player, Dave Priestman, "Vicarman" because I told him it was ridiculous for a Protestant to be called priest. I call Brendan Mullin, "Bugs Bunny" because of his smile. I also christened Harry Steele, "Stainless" for obvious reasons and Jean-Pierre Rives, now a noted sculptor, and the living proof that you don't have to be big to be a world class forward, "Je t'aime" because he had such charm with women. I called my Lansdowne club-mate Rory Moroney, "the Reverend Moroney" because he spent two years in the priesthood.'

There is, though, one nickname he is at pains to disclaim.

'Johnny Moloney was on tour with the Lions in South Africa in 1974. Near the end of the tour he was summonsed before the players' informal court [a regular occurrence when players are fined for various off-the-field misdemeanours, for example not drinking enough]. Johnny was charged with a very serious offence – he hadn't "enjoyed conjugal relations" with any woman on the tour even though he was still single at the time. In his defence Johnny said, very unconvincingly I might add, that he had in fact slept with two women. Gracer [Tom Grace] said immediately: "Shagger".

'Gracer told me about it when he came home [Tom Grace, struggling heroically to suppress a smile, emphatically denies this!] and we had a great laugh about it because no one could be less in line for that description. Shortly afterwards I saw Johnny at a reception with his girlfriend at the time, subsequently his wife, Miriam, and I shouted over at him: "How's it going, Shagger?" Miriam discreetly asked me later why I had called him Shagger. I told her that what goes on on a tour is sacred and there was no way I could disclose any intimate details about Johnny's behaviour. I can tell you Moloney had some explaining to do that night!'

Quinn is also able to tell stories against himself.

'After one international match a young autograph hunter said to me: "Can I have your autograph please, Johnny?" I didn't have the heart to tell him he had got the wrong man so I just signed it: "To Bert. Best wishes, Johnny Moloney." As he was leaving he looked up and said to me: "How do you keep playing with Mick Quinn. He plays like shit!"

'In fairness Johnny did me a favour when we played Wales in 1974. We drew 9–9. I had a bad flu before the match and was puking all over the place. The only one who knew about it was Shagger. I told him if he told anyone about it I would kill him.'

Quinn has a particular affection for another former Irish international – as much for his off-the-field activities as for his playing career.

'Johnny Murphy was a great captain of Leinster. He has a bus and hearse business and turned up for training one night in his hearse with a coffin inside. Some of us found it to be disconcerting to be doing our press-ups beside a coffin and grumbled to Johnny. He just said: "She's not going anywhere and doesn't mind waiting."

'Johnny's speeches were great, not least because he was great at taking off posh accents. His opening sentence after a Connacht match was:

"Mr President of Leinster, Mr President of Connacht, players and the rest of you hangers on." He was tremendously popular as a player. Once after we beat Ulster in Donnybrook he got up to make the speech at the dinner afterwards. Sir Ewart Bell was on one side of him and David Irwin on the other. Johnny's most controversial line was: "We stuffed the Orange banner up yer hole." Not surprisingly he was carpeted afterwards and told to clean up his act when making speeches.

'The next week we played Llanelli and beat the pants off them. We were all dying to know what Johnny would say. He began: "Well, lads, I've got to be very careful what I say this week. It was a great honour for us to have the privilege of playing against such a famous side. My only regret is that BBC's *Rugby Special* wasn't here to see us beating the shite out of ye. I know people will say ye were missing some of yer star players but don't forget we were missing one of our greatest stars – Hugo MacNeill. He couldn't get his f***ing place – I have it." The whole place was in stitches and I remember Ray Gravell in particular had to be picked off the floor he was laughing so hard.

'Ray, like a lot of the Welsh players, is really nationalistic. Once, before an international, when I was sub, I went into the toilet and I heard Ray in the next cubicle singing arias about the welcome in the hills in Wales. I told him that the only reason they welcomed us in the hills was that they were too mean to invite us into their homes! There's a limit to the amount of Ray's singing I can take so I asked him to give it a rest, but he went on and on. To shut him up I filled a bucket of cold water and threw it over him in the cubicle. I fled because he came out like a raging bull and said nothing about the incident in our dressing-room. When the Welsh team came out some of our lads remarked that Ray must have gone through an awfully heavy warm-up because the sweat was rolling off him.'

Through his involvement with the Wolfhounds, Quinn continues to have plenty of contact with the giants of international rugby.

'I met J.P.R. Williams one day at the end of 1990. It was the time Wales had gone 13 international matches without winning. He's always beating the nationalist drum going on about the rugby in the valleys in Wales and how central it is to Welsh life. It was nice, in a way, to see him eating humble pie so I asked him what his most fervent wish for Welsh rugby was in 1991. He answered: "I hope that Wales win a match." He then asked me what my most fervent wish for Irish rugby was for that year. I said: "For Ireland to win the Triple Crown, the Grand Slam and the World Cup." He said: "Ah, come on Mick, be serious." All I said to him was: "You f***ing started it."

'Gareth Chilcott earns about £35,000 a year from making speeches and about £30,000 a year doing panto. I played him once in a golf match during the Lions tour of New Zealand. At one stage my ball trickled into a pond. I could see it and asked him to hold my hand as I leaned over to retrieve it. He said he would but deliberately let me go and I toppled in. I had to take off all my clothes and try and squeeze the water out of them much to the bemusement of the women who were playing on the other greens!

'Dean Richards is the nicest guy of them all. He's loved by all rugby folk over there because he's such a down-to-earth guy. I know the media have given a hard time to Will Carling, but like Princess Diana, though for very different reasons, I have a lot of respect for him. O'Carling – he got that name on the Lions tour in 1993 when he started drinking Guinness [at a time when Mick Galwey ruled the roost on the tour in terms of social activity] – has buckets of character.

'Campo [David Campese] is a great character. He says outrageous things like: "Carling himself epitomises England's lack of skills – he has speed and bulk but plays like a castrated bull." Yet he takes the game very seriously. He gets up at 7 a.m., does his weights, has his breakfast, goes for a run, trains, and rests for the remainder of the day. His contribution to Australia's win in the 1991 World Cup was the decisive one notwithstanding the role of Nick Farr-Jones and Michael Lynagh.'

Ollie Campbell would probably be seen as the crown prince of his generation of Irish rugby. Quinn is more likely to be seen as the clown prince. And yet despite his impish streak there is a more serious side to Quinn which is reflected in his passion for coaching young players.

'My nine-year-old daughter, Elizabeth, is me in a dress, but my two boys, Michael and Mark, both play rugby in St Mary's College. My brother, Charlie, and I both train the Castleknock College team. I also trained the under-19s at Lansdowne for a while. From my point of view the ultimate coaching job in terms of satisfaction is with a school's side. You can't match the team spirit in a school's team because they are all playing to the one agenda – the good of the team. My greatest dream is to train them to win the Leinster Cup.

'I would like to think I have an eye for a young player of promise. The first time I saw John Robbie play was when he played for High School. I went over to him after he match and said: "You'll play for Ireland." Years later I won a £100 bet from him. I was playing a club match and there was a guy slagging me all through the match saying I was useless. We got a penalty 15 yards inside our half and ten yards in from the touch-line. I had the wind behind me and John bet a pound at a hundred to one that I would score, and I did.'

While Quinn's gregarious personality has won him many friends in rugby it has not always helped his career to advance.

'I played my final match for Leinster in the Sports Ground in Galway in 1984 when we were going for the Championship. It was an awful day with the wind and the rain which made it impossible for me to run the ball. There was only a handful of people in the stand, one of whom was Mick Cuddy, "the Cud", former Irish and Leinster selector. The only thing I could hear was a constant chorus from "the Cud" of: "Run the bloody ball, Leinster." I got so fed up I shouted up at him: "Cuddy, shut your f***ing mouth." He was furious and roared down at me: "That's the last time you'll play for Leinster!"'

32

PADDY REID

Reid On

As the sport needs a high degree of skill and intelligence, it is not, therefore, going to attract the lower income groups.

Anon

In Limerick, rugby is like a religion, touching a deep nerve in the psyche of the people of the city. It is recognised worldwide as one of the great cathedrals of rugby. One of the stories often told to demonstrate the love of rugby on Shannonside goes back to 1960. When a fishing boat was devoured in the flames of one of the multitude of bonfires that heralded Shannon's first Munster Senior Cup success that year, a sympathiser who offered his condolences to the owner met with an unexpected reply: 'You can buy a boat at any time, but not the Munster Cup.' One of the giants of Limerick rugby is former Irish centre, Paddy Reid.

Jim McCarthy insists that Reid should have won a hundred caps for Ireland but he 'only' wore the green jersey six times. After a distinguished schools career with Crescent College, in 1947, he followed his father onto the Garryowen side, captaining them to the Munster Cup, Munster Senior League and Charity Cup in 1947, the same year he led Munster to the Interprovincial Championships.

'My love of rugby began when I was a five-year-old when my father bought me my first rugby ball. He played for Garryowen and Munster, as did my father-in-law, Mick Kelly. I grew up in a home filled with rugby stories. One of my clearest memories is of my dad telling me about travelling to Belfast in 1911 when it was like going to the moon, because of the poor state of communications. They visited the shipyard and read a notice on one of them which stated: "Even God can't sink this ship." It was the Titanic!'

He is also an accomplished golfer having won two captain's prizes. He played hockey to a high level and won an Irish Senior Hockey Cup with Lansdowne. His wife, Cecil, also played hockey for Munster and is a former president of the Irish Ladies Hockey Union.

His international career began in 1946 in the unofficial internationals against France and Wales.

'My first match in the green jersey was a tremendous thrill. To me rugby is life. There could be no greater honour in my eyes than running out on Lansdowne Road for the first time.'

Reid was first capped in an official international against the touring Australians on 6 December 1947. It was not a fairytale debut as Ireland went down 16–3. The following New Year's Day, though, saw the opening of an unexpectedly glorious chapter in the history of Irish rugby when Ireland had a shock 13–6 victory over France at Colombes. Reid was literally at the centre of things.

'A great character in the team was Barney Mullan. The night before the game in Paris we had a team meeting, as per usual. Barney came up with the idea that if we were under pressure during the game and got a line-out he would call a short one and throw it out over the forwards' heads and lift the siege. True to plan we got a line-out on our own 25. The French players were huge. They looked like mountains to us so we needed to out-think them. Mullan threw it long and Jack Kyle grabbed it, passed it to me, I fed it to Des McKee and he returned the compliment for me to score under the posts. The glory was mine but it was Barney's tactical awareness that earned us that try.

'Travelling to Paris for us at the time was like going to the edge of the world. We were as green as grass. After our win we were invited to a reception at the Irish embassy. Of course champagne was the order of the day which was a very novel experience for most of us. We were knocking it back as if it was stout! To me the incident that best illustrated our innocence was when the Dolphin pair, Jim McCarthy and Bertie O'Hanlon, asked for red lemonade!'

The following Valentine's Day saw Ireland beat England 11–10 at Twickenham. Reid surrendered his place to Michael O'Flanagan for the match against Scotland when Ireland secured the Championship, their first since 1935, at Lansdowne Road thanks to wonderful tries from Barney Mullan and Jack Kyle.

O'Flanagan shares a unique place in Irish history with his brother, Dr Kevin O'Flanagan who won ten caps for soccer with Ireland between 1938 and 1947, playing before and after the War, was also capped on one occasion for his country on the wing at rugby against Australia in 1947. In 1946, in the successive Saturdays, he played rugby for Ireland against France, in an unofficial international, then played soccer against Scotland, and was scheduled to play international rugby the following week but had to miss out on the game. With his brother Michael, they are the only two brothers to be capped for their countries in both soccer and Rugby Union. Kevin was also a champion athlete and but for cancellations of the Olympics in 1940 and 1944, he would unquestionably have competed in the Games. He was also a noted tennis player and single-figure golfer. He was voted into the Texaco Hall of Fame in 1965 for his all-round sporting powers – the only sportsman to be voted into it for more than one sport. In 1976 he became only the third Irishman to be elected to the International Olympic Council.

Reid regained his place for the Grand Slam decider against Wales at Ravenhill. He is unwilling to blame anybody for his exclusion from the Irish team. His international colleague, Jim McCarthy, is less reticent and points out that a lot of curious selection decisions have much more to do with politics than with rugby merit – the 'you scratch my back, I'll scratch yours' syndrome. In 1948 there were two Leinster selectors, two Ulster selectors, and the other selector was a Cork man. Championing the cause of a Limerick player was not uppermost on any of their agendas.

The thirteenth of March was not to prove an unlucky date as Ireland fought a tense battle with their nerves as much as with the opposition before emerging victorious. Reid's memories of that year are vivid. He believes that the decisive moment came when Ireland lay the Welsh bogey.

'We were fortunate to have a wonderful captain in Karl Mullen. He was great for letting everyone have their say. The night before the Wales game we had a meeting. One of the people who had given us advice was

Dave O'Loughlin who had been a star Irish forward just before the Second World War. To all of us on the 1948 team he was an idol. He had played against the great Welsh scrum-half Haydn Tanner, who was still calling the shots on the Welsh team in 1948. [The previous year his late break had set up a try which robbed Ireland of the Triple Crown.] Dave told us that Tanner was the man to watch and assured us that he would make two breaks during the game. At the team meeting I suggested that Des O'Brien should be appointed as Tanner's shadow, whose job it would be to ensure that when the Welshman broke he would be quashed. I went so far as to suggest that if he didn't do his task properly in this respect he should be dropped. Des was not too happy with this part of the plan at the time but he was given the assignment nonetheless. Sure enough, as Dave had promised, Haydn broke twice. Both times Des tackled him superbly. In fact so frustrated was Tanner on the second occasion that he slammed the ball on the ground in frustration. These things don't just turn a match. I'm convinced it was the difference between victory and defeat for us in the Grand Slam.'

Did the players receive any reward for their unique achievement?

'The only thing we got was a photo of the winning team and the team crest!'

After the campaign Reid joined his international team-mate, prop-forward, Chris Daly and 'went north' to rugby League with the Huddersfield club. What prompted this move?

'I had no job and I was getting married. It was as simple as that. It was a great experience and I acquired great insights into life but on a personal level it was also a major readjustment. It was a very different world. There were a lot of Australians on the team. They were all married and went home after training and matches. There wasn't the great community spirit that there had been on the Irish team.

'I played at Wembley in front of 98,000 people but I wasn't nervous because I had taken part in big matches before. Before the game we were introduced to the Prince of Wales. As we shook hands I said to him: "Everyone at home is asking for you!" I returned to Ireland in 1950. I was always a homebird.

'I got involved in coaching youngsters as soon as I got home. There was talk that I was isolated by the IRFU because of the ban. It might be a good story but it's not the case. I never had any hassle whatsoever from anybody. In fact they were always cordial to me and turned a blind eye to my activities.'

In recent years the phrase 'Jack's army' has become a central feature of sporting parlance because of Jack Charlton's achievements with the

Irish soccer team. Reid heads the queue in Ireland's other 'Jack's army', the vast multitude who worship at the altar of Jack Kyle.

'He was a wizard. I'd be struggling to put words on him, he was such a classy player, a man apart. The strange thing about him is that for all his greatness he was such a humble man and a real team player. I would also have to say, though, that we were no one-man team. There was a great camaraderie and spirit in that side and we all pulled for each other. Bill McKay, a medical student from Queen's University, was the best wing-forward I ever saw. To me the unsung hero was full-back Dudley Higgins who of course is a past-president of the IRFU. You never had to look over your shoulder when he was on the team. He was such a great tackler he could stop a train.'

Reid continues to keep his ear very much to the ground on Ireland's fortunes at international level particularly since the appointment of his son-in-law, Pat Whelan, as Irish manager. How does he evaluate Whelan?

'He's a marvellous worker. I've never seen anybody apply himself to a task like him. He's a very sincere guy, a wonderful family man and is a great golfer. He has tremendous courage which was highlighted for me earlier this year after Ireland lost to France. Niall Hogan had a poor game that day but Pat had the guts to stand by his man, as it were, and not only keep him on the team but make him captain for the Welsh game which Ireland won handsomely. It takes a brave man to become an Irish manager because things happen out on the field that you have no control over, but you're the one that has to carry the can. I hope that we can climb the ladder soon because we have unearthed some promising new talent.'

Reid is more worried, though, about the future for the Irish club scene with the advent of professionalism in rugby.

'It's very upsetting because we don't know where we're going. I think it will take another two years before we understand the future properly. Water will find its own level. Potentially it is a very serious situation because so many of our top players have left Irish clubs for English ones. Personally I feel that in our club we all have to stand together and make it attractive for these guys to play club rugby in Ireland.'

Reid's biggest fear is that the new rugby climate might dissipate the passion for rugby in Limerick and its egalitarian structures.

'Limerick is such a stonghold of rugby because there are no class boundaries. At one stage the Garryowen front row was a doctor, docker and a lawyer.

'Rugby is more than recreation here. I went with a friend of mine to a match between Garryowen and Blackrock. Garryowen had a 16-stone player called Frank "the bull" Hayes who was what was known then as a "failed priest". We were shocked during the match when Hayes walked up behind Dave O'Leary and tapped him on the shoulder and, when he turned around, he stretchered him with a punch. Much later I asked Frank about it and told him I thought it was an awful thing for him to do. He said: "He kicked me the year before." Dave subsequently became a member of the "big five". Some years later he confirmed Frank's story for me.

'The club rivalry in Limerick is intense. To say there is no love lost between Young Munster and Garryowen is a massive understatement. The incident that best sums this up for me occurred in 1993 when Liam Hall and I travelled to Dublin to see Young Munster play St Mary's in the decisive match of the AIL Munsters won. After the game we walked past Johnny Brennan from Munsters and an elderly lady, whom I recognised immediately because of her strong connection with the club, though she never had any dealings with me. I turned around and said: "Congratulations, Johnny."

Johnny told her: "That's Paddy Reid from Garryowen."

Her reply to this information was: "I hates him!"'

33

FERGUS SLATTERY

The Magnificent Number Seven

Man is a fighting animal and rugby is a civilised (almost always, anyway) blood sport.

Wilfrid Wooller

'This is the great stuff. Phil Bennett covering, chased by Alistair Scown. Brilliant; John Williams, Bryan Williams . . . Pullin . . . John Dawes, great dummy . . . David, Tom David; the half-way line . . . brilliant by Quinnell . . . this is Gareth Edwards . . . a dramatic start. WHAT A SCORE!'

Cliff Morgan's commentary of the most talked about game of all time when the Barbarians beat New Zealand 23–11 on 27 January 1973. In the thick of the action was John Fergus Slattery, the nightmare of a generation of fly-halfs. Slattery himself scored a try in that game and made the pass to J.P.R. Williams for the final try. An auctioneer by profession he was not sold many dummies on the field.

A product of Blackrock College he was capped over 60 times for Ireland as an open-side wing forward (a world record for a flanker), between 1970 and 1984, scoring three international tries. He was part of a 19-match record back-row combination with Willie Duggan and John O'Driscoll. He captained Ireland 17 times including two overseas tours, to Australia in 1979, and to South Africa in 1981. It is recognised worldwide that 'Slats' at his best was the best because of his presence on the field. He was always first to the break-down and first to the out-half. His angles were so good that he always managed to put the opposition under pressure, forcing either the centre or out-half to release the ball. The significance of this is that when this happens it is the wing-forward

184

who is dictating the game and not vice versa. Although Slattery played his best rugby on the Lions tour of 1974 (when, with Roger Uttley and Mervyn Davies, he formed one of the finest back rows in Lions' history) as he got older he read the game so well. He put his body through extraordinary punishment.

The classic story about Slattery goes back to an African trip. After a British Lions tour fixture in Rhodesia, there was a celebratory dinner organised. The then Rhodesian Prime Minister, Ian Smith, arrived to make a speech. Shortly after, two Irish players, Dick Milliken and Slattery, decided to return to their hotel. Having consumed beverages stronger than orange juice they were feeling particularly adventurous. As they walked out they noticed just outside the entrance to the club a beautiful black-tinted-window Cadillac. They decided to borrow the car and go for a drive. After driving around for a few minutes, the partition behind the front seats slid across and the Prime Minister asked: 'Are you gentlemen looking for a job?'

In the boardroom of his business premises at Northumberland Road, Slattery's rugby brain is spinning into overdrive recalling the many golden moments in a glittering career.

'At school I played rugby and soccer for St Joseph's Sallynoggin. At the time the Irish soccer team weren't winning many games so I would go to Dalymount Park and Windsor Park to see international matches. Invariably I saw both Irelands losing!'

Slattery's first cap came against the Springboks in 1970 in an 8–8 draw. The terraces behind the goals at Lansdowne Road were empty and the playing surface cordoned off by barbed wire to prevent protesters from invading the pitch.

'It was a very controversial match. I was in UCD at the time and there was a forum before the game to debate whether or not Ireland should play South Africa. I spoke in favour and Kadar Asmal spoke against. The weather was very bad before the match and they put straw on the pitch. It was like running into a barn. Having said that, the game lost none of its impact for me because of that. Things went pretty well for us that season. We beat Scotland 16–11 and then defeated a Wales side seeking the Triple Crown 14–0.

'Selection for the Lions tour of New Zealand in 1971 was a natural progression. I was disappointed that I did not make the Test side but it was a terrific theatre of education. You're playing against the same guys every week and of course you're living and breathing rugby.

'For me touring was the best part of rugby. The best tours were the short ones. I loved touring in the south of France with Leinster. To me playing in the interprovincials was nothing but drudgery. I would have traded all my interpro appearances for one tour to France. Even though we had such great success on the Lions tour to South Africa in 1974 it got very boring at the end. You are packing your bags every three days and everything becomes very repetitive. I decided that I would never take part in a Lions tour again.

'After that tour I came back and played a lot of matches. I pushed myself too hard and my blood count went down. I see my career in two phases before and after that tour. Up to then rugby was everything for me but after that it wasn't. I had to look after my career.'

Consequently he spent a year and a half in the international wilderness. He returned and led the Irish on the successful tour down under in 1979.

'Before the Australian tour I thought we would have our work cut out to win the Tests. I think it's fair to say Australia under-performed in the first match because we caught them on the hop, but we beat them on merit in the second game.'

Surprisingly, an apparent low point of his career elicits the greatest passion.

'The 1981 tour to South Africa was a landmark in the development of the Irish side. We played out of our skins. I had captained the Irish team to Australia in 1979 but that was an experienced, powerful squad that convincingly won the series. Those who went to South Africa were very young, as in only two years we had virtually changed the entire side. It was literally a B-team, with 12 uncapped players in the party. And then we lost John Murphy, the full-back, and Ollie Campbell, whose loss was to prove very significant. Micky Quinn flew out the week before the first Test and in midweek we played a racially mixed team, scoring a lot of tries. I will always remember that Micky missed about 17 kicks at goal. Still, it was the best investment in Irish rugby that could possibly have been made. We gave a number of young players a chance to show their wares.

'We played well in the first Test and lost 23–15 but we went into the second Test without two senior players of Campbell's and Murphy's calibre and, to make it worse, we had Micky Quinn.

'In the first Test, they had out-played us in the line-out, with three giants, Stofberg, Malan and De Klerk, winning everything. All three were over six foot five inches whereas our tallest men were only six foot two and six foot three. So we decided to revert to Plan B – in other words, play many three-man and four-man variations. We would play the line-out quickly and did all sorts of things, using every trick in the book. We said that if we won 50 per cent of the possession, we would be satisfied. We also realised that South Africa's immense forwards tend to kill you when they go forward but if you turn them around, put the ball behind them and keep turning, they struggle. And we made every effort to disrupt their wheel and put-in to prevent them from getting quick ball. We were supposed to be very destructive on their ball and very creative on our own. And we certainly didn't go into the game without hope. Our loose forwards came out on top in both Tests. We knew that Rob Louw was their most potent loose forward but we managed to keep him out of the game.

'In the end it was Naas Botha who beat us. He was only the fourth man in history to drop three goals in a Test and we were out. We'd had no luck at all, missing a conversion and having a bloody good try disallowed. We were leading 10–9 when Botha got his last with a few minutes left. It left us too little time to do anything and although we tried desperately, we just could not score. I really felt sorry for the guys, their achievement was spoilt at the very last moment.'

The tour also saw one of the great wind-ups of Irish rugby. Freddie McLennan was 'duty boy' (the player in charge of informing players about travel arrangements and so on, for a particular day during a tour abroad – each player takes it in turn) one Saturday. The squad had been given the day off and had to decide how to spend it. Freddie, himself a keen golfer, offered two choices. They could either go for a game of golf or take a trip around Johannesburg harbour. Eighteen players favoured the harbour trip on the basis that they could play golf at any time but would not always get the chance to do some sightseeing in Johannesburg. The next morning the players were ready at 8 a.m. for their trip around the harbour, only to be told that since the city was 5,000 feet above sea-level it did not have a harbour, and that the nearest seaside was a massive bus trip away.

Ireland's fine performances on the tour tempted Slattery to engage in what was to be a lucrative speculation.

'When we left South Africa Willie Duggan asked me: "Fancy a bet on the Triple Crown?" The odds were a generous 14–1 and it was the first time I had ever bet on myself. Of course, I was delighted to win.'

He relinquished the captaincy to Ciaran Fitzgerald before the 1981–2 season. What prompted the move and how did he evaluate his successor?

'We had lost seven matches on the trot and needed a change. I was worried about Fitzie before the Australian tour in 1979 because he had a reputation for getting injured, but he held his own there and grew in stature from then on. He was made to lead and his record as captain speaks for itself. The only disappointment I had in 1982 was the Paris game. We went there as favourites but they hockeyed us. We haven't beaten France on their own patch since 1972. There is something wrong with the Irish psychological preparation. Our forwards in particular seem to be too easily intimidated there. If this is to change we're going to have to do something with our psychological preparation.'

Slattery is a keen observer of the evolution of modern rugby.

'Rugby has changed irrevocably, not for the worse nor for the better. It's just changed. The International Board should have acted more decisively earlier. Commercial forces have been working below the surface for years. As far back as the 1970s I was made a good offer to play in the Italian League and also one in the 1980s. At the moment, the problem is nobody knows where it's going to end. Water finds its own level. The professional ethos is creeping in at all levels. In the past, teachers didn't need to be paid for coaching in the schools but now they demand it. More is being done for players now than ever before. I don't envy the players now, even though they are making big money, because they will not have the fun I had. I think players today don't fully appreciate all the implications of signing a contract in terms of the demands that will be made on them. There are some positive developments like the formation of European League which will bring enjoyment back to the game.'

Asked about the Irish players he admired most Slattery's reply is immediate.

'The giant of Irish rugby is C.M.H. Gibson. The rest are also-rans. I would much rather play with somebody who has very little talent but total commitment rather than the reverse. I loved playing with Mossie Keane because of his great commitment. I also admired Ollie Campbell's wholesome commitment to making himself what he was – a top-class player. He is the role model you would want to hold up to younger players because of his endurance and because he developed his skills to the very maximum.'

However, he has special plaudits for his great friend and club-mate, Willie Duggan: 'Willie was both a superb player, who gave it all on the pitch, and a wonderful character.' Stories about Duggan abound. Like fellow forward Moss Keane he was an Irish national institution. A man with little enthusiasm for training, his most celebrated comment was: 'Training takes the edge off my game.' Duggan was one of a rare group of players who always made a point of bringing a pack of cigarettes with him onto the training field. Asked once in a radio interview if this was a major problem for him fitness-wise he took the broadcaster by surprise by saying that it was a positive advantage: 'Sure, if it was not for the fags I would be offside all day long.'

Another time he was having a fag in the dressing-room in Twickenham before Ireland played England. The time had come to run on the pitch but Duggan had nowhere to put out his cigarette in the dressing-room. He knew that if he ran out in the tunnel with the fag in his mouth the cameras would zoom in on him straight away. The Scottish referee, who was making his international debut, was in the dressing-room so the Irish number eight went over to him and said: 'Would you hold that for a second please'. The obliging referee said yes but Duggan promptly ran out on the pitch – leaving the ref with no option but to put out the fag. He went out to face the glare of the cameras and the first sight the television audience had of him was holding a cigarette!

Duggan was never too bothered about tactics. Asked by a journalist for the reason for a vintage Leinster performance he answered: 'We had decided to go out in the first half to soften them up and kick the proverbial shit out of them. And it went so well for us, that we had a quick word at half-time and decided to kick the shit out of them in the second half!'

In one match Duggan was playing for the Public School Wanderers when his cousin, Ned Byrne, was clobbered in the eye. Byrne turned to his relative for comfort but was instead sharply reminded: 'I told you when you hit a guy don't be watching him. Watch the guy who's coming in behind him.'

Slattery, though, has one memory which sums up his famous colleague.

'In 1983 some of the guys played in a match against the Western Province in South Africa. The match was played in mid-July. Typical of Willie, all he took with him on the trip was a small bag with his toothbrush and cigarettes. Willie was never too bothered about training at the best of times but in the middle of the summer he was totally unfit. The game passed right by him. At one stage I saw him stamping on the ground. I went over to him and asked him what the hell he was doing. He answered: "Oh, I'm stamping that bloody snail which has been following me around since the match started!"'

34

DICK SPRING

Labour of Love

> There is no such thing as 'a lack of confidence'. You either have it or you don't.
>
> Rob Andrew

Outside the front door of the Department of Foreign Affairs, Gerry Adams, Martin McGuinness and their handlers are giving a press conference. The coffee cups in the palatial conference room are still warm. All the shiny cups and saucers have harps. An old joke is taken off its life-support machine.

'Why is the harp the national emblem of Ireland?'

'Because the country is run by people pulling strings.'

Who said that the old jokes are the best? The complementary writing pads provided for all are printed on 100 per cent recycled paper.

It's been a difficult week in the peace process with a proliferation of meetings. Dick Spring is fighting manfully to disguise his exhaustion. He appears to be in some discomfort because of a back injury, which spasmodically returns to haunt him, the legacy of a bad car accident.

He has an impressive sporting pedigree. His father, Dan Spring, of Kearns O'Rahilly's, captained Kerry to All-Ireland football victory in 1940. His maternal uncles, the Laide brothers, of the Crotta O'Neills' club are considered among Kerry's finest hurlers.

'As a boy my hero was Mick O'Connell, probably the greatest Gaelic footballer of them all. In Kerry we have taken and applied the words of the Olympic motto "Higher, Faster, Stronger" for our sporting heroes. As has been said of the Jesuits: "We are tops in everything, including modesty." But modesty is not something Kerry people have had much opportunity to experience. I still follow even club football in Kerry, like the progress of Laune Rangers. Someone said they are the best side in Kerry since Tonto was their manager. This reminds me of the Galway wit who described an old Corinthians team as being the best since St Paul wrote to them!

'Sundays were spent going to either football or hurling matches with my father. In 1955, when I was five years of age, John Dowling captained Kerry to the All-Ireland and when the Sam Maguire Cup was brought home I was put sitting in it. I don't think it did me any good! My father also attempted to introduce me to Christy Ring after Cork lost a Munster final to Tipperary, but he was so disappointed at losing the game that he stormed off and wouldn't talk to anyone.

'My late father was delighted that both Donal and I played for Ireland and that my other brother, Arthur, played golf at interprovincial level and basketball at intervarsity level. Yet he always said rugby was only a game for failed Gaelic footballers.'

In 1963 Spring began his secondary education in boarding school in Roscrea. In his first year the late Gus Martin was on the teaching staff and Ned Byrne was part of the student body. Byrne, Willie Duggan's cousin, won an All-Ireland senior hurling medal with Kilkenny in 1972 playing at top of the left. His uncles, Eddie and Podge Byrne, also won All-Ireland hurling medals with Kilkenny in the 1930s. Later, as a prop-forward, Ned won six caps for Ireland.

At Roscrea, Spring was introduced into rugby but his love affair with the game was not immediate: 'For the first two and a half years I only played Gaelic football and hurling. I couldn't understand what those mad fellahs were doing playing rugby especially with all that wallowing in the muck. In my third year, though, I discovered that the rugby guys got good grub, hot showers and trips to Dublin. I was getting disillusioned with playing Gaelic games, especially after a match in Abbeyleix, where the pitch was also used for grazing sheep and cattle. You can imagine what I was covered in at the end of the match! As if that wasn't bad enough all we had in the way of washing facilities afterwards was one cold tap for the entire team.

'I take the credit for beginning an international career. When I started playing rugby I was selected at out-half because of my Gaelic football skills. Up to then the fly-half had been Mick Sherry. He was promptly given a new position as a wing-forward and never looked back, going on to play with great distinction there for Lansdowne and Ireland.

'My schoolboy memories are mainly of the matches we lost. I remember losing a quarter-final of the Junior Cup to De La Salle,

Churchtown in a high-scoring game for them – 3–0! Coincidentally they recently beat my son's Roscrea side 5–3. Some things never change. We also lost a Cup quarter-final to Newbridge. Their side featured two players who would later be my team-mates at Lansdowne; the one and only, thank God, Mick Quinn who was only up to my navel at the time and Paddy Boylan who later became one of the great stalwarts of Lansdowne.

'I went to Trinity in 1968 and decided to give rugby a try for a year. In fact rugby took up far too much of my time all through my college years. A highlight was winning my first colours match with Trinity. At the time that was a very prestigious fixture. UCD then were a star-laden team with seven or eight interprovincial players, including a number of internationals, whereas we had only two interprovincial players. They had won for the previous four years. We won 16–6 and to me there's a great lesson from that. Commitment can overcome superior skill. The win did wonders for morale in Trinity. We had John Robbie playing on the wing that day, mainly because of his contribution as a place kicker but he was brought into scrum-half when we lost our first choice through injury.'

Spring's contribution at Trinity brought him onto the Irish Universities and Munster sides against the All Blacks in 1974. The tourists were led by Andy Leslie, a back-row forward in the classic New Zealand tradition. It was to be the Universities who gave them their hardest match. The final score was 9–3 in favour of the touring side: 'In fairness they were not at their best that day. They had been enjoying the Irish hospitality a bit too much. It was some week for me. On the Wednesday I played against the All Blacks for the Irish Universities, on the Saturday I played against them for Munster and on the Sunday I played for Kerry against the reigning All-Ireland Champions, Dublin. I didn't realise at the time I was playing for the side that would win the All-Ireland the following year and would go on to become the greatest team of all time. I think that if I had devoted my energies to Gaelic football I could have made it to the very highest level in the game. At the time, though, I was sub for the Irish team and rugby had priority.'

Strangely, though, Spring's clearest memory of the time is of a match against Argentina, touring Europe for the first time.

'It was a horrendous rugby match. In the first ten minutes they put up high balls for me three times. They had a centre, called Travilagini, who was six foot plus and over 14 stone who crash-tackled me each time – before I got the ball. Another of their players seemed to think his task was to maim Barry McGann. At one stage there were so many scuffles the match was nearly called off. The only saving grace was that I had the privilege of playing against Hugo Porta, one of the greatest out-halves of all time and now Argentina's ambassador to South Africa.'

Spring's progress in rugby was to some extent put on hold because of his years spent in London and the United States: 'I played for two seasons with London Irish. The first season was a disaster but when Ken Kennedy took over the captaincy the following season we did much better. I played scrum-half in New York because I reckoned it was the only possible position a back could get the ball! Mind you, it's not easy being a left-footed scrum-half because you have to turn to get your kick in. I was offered a trial for the American side. There was no money in rugby there at the time and I would have to pay my expenses. The final trial was in Colorado and it would cost me 500 bucks to get there. I was there to make money not to spend it on internal flights so I declined the invitation. Shortly after, my small, younger brother, Donal, was picked to play for Ireland so I decided I would return home and try to emulate his achievement.

'Before I came home I had trained hard and was in good shape. I joined Lansdowne and was very annoyed to be selected on the seconds for my first match. I was on the firsts the following week. In my second year I was made captain and we won the Leinster Cup. My chief function as captain was to get Mick Quinn to pass the ball! Before that his sole tactic was to kick everything and chase it himself. More seriously I think I made a vital contribution to Lansdowne's success by persuading Paddy Boylan and Vinny Becker to come out of retirement.'

For his part Mick Quinn speaks about his former Lansdowne colleague with genuine admiration.

'Everybody remembers Dick Spring as the player who dropped the ball which lost Ireland the game against Wales in Cardiff Arms Park in 1979. But that's a mistaken impression. He was a fantastic club player but the Cardiff incident shattered his confidence on the international stage.

'His brother Donal was also a great servant to the club – though the competition between him and our international forward the other Michael Gibson, was intense. If one of them sold a dummy the other had to do the same. Gibson the younger, was a class act when he was on song and in 1979 in particular he was sensational in his four games for Ireland.'

The year 1979, though, evokes mixed feelings for Dick Spring.

'The highlight of my career was my first cap against France. That's the game I show to my kids. I can't remember what happened in the Wales game!'

Ireland's opening match of the 1979 season was a home game against France. Tony Ward kicked three penalties to tie the score at 9–9 each. Ireland's four debutants had reason to be proud of themselves. Gerry McLoughlin, the carrot-haired Shannon prop, came through his baptism of fire against the hallowed French front row very much with an enhanced reputation. Flanker Colm Tucker and full-back Spring acquitted themselves well, with Tucker bringing much of the fire that he played with in Munster's win over the All Blacks. However, a new star was born with a famous name in the tall, lean Mike Gibson. He dominated the line-out as he ranged along the line to deny France the platform to launch penetrating attacks.

After that it was off to Cardiff Arms Park. Captain Fergus Slattery brought the team to see *Adventures of a Window Cleaner* and *Adventures of a Taxi Driver*. Those films certainly took the players' minds off the game!

In normal circumstances, for an Irish side to score 21 points (and thus establish a new scoring record for an Irish side against Wales on any ground) in Cardiff Arms Park, on that most sacred soil, would have been considered a great achievement. The 1979 fixture was an exception. The problem was that Ireland gifted the home side with 15 points to lose on a scoreline of 24-21. The game was a catalogue of errors on both sides but the difference was that Ireland's were punished more severely.

After 22 minutes Ireland led 6–0, courtesy of two lengthy penalties from Ward. The dream of a win in Cardiff was starting to look as if it might be fulfilled. In the 25th minute the picture changed dramatically. Davies, the Welsh fly-half, lofted the kick towards the Irish posts but Spring was under it and there seemed to be no danger. Somehow the ball slipped through his hands and bounced over the Irish line for Alan Martin to rush on and score a try, which Steve Fenwick converted.

It had been Tony Ward's best performance to date in an Irish jersey preventing Ireland from being lost without trace and making loaves from crumbs. Although his magic moments lingered long in the memory the incident which is best remembered from the game is Spring's missed catch. While his political career has flourished he has never been allowed to forget that incident and been the butt of jokes about a safe pair of hands. Throughout the enormously popular series on RTE Radio *One Scrap Saturday*, Spring was consistently referred to as 'Butterfingers'.

'It was just the luck of the draw. Nobody who ever played with me doubted my ability under a high ball. I was caught out of position and was keeping an eye out for J.P.R. Williams. There's no question that it did affect my self-confidence from then on. The only memory people have of me is of that dropped ball. If Andy Irvine had been axed every time he dropped the ball he would have spent a lot of time on the bench. I'm not suggesting I was as good a player as Andy but I think that one ball should be kept in perspective.'

An unfortunate postscript to the match came in a subsequent article written by the Welsh flanker, Paul Ringer, for a tabloid newspaper after his defection to rugby League. Commenting on the dual standards over dirty play in Rugby Union he cited the example of an instruction five minutes before the kick-off in that match to 'sort out' Tony Ward.

'The meaning was clear and I set to it. Trouble was he was so good I couldn't lay a finger on him until late in the game but I eventually flattened him off the ball and we went on to win. I got such a booting from the Irish forwards afterwards that I couldn't get out of bed for two days. After I'd laid out Ward that time he turned up late at the after-match reception with a massively swollen eye.'

Two weeks later Ireland had a welcome opportunity to redeem themselves with a home game against England. The clash with the 'auld enemy' was a bruising battle that had the Lansdowne Road crowd at fever pitch. Ireland won 12–7. Before the next game Spring was dropped to make way for Bangor's Ronnie Elliott. The call of politics deprived Spring of an opportunity for rehabilitation at international level.

'I was invited by the IRFU to go on the Australian tour in 1979 but I was trying to establish my new law practice and I didn't feel I could afford the time from work. There was another reason for my refusal. There were local elections on that year and I had indicated my wish to run in Tralee. I was elected but decided to play on for a year in Lansdowne out of loyalty to Paddy Boylan, who had succeeded me as captain. The next year, though, I played junior rugby with Tralee. We reached five finals but lost them all. In 1981 there was a general election and I was elected TD and was immediately made a junior minister. I played two rugby games in that capacity. In the second I was caught in a ruck and I heard two of the opposing forwards arguing over who would be the first to kick the minister's head in. It was then I decided it was time for me to retire.'

Spring is not the only Irish political leader to have a bad sporting accident. A sudden transformation occurs when Bertie Ahern recounts his most memorable moment of his soccer career. He shifts uncomfortably in his chair, wincing at the memory. His eyes are deep pools of pain.

'In the early 1970s there was a few bob to be made in the summer seven-a-sides. Because of that it was a very serious business indeed. As a result the cream of the League of Ireland players were involved, like Ben Hannigan and Eric Barber. It was shortly before I got married and I was working as an accountant in the Mater Hospital at the time. I didn't have time to go home for my gear. All I had was a pair of squash shorts with a fly and a zip. Disaster struck in the dressing-room. I got my zip stuck in my foreskin. I was in agony. [The wounded tone of his voice leaves no room for doubt about the veracity of this claim.]

'There was a fellah from Cork in the dressing-room called Barry. I can't remember his surname but I will never forget him to my dying day. He was a soldier and had served in Vietnam. At first he suggested that I go to the Mater but there was no way I would agree to that because I worked there. Barry rustled up a jar of Vaseline and a knife and went to work to untangle me . . . if that's the right word!'

The saga of the zip, Vaseline and the knife is not for the squeamish nor for those about to eat. Suffice to say that the delicate operation was completed successfully, if very painfully, and the future Fianna Fail leader was spared the nickname Bertie Bobbit!

'I had taken part in the kick-about before the game and my team-mates had no idea why I didn't take my place on the pitch. They played on with six men but I came back on for the second half. That's dedication for you! We won 2–1 but the lads never knew why I missed the first half.'

Was Spring's rugby background an advantage to him in politics?

'There are no votes in rugby, certainly not in Kerry. To the best of my knowledge I'm the only ex-Irish international to have become a TD so there's not exactly a political rugby fraternity.

'Occasionally it comes in handy when I'm giving speeches. Sometimes when I want to get an audience's attention I say Fergus Slattery, Tom Kiernan, Willie John McBride and myself have 153 international caps. I don't mention that I only got three of them! Another trick I used recently when I gave a speech to a rugby audience in Wales to get their attention was to start by speaking for the first three minutes in Irish. By the time I started speaking in English they were ready to hang on to my every word!

'John Major was quite impressed when he heard I played for Ireland. He played rugby himself when he was very young but didn't prosper at the game because at that time he was too small. I found that quite surprising because he's a tall man now. John's great passion is cricket and his mood fluctuates a lot depending on the fate of the English team. I'm always wary about having sensitive negotiations about the peace process with John when England are playing. The best time to negotiate with him is when England are doing very well – mind you that doesn't happen very often!'

Despite his hectic schedule Spring still has sporting ambitions: 'My raging obsession is to play a good round of golf in Kerry!'

Although Spring's international record is not the one he would have wished for he still has many happy memories of his rugby days.

'Barry McGann and I had been out for the night. The next day we were training for Munster and neither of us were feeling the best. Tom Kiernan was training the side at the time. An awkward high ball was pumped in between us and both of us shouted "Yours". Tom intervened immediately and said: "Gentlemen. There's only one call in rugby: Mine!"

'Like so many others I have my own particular stories of Moss Keane. Moss hates flying. Once I was a sub for a match at Twickenham. When we returned home we had a very late night session in St Mary's rugby club. I stayed in Moss's "high class" flat in Rathmines. We woke up the next day at midday very much the worse for wear and went to "Joe's Steakhouse" for some food. Moss ordered a mixed grill. My tastes were more modest and I just asked for plaice and chips. When the food arrived Moss looked a bit queasy. He looked up and said: "Springer, would you ever mind swapping?" I duly obliged. I'd say it was the only time in his life he turned his back on a big meal!

'Another time we were together for a match in London. We were both starving on the Saturday night. The two of us crept into the kitchen and sought out some food. Suddenly we were caught in the act. We expected to have the face eaten off us. After a dramatic pause he said: "You know ye're lucky lads. There's now three Kerry men in the room." We got the meal of our lives!'

35

TONY WARD

The Good, the Bad and Ollie

What lovely legs he has.

Barry McGann on Tony Ward

No Irish sports star, apart from George Best, has filled more newspaper columns than Tony Ward. In his first two seasons of international rugby (1978 and 1979) Ward was heralded the most exciting find in the British Isles since Gareth Edwards. He became an instant pin-up in a sport that historically preferred to play down its heroes. He was regularly spoken of in the same breath and awed tones as Barry John and Phil Bennet and was hailed internationally as the best out-half in the world. It is astonishing that a player of his talents only won 19 caps. In fact it is surprising that he never got the nickname 'the judge' as he spent so much time on the bench. However, Ward's tendency to earn awards was to draw the ire of the IRFU.

'When it came to my acceptance in London of the Player of the Season award in a rugby writers' poll, the IRFU stepped in. The dinner was fixed for Lingfield racecourse and it was graced by some of the most famous players of that era, including Terry Holmes (Wales), Andy Irvine (Scotland) and Jean-Pierre Rives (France). Before I departed for London, I received an instruction from the IRFU that I wasn't to accept the award, though I could attend the dinner itself. We then had the ludicrous situation where I walked up to the applause of fellow internationals, shook hands with the person making the presentation but couldn't even touch the actual trophy. It eventually went to Sunshine homes and I had the satisfaction that, indirectly, I was helping the cause of underprivileged children.'

Then Ward was sensationally dropped from the Irish team on a tour to Australia in 1979. He clearly remembers the chain of events as if they were yesterday.

'Before departing for Australia, at a squad session at Lansdowne Road, Noel Murphy [the coach] kept emphasising that there was going to be no star system and that, in effect, everything was to be subjugated to the needs of the team. He stressed also that no player must think that he was automatically assured of a place. I am very sensitive in such matters. I couldn't escape the feeling that such comments were aimed specifically in my direction.

'The last game before the first Test against Australia was against Queensland in Brisbane. Ollie Campbell was selected at out-half. He scored Ireland's total of 18 points in an 18–15 triumph. It was suggested by some writers that Ollie would be selected in the centre for the first Test and that I would be the choice at out-half, that in view of my 19 points against New South Wales and his record against Queensland, the selectors would make room for both of us.

'It is not just the 19 points that I had scored that made me satisfied with my performance against New South Wales. I always knew when I played well and when I had an indifferent game. I don't have to wait to read the papers to come to that conclusion. I knew deep down that I had played extremely well, just as Ollie did against Queensland. What rankled and hurt me deeply was that I had no inkling that I was going to be passed over. In later years, there would be times when I hoped to be recalled but I wouldn't be disappointed when I wasn't named. In Australia in 1979 it was different.

'Noel Murphy admitted to Irish rugby correspondents covering the tour that he had grave reservations about omitting me and that he had a few sleepless nights wondering if he had made the right decision, and he was quoted as saying: "I knew that if we had lost there would be a terrific outcry at the dropping of Tony Ward."

'There is one point I will never concede – that the selection of Ollie Campbell before me for the first Test was justified. I know that my critics will contend that the end justified the means – that Ollie won both Tests for us. However, when they made their decision the evidence they had before them hardly warranted dropping me. There was no guarantee that Ollie would produce the goods. They must have known that they were taking a gamble and a big one at that. I am convinced that I was dropped because of all the hype at home and in the Australian media.'

As always, looking straight into the eye of anyone to whom he is talking, Ward chooses his words with deliberate care. The scars from

Australia have never been entirely healed. 'I could never be accused of having an arrogant or cocky personality. But I must confess that I bordered on arrogance where rugby was concerned. I know that sounds strange but let me explain. I used to worry dreadfully before big games and especially before international matches, but once I stepped on the field of play I became totally self-confident. I loved the atmosphere of big matches. I liked nothing better than coming out at Lansdowne Road and hearing the "Irish roar". The bigger the occasion, the more I loved it and the more I seemed to become inspired. It seemed as if my game lifted with the tide that the surging atmosphere of great occasions created, both at home and abroad.

'What the Australian experience did for me was to undermine my self-confidence. The Ward v. Campbell saga took off. My game and my approach to rugby was analysed and dissected. I couldn't pick up a paper but the hype was there in cold print. At one stage of my career I did not think about my game. I was an intuitive, instinctive player. It had all seemed to come naturally to me. After Australia I began to believe what I was reading. It reached a point where I sat down one evening and asked myself – can I really play rugby at all? My confidence just went. And went almost totally.

'It's all right for people to say that you shouldn't worry about what the papers say, that much of what is written is meaningless anyway. I don't think players who exclaim loudly to the heavens that they "never read a paper" are telling the truth. The papers reflect public thinking and fashion it. And in the Ward v. Campbell debate everyone seemed to be taking sides. There were no neutrals.'

During his time as national coach, Mick Doyle was guest speaker at a luncheon of the Irish Business Association in the London Metropole Hotel and was quoted as attacking newspaper reporting of rugby as 'insensitive', 'wildly inaccurate' and 'pseudo-aggressive'. He made particular reference to the harsh treatment given by newspaper reporters to the Irish selectors because of their failure to pick Tony Ward. As an example of the distortions in the print media he told the 'parable' of an Irishman who fell under a tube train in London and was killed. The London *Times* reported it straight, *The Sun* that an Irish terrorist had disrupted British Rail schedules, *The Irish Independent* that a Scotsman had been killed at Heathrow, *The Irish Press* that British Rail had murdered an innocent Irishman and *The Irish Times* that Tony Ward had his travel schedule disrupted because of a mishap on British Rail.

For Ward the 'Australian Experience' was the defining moment of his career.

'It took me two years to get over it even though I played in the International Championship in 1981. I came through it and it taught me a lot about life and human relationships. My values in life changed and rightly took on a different perspective. I became much more philosophical about life in general. Sometimes, though, my mind goes back to a dressing-room in Sydney in 1979 and I can hear Jack Coffey [team manager] saying to me as clearly as if it was only yesterday: "It's crazy what's going on, all this media stuff . . . I suggest you stay away from those fellows altogether."'

Ward also found himself at the centre of a storm when he was one of four sports personalities who appeared in an advertisement for CIE. He did not put up much of a fight when he was accused of transgressing the amateur rules.

'I can put my hand on my heart and say I never got a penny from the game but I never defended myself in public from the innuendo about me. It was the fear factor. The Church ruled with an iron fist, but that's now changing. It was the same with the IRFU. Last year when you had all the controversy about Bishop Comiskey's comments I could see parallels with the IRFU's attitudes to changes and the celibacy debate in the Church.

'Individually I never had a problem with the IRFU hierarchy but something seemed to change when they got together in a room. I was lucky that I was being tipped off in advance about what was happening next, but what a way to have to carry on with your career? I should have been able to concentrate on the game.

'There was increased TV coverage for players like me. Some of the diehards running the game begrudged this kind of exposure. Deep down inside me I feel bitter about the way I was treated by the people who run the game and in many ways still run the game. Rugby football administrators are self-perpetuating, they don't move with the times.

'When I arrived on the scene, they had just moved on from the stage where, for the privilege of playing for your country, you no longer had to buy your own rugby jersey. For home rugby international weekends we stayed in the Shelbourne hotel. It was strictly for the boys, and spouses and girlfriends were not catered for at all. There was no after-match meal for the partners. They were allowed to come in for the dance. The system of putting two players in a double room also excluded partners. If I was rooming with Moss Keane, for instance, we had a system that he would stay [in the room] for one of the internationals and I would stay for the next. Even the choice of music was wrong. The band were playing music from way back when. Out of courtesy we'd stay for a few minutes and then go out and do our own thing.

'In the interim much has changed. The IRFU is now accommodating partners, giving them meals after matches and booking twice the number of rooms. Players are given telephone call cards on away matches. I'm absolutely delighted that players are getting rewarded for the effort and the time they are putting in. I don't begrudge them for the money they will get.

'I'm not convinced that all the changes are good ones. During last year's World Cup I was watching Sky News and saw the South African players on their mobile phones; they were probably onto their agents. I wondered to myself if this was the same game I had played less than 10 years before.

'I think it is sad that the game as we know it is changing. I don't know where the game is going. I don't think anybody knows. The saddest thing from an Irish point of view is that I don't think the IRFU knows where it's going. It was sad reading the statements last year when the rules on amateurism were transformed that they were being dragged along kicking and screaming.

'One example from last year illustrates this perfectly for me. Rugby League organised a major showcase event in the RDS. There were two games, Wigan and Leeds, while Ireland took on Scotland. They were using the Shamrock Rovers' facilities but there weren't enough showers to accommodate all four teams. The rugby League organisers asked Belvedere rugby club, which backs on to the RDS, to use their facilities and the club agreed.

'On the Thursday week before the game Belvedere got a call from the IRFU whose spokesman said that it was entirely inappropriate for the facilities to be used for Rugby League. Can you believe this kind of thing is still going on? Surely the point is to provide youngsters with as many sporting opportunities as possible rather than having them messing up their lives with drugs or whatever.

'Yet the same organisation allows soccer to be played on their national grounds. Last year, they kicked the two resident clubs, Lansdowne and Wanderers, off just nine days before Ireland was due to play Austria, because Jack Charlton wanted the pitch ready. It's the power of the pound, that's the hypocrisy of it. I find it stomach-turning.

'When people get together in a room, it's incredible the decisions that come out of it. Really, you have to wonder if the grassroots feelings are being represented by the IRFU. I doubt it. I'd say 99.99 per cent of rugby fans would be appalled about that Belvedere episode.'

36

PAT WHELAN

Whelan and Dealing

Q: What's new about the big Irish Softie?
A: He's getting paid for playing rugby.

graffiti on Dublin wall

Outside the Berkeley Court hotel a hoar frost lays on the lawns and the hedgerows are hung with the lace trimmings of what seem to be a thousand spiders' webs. The trees appear to be standing and shivering together, hugging bare limbs and grumbling about the cold. A few tattered leaves make a flimsy blanket on the frozen earth. The faint horizontal threads of clouds are growing a fiercer red against the still grey sky, the streaks intensifying to scarlet and to orange and to gold, until the whole sky is a breathtaking symphony of colour. Sunrise so raises the spirits that it is easy to understand why dawn worship was a powerful primitive belief.

In the lobby of the hotel a little girl is mesmerised by the Christmas tree. It is decked out with lovely stars, baubles red and green and gold, crisscrossing in a kaleidoscopic display of colour. There are little silver balls, lights like tiny stars and pale-coloured tinsel threaded among the branches. Round the bottom are set boxes of presents done up in pretty paper, tied with red ribbon. The little girl is a portrait of mystery, magic, hope and above all innocence. Despite the early hour the atmosphere is as Dickensian as Scrooge after the ghosts.

In marked contrast on the Sunday morning before Christmas, Pat Whelan is not yet in festive mood. His early morning on the second floor of the hotel is something of a game of musical chairs.

Scene One: 9 a.m. The Donnelly Room 2. The cognoscenti, that is, the rugby correspondents have assembled for the announcement of the squad who will usher in 1996 by making the trip to the United States for a friendly international. A liberal supply of croissants and Danish pastries is provided with the coffee. RTE radio's Tom Rooney wants to know why only two out-halfs have been selected for the trip when there are three scrum-halfs and hookers. Whelan takes this and subsequent questions in his stride. Everybody goes away reasonably content.

Scene Two: 10.00 a.m. The Donnelly Room 1. Whelan joins Murray Kidd and a small group of top IRFU officials for a detailed meeting about the fine details of the tour: travel, accommodation, players cover for medical and dental care, the post-match reception, the complications caused by the fact that the televising of the match is part of a franchise deal, and so on.

Scene Three: 10.45 a.m. The Donnelly Room 2. Whelan is joined by Murray Kidd for a private meeting.

Scene Four: 11.10 a.m. The Donnelly Room 1. Whelan and Kidd rejoin the officials to tease out a few practical questions about training facilities. Is a scrummaging machine essential? The Irish team manager answers in the affirmative.

Scene Five: 11.20 a.m. The Donnelly Room 2. Whelan is interviewed for this book.

It is surprising that Pat Whelan never captained Ireland because he had an incredible will to win. Like most hookers he was not afraid to get physically involved. It has been suggested that the phrase 'You live by the sword' was his motto. Whelan's preparation for big matches was unusual. He spent the afternoons before internationals in bed. The initial impression of a tough businessman softens dramatically as his rugby memories return to him like an old friend. Suddenly he is entangled in the clinging cobwebs of childhood.

'I think I acquired my passion in rugby from my uncle, Kevin Frost, who was a great Young Munster fan. He owned Frost's bar which was a mecca for young people in Limerick. I still remember him taking me to Cork when I was ten years of age to see Shannon play in a Munster Cup final.'

Another formative influence on Whelan was his father-in-law, and member of the 1948 Grand Slam winning side, Paddy Reid.

'He didn't have a direct influence on the way I played rugby but where his influence was crucial was on my character. He created an atmosphere. Probably the best way to put it was that my "ambition ethos" became very strong after I started going out with his daughter.'

Whelan's international career saw as many lows as highs.

'The highlight of my career was definitely my first cap against England at Lansdowne Road. Running onto the pitch for the first time is a moment that will live with me until I go to my grave.'

Ireland won 12–9 in a match that also marked Willie Duggan's international debut. However, the fairytale went sour in the next international at Murrayfield as Ireland lost 20–13 and Whelan lost his place.

'I was dropped three times from the Irish team. All were intensely disappointing and the low points of my career – though it was also a huge disappointment for me to have to miss the South African tour with Ireland in 1981 because of injury. Losing Cup finals with Garryowen were always crushing experiences for me. In that match against Scotland we were up against what were certainly the best front five in the business at the time. We only lost two balls in the scrum so I didn't anticipate I would be dropped – but I was and Ken Kennedy was recalled. Even now I can still recall that "downer" especially after winning only two caps.'

Leinster's John Cantrell then grabbed the hooker's slot, though Whelan reclaimed it on the tour to New Zealand in 1976. In 1977 he was one of only six players (with Willie Duggan, Tom Grace, Mike Gibson, Moss Keane and Phil Orr) to play in all four of Ireland's internationals. The following season saw the second biggest highlight of Whelan's career: the defeat of the All Blacks. Munster rounded off a magnificent season by beating Leinster 12–3 in Lansdowne Road in December, to win their first Grand Slam since 1968, their first Championship outright since 1973 and to record their first win at Lansdowne Road since 1972.

'That game was played on a Sunday. The previous day the All Blacks were playing against the Barbarians and the Munster team watched the match in the hotel together. The All Blacks only won with a late drop goal and I still remember the roar that went up when they got that score because it meant that the All Blacks had won 17 out of 18, highlighting the uniqueness of Munster's achievement. It set us up for the performance the next day, without question Munster's finest season. The magnitude of our achievement in defeating the All Blacks only sunk in years afterwards.'

In 1979 Whelan was to find himself out in the cold on the Australian tour. He lost his place to Ciaran Fitzgerald. In the storm of controversy generated by the shock decision to drop Tony Ward in favour of Ollie Campbell, Whelan's omission went largely unnoticed. Whelan had been tipped off by a journalist of the imminent changes. It was he who prepared Ward for the biggest shock of his life on a coach journey to an idyllic spot called Paradise Bay, just outside Brisbane, for a training session. Whelan simply whispered: 'Prepare yourself.'

An injury to Ciaran Fitzgerald saw Whelan back in the Irish shirt for the opening match against France in 1981. Most of his happiest memories are of off-the-field activities: 'I was fortunate in that my international days coincided with that of three of my Garryowen friends: Shay Dennison, Larry Moloney and Shay Deering. It's very difficult to talk about Shay Deering to somebody who never met him. Anyone who played with him or against him will never, ever forget him – as a rugby player or as a man. He was a breed apart – someone you would walk on water for. It's one of the great mysteries of Irish rugby that he didn't win scores of caps. I'd say most players of his era who were asked about the giants of Irish rugby would have him at the very top of their list. The four of us travelled up to Dublin together for squad sessions. On the way home we had a number of stops for "light refreshments". We came home at all hours of the day and night. My wife could never understand how a training session could last 24 hours!'

Whelan was determined to learn the lessons from his experiences as a player when he took on the position of manager of the Irish team in 1995.

'I know how important it is now to treat players properly. In my playing days it was not the norm to ring players beforehand if they were to be dropped. They never got any prior warning nor any explanation. Nowadays, as a manager it's essential to be very communicative with players and to keep in constant touch with them. If a player's form is slipping and he runs the risk of getting dropped he should know about it. If players understand, it is much more easy to accept it.'

Particularly in the light of what happened to Mick Doyle's and Ciaran Fitzgerald's business interests while they were in charge of the Irish team he was anxious not to repeat their experiences.

'After I was appointed I took on an experienced project manager. He is taking care of a lot of my responsibilities. I'm not sure how long I can continue in the job. It is costing me a lot because the position of manager is an honorary position.'

Whelan is a child of his times – conditioned by rugby's social climate and personifying its prevalent ethos. Efficiency and pragmatism are the virtues he lives by. He stands for what is deemed necessary for success in rugby today – hard-headed, tough no-nonsense realism in place of romanticism and sentimentality. How would he react to the idea which is increasingly floated of having just one man in charge of the Irish set-up?

'In my situation that just would not be on. With the five-man selection committee system we have today there is a very clear allocation of responsibilities.'

Whelan walked into the job with his eyes wide open, knowing that he would almost certainly be faced with a flurry of criticisms.

'I don't have any problem with anybody criticising me – providing it is constructive, fair and as long as my family are left out of it. The excitement in the job for me is that I have identified that there is a significant amount of new, young talent out there and the thrill is bringing it through. I believe there is a great future for Irish rugby if we embrace the professional era properly. To be honest I think the IRFU are way ahead of the other "home countries" in the speed with which they have moved to resolve the contracts' issue. They have also gone the right way by appointing a full-time coach.'

Whatever the future brings, Whelan will always have a vast reservoir of happy memories from his playing days to draw on, especially about the personalities he played with.

'I suppose one of, if not the, greatest character(s) of them all was Phil O'Callaghan, even though I once thought he cost me my place on the Irish team. Munster were playing the Wolfhounds shortly before my first cap. The Irish selectors were there so I was all fired up to give the performance of my life, especially as my immediate opponent was the then French hooker. At one stage we had their scrum pinned back and I was about to win a strike against the head. For a second I could almost taste my first cap. Then, inexplicably, Philo put in his hand and pulled back the ball. Instead of getting a heel against the head, Ireland were penalised. I can laugh at it now but at the time I could have throttled him.

'On our tour to New Zealand in 1976 Philo came to me and said that the team needed more "bite" and that the only way we could get onto the team was to show that bite. He was absolutely correct. When we played Auckland both of us scored extremely high on the "bite stakes" and got into the Test side.

'I scored the first try of the tour when I flopped over from five yards. I really enjoyed that experience, especially the competitive way the New Zealanders played their rugby. There was also plenty of *craic* off the field. I was rooming with Mossie Keane the morning after a match. Ned Van Esbeck came into our room, to call us for Mass at what seemed to us in our "tired and emotional" state, to be an ungodly hour. All I can say is that Mossie escorted him out of our room in "typical Moss fashion". I'm not prepared to elaborate any further!'

37

TOM CLIFFORD

The Garden of Get Somebody
(Jim McCarthy's choice)

> The only doubt in my mind was whether rugby isn't too
> dangerous a game – for the spectators.
>
> Robert Lynd

The crowds had been gathering since lunch-time in Thomond Park for
the Munster Cup final between Shannon and Young Munster. One of
the first into the stand was a man who had presented two tickets on
arrival. With only five minutes to go before the match the seat beside
him remained unoccupied. This aroused the curiosity of the person on
his other side. 'Are you waiting on someone?' he inquired. 'Ah, no,'
replied the Young Munster fan. 'We've had a death in the family since I
bought the tickets. In fact, to tell you the truth, it was my wife that died.'

'I'm very sorry for your trouble,' said the other, 'but could you not get
anyone else from the family to come along with you?'

'Yerrah, not at all, sure they all wanted to go to her funeral!'

This story is just a small indicator of how seriously they take their
rugby in Young Munster. No one encapsulated their passion for the
game better than Tom Clifford. He was first capped for Ireland against
France in 1949 and was a key part of the Triple Crown victory in that
season and toured with the Lions to New Zealand in 1950. His name
lives on through 'Tom Clifford Park', a ground which had been
variously described as 'The Killing Fields', 'The Garden of Get
Somebody' and 'Jurassic Park'.

Rugby is to Limerick what films are to Hollywood; a city-wide
obsession that sets a pecking order, discussed endlessly and by everyone,
complete with its own arcane laws and rituals. Pubs are the churches of

this strange sporting religion and its gurus are anyone who can hold an audience. This art's greatest prince was Tom Clifford.

One of his favourite stories was about the two Young Munster fans sitting at a bar counter, reliving the latest game they had seen. After a brief lull in the conversation, one said to the other: 'I wonder if there is rugby in heaven?' His friend said that nobody knew for sure, but suggested that they should make a pact there and then that whichever of them died first would come back and tell the other. They both agreed and the pact was soon sealed with another round of drinks. In due course one of the men died and the day after being buried he turned up at the foot of his friend's bed as arranged. The man in the bed almost died himself with fright, but soon remembered the purpose of the visit. He sat up immediately, eager to hear the news. 'Tell me quick,' he said, 'is there rugby in heaven?' The dead man replied: 'Well, I have good news and I have bad news. The good news is that, yes, there's rugby in heaven alright. But the bad news is that there's a game next Saturday and you're playing scrum-half!'

Everybody in Limerick knew Clifford's bike. He never locked it because no one would dare touch it. Once he was speaking to an ever-increasing circle of Young Munster fans about a big match when he held his bicycle in the air. When asked by an onlooker what he was doing he replied: 'I'm holding a Raleigh!'

For Jim McCarthy, Clifford was not only one of the great props but perhaps the greatest character in Irish rugby.

'When I look back it's the matches with Munster that stand out for me. Bill Shankly's famous saying that football is not a matter of life or death but more important applies to rugby in Munster, especially in Limerick. For me the person that encapsulated that feeling was the late, great Tom Clifford. He was the character among characters. I'll never forget his funeral. The church was teeming with rugby folk. The priest giving the homily had been a lifelong friend of Tom's and told us how he had invited the giant of Irish rugby to his ordination Mass. After the ceremony he asked Tom what he thought of it. Tom replied: "You spoke too long. The next time, if you go on for longer than ten minutes, I'll set off an alarm clock in the church." The next Sunday the priest saw Tom arriving in at the church and noticed he had a bulge in his overcoat. When Tom caught his eye he pulled out an alarm clock!

'As there was such a massive attendance of sports personalities at the funeral the priest went on to compare it with the funeral of the Welsh boxer, Tommy Farr. Tommy had fought Joe Louis for the world title in 1936 and had been destroyed, but he was such a hero in Wales the

Welsh all claimed he was robbed. When he died his funeral service was attended almost exclusively by ex-boxers, with severely disfigured noses, cauliflower ears and a lot of them were in a pretty bad mental state, sparring with themselves. The minister was afraid of a riot and before the service started he called over the altar boy and said: "Brown, whatever I say and whatever I do don't ring that bell or they'll start the mother of all fights!"

'I was on the Lions tour with Tom in 1950. We were two of nine Irish players on the tour as well as George Norton, Michael Lane, Noel Henderson, Jack Kyle, Jimmy Nelson, Bill McKay and the captain of the Lions, Karl Mullen. Tom was a larger-than-life figure especially when he sang his party piece, *O'Reilly's Daughter*. His only rival in the character stakes was probably Cliff Davies, a Welsh coalminer. Cliff was greeted by the New Zealand Prime Minister, S.G. Holland, who said: "Glad to meet you, Cliff." Cliff retorted: "Glad to meet you, Sid."

'Another typical Munster forward was Starry Crowley, a hooker. At one stage we were playing in a ferocious match when he "made contact" with a player. He explained his motivation to me afterwards: "I was running across the pitch and I saw a head lying on the ground and I kicked not to maim but to kill."

'That kind of commitment is essential if you are to win matches. There's no doubt in my mind that if you look back to the 1995 World Cup, South Africa were the fourth best team after the Wallabies, the All Blacks and France but they were that bit hungrier which allowed them to win the tournament. No one I knew played with more hunger than Tom Clifford.

'My clearest memory is of Tom playing for Munster against the Wallabies in 1948. Munster had a very simple way of dealing with touring sides. That was as soon as possible to bring them down to our level and then it was an even match! Tom was in the front row packing against Nick Shehadie, one of the stars of the Australian side, and said: "Come in here son. You may as well die here as in f***ing Sydney!"'

38

SHAY DEERING

The Player's Player
(Tony Ward's Choice)

A leader is a man who has the ability to get other people to do what they don't want to do and like it.

Harry Truman

When Ireland drew 9–9 with Wales in 1974 the late Shay Deering, 'Deero', made his international debut. His selection continued a great family tradition. His father, Seamus, was a distinguished Irish forward of the 1930s, and his uncle Mark (both from Bective Rangers) also played for Ireland. Deero was a colossus of a forward with awesome power who had the honour of captaining his country. Few people have made a greater impression on and off the field on those who knew him.

A new range of emotions come into Tony Ward's voice and facial expression as he talks about the man who was, and is, his inspiration. He speaks with even more intensity than normal.

'For me the best Irish player by far in his position was Shay Deering. He was the ultimate personification of bravery. His biggest problem was his lack of fear. He would stick his head in where most people would stick their boot. Fergus Slattery would be the first to admit that the way he and Shay complimented each other for UCD and Leinster was a significant factor in Slats's progression to the top.

'His caps were a paltry return relative to his ability and commitment. He was one of those players who oozed, and I mean oozed, physical presence and charisma. He was the original gentleman off the pitch but boy was he a hard man on it. He particularly loved showing a gap to an outside-half or scrum-half and then when the player took the bait he pounced on him. My favourite rugby player of all time is Gerald Davies, but my all time hero is Shay Deering. He will always have a special place in my heart.

'I first got to know Deero as a starry-eyed schoolboy in St Mary's in 1966. Shay was in sixth year and captain of the school winning cup-winning senior side. He became my instant hero and he has remained so to this day. With the arrival of his twin brothers, Kevin and David, in my class I was to get to know Seamus on a more intimate basis and many times, as the years progressed, not only were our paths to cross but they became very much one and the same. We played together for club [St Mary's and Garryowen], for province [Munster] and for country and I will be forever grateful that it was with, rather than against, him I played.

'He won eight caps for Ireland between 1974 and 1978, captaining his country in his final appearance. He won Munster and Leinster Cup medals, a Leinster League medal and was capped for both provinces. He had a most distinguished career but long after the cups and caps have been counted, it is the friendships he made along the way that mattered the most. Shay was quite simply the player's player.'

For Johnny Moloney, Deering was a brilliant constellation in an otherwise gloomy sporting sky.

'He was a very sympathetic personality off the field but hard as nails on it. In 1995 I saw his son, Shane, helping Westmeath win the All-Ireland minor football title. At one stage he brought off a rugby tackle which his father would have been proud of. I hope Shane will keep the Deering name in lights.'

Ward's admiration for Deering is almost matched by Mick Quinn.

'He was such a charismatic man. His smile signalled friendship but when he hit you in a tackle, friendship went out the window. He was a great teacher and leader and you would have died for him. We all knew about his medical condition so we organised a golf classic to help him out a bit. Four days before he died he carried around his bag and played nine holes of the course. I remember Stewart McKinney who was his rival for the Irish jersey was in tears and how upset Slats [Fergus Slattery] and people like that were. His funeral will live with me forever. I gave the homily at the Mass. Gracer [Tom Grace], who wouldn't be my biggest fan by any means, told me afterwards that it was the best speech I ever made. I think it was for the emotion as much as the content.'

For his part Tom Grace finds it very difficult to talk about his great friend's death but his respect for Shay, both as a player and as a man knows no limits. 'If someone asked me for a definition of the player's player I would simply have two words to say – Shay Deering.'

Like so many others Mick English is totally bemused that Deering only won eight caps, particularly since Ireland were trawling along the rocky bottom of international rugby that had been their all-too-familiar habitat when he was in his prime. 'He was one of the best forwards I ever saw. No one could surpass his commitment. He was one of the few genuinely unforgettable people I ever met.'

Deering's heady mixture of athleticism, speed, aggression, power, skill and bravery won him incredible respect from his peers but in his final years it was his bravery that provided an enduring memory for Tony Ward.

'That he was brave on the field is beyond dispute but in his final years his bravery was stretched to the limits in the face of his battle against a terminal illness. He displayed courage and fighting qualities that one would expect only of him. His passing has left the game he loved much poorer.

'In recent years I think of him regularly, particularly whenever I hear the Bette Midler song *Wind Beneath My Wings*, from the film *Beaches*, because of the line: "Did you ever know you were my hero?" Every time I hear that song Deero flashes into my mind.'

To no former Irish player does the adage 'gone but not forgotten' apply more to than Shay Deering:

> The life that I have is all that I have,
> The life that I have is yours.
> The love that I have of the life that I have,
> Is yours and yours and yours.
> A sleep I shall have, a rest I shall have,
> Yet death will be but a pause.
> For the peace of my years, in the long green grass,
> Will be yours and yours and yours.

39

MIKE GIBSON

Glory Days
(Mick Quinn's choice)

After 162 years, rugby union still doesn't know what it wants to be when it grows up.

Geoffrey Nicholson in 1985

When Ireland toured Australia in 1979 press attention centred on the elder statesman of Irish rugby, Mike Gibson, the most capped international of all time. Gibson was then 36 but still feared because, although his flesh was not as willing as the golden days of his prime that made him one of the most outstanding players in rugby union, his keen brain and polished skills still functioned unimpaired. It was widely expected that the tour would mark his swansong and the press looked forward to one last hurrah in which he would weave his magic just one more time. He made two Test appearances on the tour which added to his 12 Lions' Test appearances, edged him one ahead of Bill McBride (63 and 17) on the overall international match list with 81 (69 Irish caps). For Mick Quinn, Mike Gibson was Ireland's and the world's greatest player.

'When we trained with the Irish squad Mike Gibson, John Robbie and I were always at the front when we ran. Once Gibbo invited me up North to train with him at the Mary Peters track. I considered it a great honour. When you are training with rugby players you only get as fit as the unfittest player on the team. When you have finished running you have to wait for the slowest runner to complete his run before starting again. When I went to train with Gibbo I learned that if you wanted to be really fit you had to train like an athlete and on your own. After that I trained in Trinity College every lunch-time with former international athletes Noel Carroll and Brendan Murphy. Noel always told me that rugby players hadn't got a clue how to train. He's probably right.

'The one thing we didn't do then that players do today was to be very careful about our diet. I was a steak man. I never smoked nor drank which helped. I had to train very, very hard myself because the competition with Tony Ward and Ollie Campbell on the scene was so intense. I even trained on Christmas morning. The thought that kept me going then was that the two lads were in bed and I had one up on them! Today I hear players talking about all the sacrifices they make. I don't begrudge them the money they get in this professional era but I really get sick when I hear it suggested that the current players are more committed than we were. I doubt if any player, professional or not, today trains harder than Gibbo did. I certainly learned a lot just by watching him train and playing with him was an education in itself.

'I like to think that I played my part in Gibbo's great displays for Ireland. I always blessed myself with Lourdes water before matches. The only players who would come looking for some off me were Moss Keane and Willie Duggan. Moss would sneak over when he thought no one was looking and ask me for some of that "firewater". I always splashed some on Gibbo's legs when he wasn't looking and he went out and played like a genius!

'It wouldn't be accurate to say we were an ecumenical bunch but there were times religion brought us together. On the tour to New Zealand in 1976 the team doctor, Dr Bob O'Connell, organised Mass for us on a holy day of obligation for Catholics at Palmerston North. We could not get Mass anywhere so it was decided to invite a priest in to us and that everybody would go to Mass. The Catholics knew to bring change for the collection but the others didn't, with the result that the priest got a silent collection from the Protestants. He was thrilled and wrote to all the Irish papers telling them what a wonderful bunch the Irish squad were and such fabulous ambassadors for their country!

'Another thing I learned from Gibbo was what you might call a philosophy of the game. One statement in particular stands out and it's one I constantly repeat when I'm coaching kids: "The guys who are the best are the guys who can do the simple things, kicking, passing, running, better than anybody else. Work on the basics, everything else will fall into place."

'I remember telling a ballboy that, once, in a dressing-room when I played in a charity match for Public School Wanderers at West Hartlepool. I didn't think much more about that incident until 1984 when I was in Cardiff with my close friend, Brendan Mullin, who was playing for a Lions' selection against the Southern Hemisphere. I was in the lobby of the Angel hotel with him. I would consider Brendan to be the best Irish player since Mike Gibson. Who walks in but Rory Underwood. I was dumbfounded when he walked up to me and said: "Hello Mick". I asked him how he knew me. He told me that he had been the ballboy I talked to all those years before and that I had been the only player to talk to him that day. We became good friends.

'Some years later I got mini-rugby going in Lansdowne. We would have 150 kids every Sunday. At one stage we organised an under-12 tour to England. Rory is a pilot with the RAF and I got him to arrange a tour of the RAF base for the kids. It was great for them to see all the fighter jets and have the guys at the gate salute them and address them as sir. Rory also arranged for us to be taken into the briefing room before the pilots went on a mission to Scotland. Rory told me that he never forgot what I told him about doing the simple things well. I suppose Gibbo and myself must take some of the blame for all of those tries Rory has scored against Ireland! I call Rory "The Chinese Takeaway".

'Gibbo was such a meticulous single-minded player. I think the only player who could match him in that respect was Ollie Campbell. Mind you, Ollie has lightened up since he retired. Ollie is married to rugby, though there were many girls who would have been happy to be Mrs Ollie Campbell. He's brilliant with kids and would be a fantastic father. To get to the highest level you have to be very dedicated, and both Ollie and Gibson had phenomenal dedication.

'Gibbo had a great temperament. The only time I ever saw him rattled was on the tour to New Zealand in 1976. We were really up against it in some of the matches. I remember Tom Grace saying at breakfast: "Quinner, do you think we'll get out of the place before they realise we're afraid of them." We laughed at the time but I wonder! Barry McGann did not share the general concern. He was playing at out-half that day and was kicking everything, and I mean everything. At one stage Gibbo yelled for a pass but Barry said: "Listen, Mike, when I meet a player who can run as fast as I can kick it then I'll think about passing it!"'

40

KARL MULLEN

Captain Fantastic

(Des O'Brien's choice)

Wanting to win is everything, but winning itself is nothing.

Maxim of the real sportsman

A lovely moment in the 1995 World Cup in South Africa occurred when scrum-half Niall Hogan was conferred with his doctor's degree by the College of Surgeons in a special ceremony. He is one of the many medics who have played for Ireland.

He only won five caps, between 1879 and 1881 and only scored one drop goal. Yet the contribution of Dr John Christopher Bagot to Irish rugby was significant. In his final appearance in the green shirt his drop goal in the dying minutes of Ireland's 1881 victory over Scotland secured Ireland's first international victory after ten defeats.

Dr William Neville is one of a select few who captained Ireland in their debut international, doing so against England in 1879. Dr Joseph James Barnett was capped twelve times in the centre for Ireland between 1899 and 1903. He has the distinction of being Ireland's first scorer in the twentieth century – when he dropped a goal against England in 1900, Ireland's only score that season. At the tender age of 18 he won his first cap for Ireland, while he was still at Campbell College school, as Ireland went on to win the Triple Crown that season – though he was forced to miss the final match against Wales because of mumps. To this day he is the youngest player to have won a Triple Crown with Ireland. He died at the age of 26, in 1907.

Dr Hercules John Knox won ten caps in the Irish forward line between 1904 and 1908. He changed his surname by deed poll in 1912 to Beresford-Knox. Dr Paddy Stokes is one of only eight players who was capped before and after World War One – winning 12 caps in all.

Dr Thomas Wallace has the unique honour of captaining two different countries at rugby. He captained Ireland in 1920, while working in Wales. In the light of his distinguished service to Cardiff club he captained a Wales XV in an unofficial match against the English Civil Service.

Doctors also played a prominent part in the golden era of Irish rugby. Apart from the peerless Jackie Kyle there was team captain, Old Belvedere's Karl Mullen. Mullen is Ireland's most successful captain leading Ireland to their only Grand Slam in 1948, the Triple Crown in 1949 and the Championship in 1951. He also led the Lions in Australia and New Zealand in 1950.

Another doctor who contributed to Ireland's success was prop-forward Dr Arthur McConnell. The Collegians player was as tough as teak. Dr Bill McKay won 23 international caps for Ireland, scoring three international tries. He was a brilliant tackler and scored a try against England in the Grand Slam year and toured with the Lions to Australia and New Zealand in 1950, and was the leading forward try-scorer on the tour with ten tries. A wartime commando, he emigrated to New Zealand.

The year 1949 saw Karl Mullen team up with a player who made history. Fr Tom Gavin played twice in the centre for Ireland that year against France and England. A headmaster, and product of Cotton College in Staffordshire and Cambridge University, he has a unique claim to fame in the annals of Irish rugby: he is the only practising Roman Catholic priest to play for Ireland. However, he is not the only clerical connection with Irish rugby. Before Thomas Arnold Harvey became Bishop of Cashel he won eight international caps in the pack between 1900 and 1903 and made two international cricket appearances, scoring 113 runs and taking two wickets. Two of his rugby playing brothers, George and Frederick (who received the Victoria Cross in World War One), were also capped for Ireland. Marney Cunningham was capped seven times on the flank for Ireland in 1955 and 1956, scoring a try against Wales in his final international against Wales. He later became a priest. Charles Vaughan Rooke was capped 19 times for Ireland in the 1880s and is considered to be one of the initiators of flank forward play. He was secretary to the Leinster Branch of the IRFU for a time, later becoming an Anglican Minister in New Zealand. Ernie Strathdee, a strong player with an accurate pass was Jack Kyle's partner (and club-mate) at scrum-half in the 1948 and 1949 season. He won nine caps for Ireland. A Presbyterian minister and TV sports journalist, he died in a hotel fire in Belfast in 1971.

For Jack Kyle, Mullen was an inspirational force.

'Karl Mullen was a wonderful captain. His greatest gift was to let the players play to the best of their potential. There were times, though, when he showed great tactical awareness. Before we played Wales in Swansea in 1949 he gathered us around and said: "We're going to run them into the ground." We had such a fit and fast back row in particular at the time that he knew we could wear them down and we did. There's a lot of talk today that "forward supremacy is the key" but at that time we were always able to win the battle of the packs which made our job in the backs all that much easier.

'I especially remember the game against Wales at Ravenhill in front of a capacity crowd of 30,000. I'd say they could have taken four times as many had there been place for them. We were all understandably a bit apprehensive but deep down felt we could win. Karl made a point of getting the team to discuss tactics and the strengths and weaknesses of our opponents before matches. He made sure that every man had his say and it was an important part of the pre-match preparations from the point of view of contributing to the great team spirit. We also had "a council of war" at half-time and Karl kept us on the straight and narrow.'

Des O'Brien has a very personal memory of Mullen.

'I won my first cap against England in 1948. Karl came to me on the team bus and asked me if I would be a leader of the pack. I told him I didn't feel up to it because I didn't know any of the forwards as I was a London Irish player at the time. He said: "We can soon fix that," and then he took me on the bus and introduced me to the forwards. Karl was a great player. The laws of the game were different then and he was very capable of winning a heel against the head when the ball was in the opposition's back row of the scrum. I would sum him up as a great captain and an exceptional hooker.'

APPENDIX

The focus of this book was primarily on players I had access to in terms of interviews. This precluded me from featuring many of the deceased stars of the past. The first Irish-born player to play a part in a Triple Crown win was Wilfred Nash Bolton, who was part of the 1884 English Triple Crown winning team. On the way he scored a try against his native country. Dr Tommy Crean was an ever present in Ireland's first ever Triple Crown winning side in 1894 and was on the first ever Lions tour to South Africa in 1896, playing in all matches. He has the distinction of being the first Irish player to captain the Lions in a Test match. In 1901 he won a Victoria Cross for his services as a Surgeon Captain in the Boer War.

Dr Ernest Duncan was capped 13 times at scrum-half for Ireland between 1904 and 1908, scoring two tries. He served in World War One and received the Military Cross. Dr Samuel Campbell won 12 international caps for Ireland between 1911 and 1913 and also earned a Military Cross in World War One.

Andrew Todd won three consecutive international caps at full-back for Ireland in 1913 and 1914. Each match was played on a different day of the week. A major in the RAMC he was awarded the Military Cross for his services during World War One. His son, the Dublin-born actor Richard Todd, was nominated for an Oscar. Sir William Tyrell won nine caps for Ireland before becoming an Air Vice-Marshall with the RAF in World War One when he won a DSO with a bar and a Belgian Croix de Guerre.

In his ten caps for Ireland between 1904 and 1907, Thomas Trevor Hull Robinson scored one international try. He won a DSO in World War One. Joseph Patrick Quinn scored nine tries in his 15 internationals on the wing for Ireland, captaining the side in his final appearance in 1914. He later won the Military Cross. His son, also J.P., won five caps for England in the centre in the mid 1950s.

Robertson Stewart Smyth was capped by Ireland in 1903 and won three Test places on the Lions tour of South Africa. He was killed in World War One – at the age of 36. The first man to swim Belfast Lough was William Victor Edwards, an Irish 200-yard swimming champion and water polo star. He won two caps for Ireland in the pack in 1912. The Great War claimed his life when he was killed in action in Jerusalem in 1917.

Another Irish-born player, Dave Gallagher, emigrated from the hills of Donegal at an early age to New Zealand. He went on to become the All Blacks' first ever captain, in their international against Australia in 1903. He was also appointed captain of the first touring All Blacks side to the British Isles in 1905–6, though injury caused him to miss their clash with Ireland. In 1917 he lost his life in World War One at Passchendale.

George St Leger Fagan won one international rugby cap for Ireland against England in 1878. Nine years later his younger brother, Arthur, was capped for England, bringing them the unique honour of being the first pair of brothers to play rugby for different countries. Hugh Ferris was capped four times for Ireland in 1900, 1901, and in 1903 he was capped for South Africa against the Lions. He is one of only three players to be capped for Ireland and later for another country.

C.V. MacIvor, West Indies-born, played seven international matches for Ireland between 1912 and 1913 scoring one international try, when he was killed in training at Trinity by a kick, in October 1913. He was just 22 years of age.

James Cecil Parke won 20 international caps for Ireland between 1903 and 1907, three of them as captain. He is probably more famous, though, for his exploits on the tennis courts where he was once ranked number four in the world, winning the Wimbledon Mixed Doubles title in 1914, was a singles semi-finalist in 1910 and 1913, and won an Olympic silver medal in the Men's Doubles with Britain's Josiah Ritchie at the 1908 Olympics in London. In 1912 he won both the Australian Men's Singles and Doubles. He also twice represented Ireland at golf.

When Dr George Harman died in 1975 at the age of 101 years and 191 days he became the longest lived rugby international ever. He was part of the Triple Crown winning side in 1899. He also played first class cricket with Trinity College. His brother, William, played once for Ireland in 1907 in a cricket international.

Lucius Gwynn won seven caps for Ireland on the wing in the 1890s. He was also recognised as Ireland's finest batsman of his generation in his 11 international cricket matches for Ireland. He has the best average runs-per-innings of any pre-World War Two cricketer and also took fourteen wickets for Ireland and scored 80 runs in his one appearance for the Gentlemen of England. His brother, Arthur, was also a dual Irish international in rugby and cricket.

Henry Hagarty Corley won nine caps for Ireland, including three as a captain, between 1902 and 1904. As a right-hand bat cricketer he played four times for Ireland between 1907 and 1909, scoring 50 runs.

Dickie Lloyd was capped ten times for Ireland between 1910 and 1920. A prodigious kicker, he kicked seven drop goals for Ireland which stood as an Irish record until 1982. He led his country 11 times, notably to the International Championship in 1912. He also reached the heights in the cricket world, once setting Trinity's highest ever stand, 323, along with H.M. Read. Read went one better. Not only did he represent Ireland at cricket and rugby (13 caps) but he also reached international standard in tennis.

Robert James Barnes scored a try against Wales in his only international for Ireland in 1933. He also played for Ireland in cricket eight times, scoring 433 runs for his country. His younger brother, J.H., also played cricket for Ireland.

Noel 'Ham' Lambert won two caps in the Irish three-quarter line, against Scotland and Wales in 1934. He subsequently refereed 11 international matches. As a right-hand bat cricketer he played 21 matches for Ireland, scoring one international century. His father, Bob, also played 52 times for Ireland at cricket and was capped 11 times for his country at badminton.

William Raymond Hunter won ten caps for Ireland as a winger and centre in the 1960s and even made the Lions tour to South Africa in 1962. He also took 33 wickets in his 28 international cricket matches for Ireland. His brother, Laurence, also won two rugby caps for Ireland.

In 1885 Ned Walsh defeated American Malcolm Ford to become world champion in the 120 yards hurdles. He also won seven international rugby caps with Ireland. Ernest H. 'The Swallow' Greene was Irish sprint champion in 1885 but is best known for his rugby career when he won five caps on the wing for Ireland between 1882 and 1886. He scored one international try. His characteristic trademark was a magnificent swerve.

In the 1930s Freddie Moran won nine caps on the wing for Ireland, scoring six tries. But for the intervention of the Great War he would have won many more. He was also an Irish international sprint champion and joined a select group who have competed for Ireland at three sports when he represented his country at clay-pigeon shooting.

Thomas St George McCarthy was capped at rugby in 1882 against Wales. Two years later he was involved in the famous meeting in Hayes Hotel in Thurles which led to the establishment of the GAA.

Jack Doyle scored a try against Wales in his only appearance for Ireland in 1935. Although he was also a champion sprinter he is best known as one of the most colourful characters in the Irish horse industry as jockey, trainer, buyer and bloodstock agent. One of his 'clients' was Mill House who has an assured place in sporting history because of his epic duel with Arkle.

Dr Andrew Clinch was the first pupil of Belvedere College to be capped for Ireland. He played ten times on the wing between 1892 and 1897 and in all four Test matches in 1896 on the Lions tour of South Africa. His son, Jammie, one of the great characters of the game, was capped 30 times for Ireland as a wing-forward. He also toured South Africa with the Lions in 1924, even playing once as an emergency full-back, and ensuring a record of being part of the only Irish father and son to represent the Lions. Jammie's son and grandson both won colours for Trinity, making them, uniquely, four generations to do so.

Dick Collopy won 13 international caps in the Irish forward line in the 1920s, playing seven times with his brother Billy. Not only did Billy win 19 caps and captain his country but he was one of a select group of Irish players to play for Ireland before and after World War One. His father, George, was also capped twice for Ireland in 1891 and 1892. The second set of father and two sons to play for Ireland were the McKibbins. Harry McKibbin won four caps for Ireland in the 1938–9 season and toured with the Lions to South Africa in 1938. His son, Alistair, was capped 14 times between 1977 and 1980 and another Harry was capped as a reserve full-back against Scotland in 1976. Harry Snr's brother, Des, was also capped eight times for Ireland. Both have been president of the IRFU.

Charles Beamish carved his niche in Irish rugby history when he became the first Irishman to score a try against the All Blacks in a 17–9 defeat in 1935. A prop-forward he won 12 caps for Ireland while his older brother, Sir George, was capped 25 times, winning his first cap at the age of 19, between 1925 and 1933. In his prime, George was considered the finest forward in the game, captaining Ireland to a share in the International Championship in 1931, when Ireland won at Cardiff for what turned out to be the last time for 31 years. That same year he also captained the Midland Counties to a celebrated 30–21 win over the touring Springboks – the Boks' only tour defeat that season. The previous year he had played the most games, 21, on the Lions tour. In 1942 he was awarded the CBE and 13 years later the KCB. Another famous threesome were the Moore brothers, Malcolm, Frank and Frederick (who was knighted in 1911), who won two, three and four caps respectively in the 1880s.

Brian Curtis was born in Shanghai but won three caps for Ireland in the back row in 1950 (five years after he won the Distinguished Flying Cross), before emigrating to South Africa. His son, David, won a Blue for Oxford in both rugby and cricket and was first capped for Ireland in the centre in 1991.